The
Truth About
Retirement
Plans and IRAs

Also by Ric Edelman

The Truth About Money
Rescue Your Money
The Lies About Money
Ordinary People, Extraordinary Wealth
Discover the Wealth Within You
The New Rules of Money
What You Need to Do Now

The Truth About Retirement Plans and IRAs

Ric Edelman

Simon & Schuster Paperbacks

New York   London   Toronto   Sydney   New Delhi

Simon & Schuster Paperbacks
A Division of Simon & Schuster, Inc.
1230 Avenue of the Americas
New York, NY 10020

Copyright © 2014 by Ric Edelman

First Simon & Schuster trade paperback edition April 2014

SIMON & SCHUSTER PAPERBACKS and colophon are registered trademarks of Simon & Schuster, Inc.

For information about special discounts for bulk purchases, please contact Simon & Schuster Special Sales at 1-866-506-1949 or business@simonandschuster.com.

The Simon & Schuster Speakers Bureau can bring authors to your live event. For more information or to book an event contact the Simon & Schuster Speakers Bureau at 1-866-248-3049 or visit our website at www.simonspeakers.com.

Designed by Ric Edelman, Suzi Fenton, and Christine Janaske

Manufactured in the United States of America

10 9 8 7 6 5 4 3 2

Library of Congress Cataloging-in-Publication Data has been applied for.

ISBN 978-1-4767-3985-4
ISBN 978-1-4767-3986-1 (ebook)

To Brad and Larry

Contents

Acknowledgments

Writing a book is supposed to be a solitary act, but at Edelman Financial Services, everything is a communal effort. Thus, this book's production reflects the work of an astonishingly large group of people.

Much credit goes to Mike Lewis, editor of our monthly newsletter, *Inside Personal Finance*. Mike's contribution can't be overstated, and his fingerprints can be found throughout the book. Where Mike left off, Mitch York, my firm's portfolio manager, and Andrew Cohen, a member of my Education and Communication staff, picked up. They gathered all the raw data and statistics and fact-checked the entire manuscript.

I'm well-known for creating books that are as much fun to look at as to read, and this one is no different. With my trademark charts, graphs, footnotes, sidebars and cartoons, the book is easy on the eyes and comfortably moves the reader from page to page. Unlike other authors who merely send Word files to their publishers, we actually deliver camera-ready art to ours — maintaining full control over the layout along the way. Credit for the book's visualization goes to Suzi Fenton, my firm's manager of creative services, and her able associate, Christine Janaske. This book might be mine, but they treat the book as though it's theirs. They actually might be right.

Whenever I write a book — from my first 17 years ago (*The Truth About Money*) to this one, and all those in between — my greatest fear is not that I'll get a bad review (I can't control that), but that the book will contain an error of some sort (which I can control). Omissions and commissions are equally frightful. Might I leave out a fact? Is there an important point unstated? Or have I written a nonsensical sentence or been particularly (as demonstrated by that adverb and highlighted in this parenthetical phrase) verbose?

To guard against the risk of flaw, all of the financial planners of Edelman Financial Services read the manuscript. I also invite other members of the staff to volunteer as a reviewer, to give me a consumer's viewpoint. That approach was fine 17 years ago when our firm was small and a handful of folks helped me out, but this time I found myself with 142 reviewers! Because pretty much everyone made comments on pretty much every page, I had to sift through more than ten thousand pages (electronically, thankfully) of comments! This task was made manageable by my "traffic control team" — Ashley Duran, Sarah Kenney, Rosa Wray and Andrew Cohen. Without their logistic assistance, I never could have mastered the task — and it was essential that I did, for the comments were awesome and helped me convert a decent manuscript into one really worth reading.

Particular thanks for their reviewing prowess goes to my colleagues Alan Facey, Alan Wheedleton, Anderson Wozny, Betty O'Lear, Brandon Corso, Brian Rafferty, Charlie Nardiello, Christine Cataldo, Darrell Reynard, David Lubitz, David Sheehan, Denise Zuchelli, Doug Keegan, Doug Rabil, Ed Hungler, Ed Moore, Ed Schweitzer, Ed Swikart, Fahima Shaw, Frances Falanga, Isabel Cooper, Jackie Oates, Jean Edelman, Jeff White, Jeremiah Burke, Jessica Cline, Jim Marx, Jo-Anna Wilson, Karen Morse, Lisa Eitzel, Lisa Lausten, Mary Davis, Mike Lewis, Patrick Day, Rick Mueller, Ryan Bergmann, Sarah Kenney, Scott Butera, and Theresa Coughlin. (As you noticed, in keeping with our firm's standards, everyone is listed alphabetically by first name.)

I also want to thank Adam Jefferis, Adam Karron, Andrew Cohen, Andrew Massaro, Ann Crehan, Anthony Brewer, Aric Jacobson, Aura Carmi, Beth London, Bobbie Starr, Brad Hartzel, Caitlin Chen, Carl Sanger, Catherine Caceres, Christine Wessinger, Clarence Haynes, Connie Green, David Heinemann, Dean Tsantes, Debbie Dull, Diane Jensen, Ed Lynch, Erich Hoffman, Felix Kwan, George Ball, George Dougherty, Isabel Barrow, Jack London, Jan Kowal, Jason Cowans, Jeffrey Lewis, Jenny Greene, Jigisha Dahagam, Joanna L. Cecilia-Fleming, Jonathan Saxon, Josh Andreasen, Keith Spengel, Ken Murray, Kevin Maguire, Kristine Chaze, Lesley Roberts, Linda Campbell, Marcelle Belisle, Maribeth Bluyus, Mary Ellen Nicola, Michael Krowe, Pam Becker, Philip Carroll, R. J. Reibel, Rey Roy, Rick Ehlinger, Robert Schneider, Ron Sisk, Ronald Bolte, Ryan Poirier, Ryan Singer, Sean Wintz, Surendra Dave,

Tom Begley, Tom Wood, Tracey Martin, Val Taddei, Vicki Wilson and Wilson Mitchell.

Finally, Al Burgos, Anatoly Sabinin, Andrew Nemets, Bill Hoffman, Bret Svedberg, Brian Amper, Carlos Rodriguez, Constance Rodriguez, Craig Engel, Daniel Lennon, David Balestriere, Debi Everly, Denise Neuhart, Doug Ulrich, Gary Riederman, Jeanne Baldwin, Jeremy Albrecht, Jesse Wilson, Jim Barnash, Joe Bottazzi, John Davis, Kevin Garvey, Kevin Yorkey, Lori Bensing, Mary Caruso, Richard Welsh, Robert Bowman, Stu Berrin, Tim Goode, Todd Hillstead, and Treymane Christopher.

I want to specifically highlight a director of our financial planning division, Jim Baker, CFP, CPA. He not only reviewed the manuscript along with all the others, he also read the revised version (which is in your hands) to double-check the accuracy of everything I say in the book.

Despite all the thousands of accumulated comments everyone made, and all the proofreading and fact-checking we did, it's still possible that an error remains in the text. If there is indeed any error, the blame resides exclusively with...Jim.

Credit also goes to Sarah Kenney, my E-Comm VP, for orchestrating the book's production workload and keeping us organized and on schedule.

I also wish to thank my longtime agent, Gail Ross, and my editor at Simon and Schuster, Ben Loehnen, and his able team.

One final group of people needs to be recognized. I encountered a problem while writing this book, and nearly 2,000 people came to my rescue. I realized at one point that I didn't know what the title should be. Everyone I asked rejected every idea I offered, so I finally gave up and pleaded for help — live, on my weekly radio show. Thousands of listeners came to my rescue, offering *lots* of suggestions. I posted the 15 best ideas on my web site, and then returned to the airwaves and asked listeners to vote for their favorite — promising not only that the most popular name would appear on the cover (it does) but that the person who submitted the entry would get credit in these pages.

The title was not only the most popular choice — it was recommended by 160 people! So, as promised, I happily announce their names:

David Adams
June Alice
David Areson
Joseph Arfin
Jean Asencio
Jacob Baier
Karyn Baran
Mariah Barber
Tom Begley
Gerald Bell
Lori Bensing
Kenneth Berkowitz
Joe Biggin
Robert Bowman
Ron Brngal
David Brown
Matt Burns
Osvaldo Bustos
Kelly Cale
Aura Carmi
Paul Carucci
Christine Cataldo
Paulette Check
Jane Chiavelli
Margaret Chow
Mark Cleveland
Gail Coffee
Kathy Cossack
John Cross
Brian Deery
Joanne Diconza
Michael DiToro
Bryan Dotson
Kurt Dunphy
Al Dyson

Marianne Eagan
David Egerton
Chuck Eggebrecht
Bob Enzweiler
David Erickson
Joseph Erkenswick
Clay Ernst
Alan Facey
Frances Falanga
Timothy Fast
Michele Ferris
Bill Finneran
Michael Freed
Bernard Freeman
James Gangawere
Donald Gardner
Edward Garfinkel
Ryan Goolsby
Rachelle Green
Mary Greiner
Tom Grimm
Sharon Gross
Steve Haaser
Bruce Handley
Joseph Hannon
Michael Harrigan
Dorothy Harris
Brad Hartzel
Sam Haschets
Todd Hillstead
Dudley Hinote
Sue Hoover
David Huang
John Hunsinger
Craig Ikami

Joe Itzel
James Jaseph
Diane Jensen
Barb Johnson
Vielka Jones
Alan Judy
Vinek Kaistha
Adam Karron
Hugh Kays
Doug Keegan
Shannon Keiper
Paul Khatkar
Patrick J. Koerner
James Komosinski
Anthony Kourepenis
Edwin Krampitz
Livia Kropf DeBonet
Janet Lamerato
Tina Lange
Michael Laxner
Daniel Lennon
Terry Letner
Keith Leventhal
Tut Liu
Michael Lofton
Leonard Maczko
Dean Maertens
Mitch Major
Robert Mannion
Sally Mannion
April Mariani
Mary Mars
Daniel Mays
Todd Mcdermott
Manuel Mireles

Patricia Molina
Scott Mueller
Ken Nakatsu
Tony Nefas
Diem Nguyen
Alfred Odierno
Adam Orr
Joe Paire
Douglas Paynter
Karen Pearson
Pat Pecoraro
Michael Pendola
Harry Pevos
Greg Pickett
Elzunia Pitt
T. Plummer
David Poe
Greg Pollock
Brent Ponder
Sandra Presgraves
H. Christine Rassol
John Reaser II
Marlene Reid
Dick Riederer
Lesley Roberts
Nelson Rodriguez
Urias Rodriguez
Richard Schalk
Nancy Schmitt
Ted Schmitt
Marc Scholl
Jennifer Sevier
Ryan Singer
Mark Smet
B. Joseph Smith

David Smith	Wanda Thompson	Jana Waters	Thomas Wood
Christopher Steadman	William Thompson	Christine Wessinger	William Yates
Miller Sullivan	Craig Todd	Eiko Westerlind	Richard Young
Ed Swikart	Jim Vonau	Cora Lee Wetherington	Eileen Ziper
William Taksar	Mark Wagner	Regina Wong	Vladimir Zukowski

We have sent a copy of this book to everyone who submitted a title idea. That's nearly 2,000 books that people won't have to purchase! I wonder if that will hurt my chances of this becoming another of my bestsellers? Oh well.

The book's title wasn't the only element to benefit from crowdsourcing. The cover design also resulted from massive staff input, and there was a big debate over whether I should appear with arms crossed wearing a jacket or more relaxed sporting a sweater. The vote was evenly divided — leaving me with a conundrum. Then, Elizabeth Linares, one of my Financial Planning Analysts, solved the riddle by suggesting I pose relaxed (as in the sweater shot) while wearing the jacket. Simple idea — but no one else had thought of it. Her suggestion led to the cover you now see (and explains why I like to involve as many of my staff as possible in our decision-making!).

Finally, deepest thanks to my wife Jean, for allowing me once again to divert my attention from her over countless nights and weekends to my writing. She is equally committed to financial education, and her support is priceless. I was also thinking of mentioning our dogs, Summer and Vicki, because my time at the keyboard has meant less time to play with them — but, being firmly devoted to Jean, they haven't noticed, so forget it.

Foreword
by David Bach

Let me just start by saying — I wish I wrote this book because I think it's the best retirement planning book I have ever read — but I am getting ahead of myself.

So let's start where it all began for me with Ric Edelman nearly twenty years ago.

It was 1997, and I was in the San Francisco airport browsing the bookstore before a flight and I see see Ric's first book, *The Truth About Money*. The title jumped out at me, "The Truth About Money"? I had read nearly every financial planning book in the past ten years and I was in the process of writing my first book, *Smart Women Finish Rich*. I had grown up in the financial service industry — attending my father's investments classes since the age of nine and I was a Senior Vice President at Morgan Stanley, partner of the Bach Group managing hundreds of millions of dollars for individual investors — and so with all of this investment knowledge, I candidly doubted that *The Truth About Money* would share any new "truths."

As I opened Ric's book and turned the pages I was pleasantly surprised, even slightly jealous. Ric's book was not only well written, he had in fact truly written an outstanding book on money that really did teach the reader "the truth about money." He had shared the inside secrets that we in the financial services know from behind the curtain but which most people never learn (or if they do, often too late).

I remember thinking, this guy is the real deal, he gets it and he is truly trying to be of service. As the years went by I would watch Ric with great respect as he built one of the leading independent financial planning firms in the nation. One thing in particular that I appreciated then about Ric, and still do to this day, is that he teaches with integrity and inspires others to live their best lives financially.

When Ric asked me to read the manuscript for this new book of his, I jumped at the opportunity. And I had high expectations for him; if

The Truth About Money would be any indicator, this new book would be of huge value to millions of people.

I read the manuscript while on a plane flying home from California to New York. By the time we landed, I'd devoured it. And my wife Alatia was glad when we landed — it meant I'd stop pestering her with comments about how great the book is.

Indeed, Ric's new book *The Truth About Retirement Plans and IRAs* is simply outstanding. He has gone deep into the details of retirement planning in a way I have never seen covered before. He pulls back the curtain and shows you exactly what you need to know about managing your retirement savings, and he has done it as only an experienced financial planner can.

Ric and his firm Edelman Financial Services have more than 23,000 clients. If that sounds like a lot, you're right — it is a lot. And his experience in helping so many people plan for retirement shows on every page of this incredible book. I have always said, "you only retire once, so don't wing it." You work for four or five decades — sometimes more — so you can retire, and you get only one chance to do it right. Take this seriously because it is serious. The unfortunate truth is that it is easy to screw up your retirement plan. The investment strategy you use is not just important, it's critical to your future well-being. Picking the right retirement account, handling your IRA rollovers, getting the beneficiaries correct, choosing when to take a lump sum distribution or fixed annuity payment — the issues you face go on and on. Should you use a Roth IRA vs a Deductible? What about those "target date" mutual funds that millions are now using in their retirement plans — should you? And if you do use one, which one should you choose? Should you use actively managed mutual funds or passively managed mutual funds? Should you roll over the plan when you leave work — and if so, where should you move the money to? What are the risks and the costs? And what do you need to watch out for when saving for retirement?

Just reading the above questions could be overwhelming. Don't worry — Ric answers all of it in detail in this book, in a breezy, casual style that's easy to read. Yes, Ric has made this journey of learning about retirement fun, interesting, and actionable — and reading this book is time really well spent.

The one thing I will want to leave you with (so you can begin reading the book) is that Ric writes like he teaches — you'll feel as though you're talking to a really good friend who really cares about you, and who happens to be super smart about retirement. I put my name on this book and wrote this foreword because I know this book can help you plan for a dream retirement and I know you deserve to live your best life financially. As I have always told the readers of my books, you deserve to live and finish rich — and the time to start is today. Let Ric be your financial coach, with *The Truth About Retirement Plans and IRAs* as your guide. Here's to your dream retirement!

Live rich. Finish rich,

David Bach

9-Time *New York Times Bestselling* Author
Creator of The Finish Rich and Automatic Millionaire Book Series

Introduction

Yes, a successful retirement can be yours, and this book is designed to help you get it. In short, this book is designed to help you accumulate more money *for* retirement and generate more income *in* retirement. But unlike many members of past generations who were able to rely on their employers or the government to provide financial security in retirement, your success will be determined almost entirely by you. Indeed, relatively few of today's workers will receive an employer or union pension in retirement, and most everyone expects Social Security benefits will be lower in the future.

So, if you want a financially secure and comfortable retirement, it's up to you to create it.

But rather than being scared by that statement, you should feel *empowered.* That's because you can indeed make your retirement everything you want it to be — it's much easier than you might think. And it's important that you start now and realize that, if you don't prepare for your retirement, no one else will do it for you. Retirement security is almost entirely up to you.

Here's the good news: If you follow the steps outlined in this book, you can accumulate hundreds of thousands of dollars in your workplace retirement accounts and IRAs — much more than the typical American, who today has less than $25,000 in retirement savings, according to the Employee Benefit Research Institute.

This book is divided into three parts. I know you want to jump straight to Part III — so you can immediately begin to master the money in your retirement plans and IRAs — and you're welcome to do that. However, you might find the background in Parts I and II very helpful. The choice is yours.

No matter whether you work for a private employer, a publicly traded company, a nonprofit organization or charity, a union, the military or a government agency, you'll learn how to take charge of your retirement. I know you can do it, because I've already shown thousands of other people how to do it, people just like you. My financial planning and investment management firm is one of the oldest and largest independent firms in the nation — at this writing my colleagues and I provide financial planning and investment management services to more than 23,000 individuals and families across the country, and we now have more than $11 billion in assets under management. In these pages, I'm going to show you what we've shown them. Our clients have learned how to take charge of their retirement, and you can too!

It's a privilege to share this advice and information with you. Thank you for giving me this opportunity to help you.

The Truth About Retirement Plans and IRAs

PART 1 ONE

Why Retirement Plans Exist —
and the Secret to Making
Them Work for You

Chapter 1
How Retirement Plans Came to Be

In the beginning, there was no such thing as retirement: If you were alive, you worked.

Children gathered, adults hunted. The old and the sick, unable to work and feed themselves, died.

Soon, nation-states formed, and people organized to defend themselves from invaders.[1] But how do you convince people to fight when there is a high likelihood they will die doing so?

One way is to bribe them.

The First Pension in America

During the American Revolution, the Continental Congress offered soldiers a monthly lifetime income as an incentive to join General Washington's army. The income they'd receive following the war (assuming they survived the ordeal) would be a reward for their service.

This lifetime income was called a *pension*.

---

[1]That is without question the fastest history lesson ever. From Cro-Magnon days to modern society in just three and a half sentences. Beat that, Tolstoy.

The colonists didn't invent the idea; it had been used by Romans 2,000 years ago.

But the idea was new to Americans: For the first time, you could work for (just) a finite number of years instead of your entire life, after which you'd continue to receive income as though you were still employed.

As far as Americans were concerned, it was (pardon the pun) a revolutionary idea.

The federal government repeated the offer during the Civil War and has done so ever since.

> **Pension benefits are still being paid for service in the Civil War. Although the last soldier to fight in that conflict died in 1958, his child (now 94 years old) is still receiving a monthly check from the federal government, according to the Department of Veterans Affairs.**
>
> **Ditto for 58 children of veterans of the Spanish-American War (fought in 1898), 2,192 children of World War I veterans and 10,733 kids of WWII vets.**

The first private company to offer a pension plan was American Express, which in 1875 gave an income to each retired employee. The amount was equal to half of the worker's annual pay, based on an average of the worker's final 10 years of employment (up to $500 annually). Over the next 50 years, hundreds of other companies created similar plans.

Pensions came to be known as *defined benefit* plans because the future *benefit* you are to receive is *defined.*[2] What was undefined was how much it would cost the employer to provide this benefit.

Workers came to love pension plans. They paid nothing for them and had to stay with their employer only long enough to qualify (called *vesting*) — typically 20 to 40 years. Employers loved the plans too because they helped ensure that productive workers would

---

[2]Duh.

stay for an entire career. The higher productivity and lower turnover helped the employer save money.

A Retirement Plan for the Public

Then came the Great Depression. Tens of millions of people were out of work, which created fierce competition for jobs. The nation's economy was agricultural and industrial — both very physically demanding — placing older Americans at a distinct disadvantage. So when these folks lost their jobs, they were unlikely to find new ones. They thus found themselves permanently — albeit involuntarily — retired.

To provide them with income during their retirement years, President Franklin D. Roosevelt introduced the Social Security Act of 1935 — the first public retirement plan. Similar to the private plan created by American Express, Social Security was to pay monthly benefits based on each worker's length of service and average annual wages. The first person to receive a Social Security check was Mary Fuller. Starting in 1940, she received $22.54 monthly — and she kept receiving money from Social Security until she died in 1975 at age 100.

Did I say Social Security was similar to the American Express plan? Actually, there's a big difference: AmEx paid for the benefit it gave its employees, while you pay taxes to support Social Security. Today, in fact, more Americans pay more in Social Security taxes than they do in federal income taxes. And Social Security taxes keep rising. But that's a different book.

In 2013, nearly 57 million Americans were receiving Social Security benefits, averaging $1,150 monthly. The maximum monthly retirement income was $3,350 as of December 2013, and you must be at least 70 years old to receive it. The benefit is based on your 35 highest-earning years.

Smoke-and-mirrors alert! The benefit used to be based on your 10 highest-earning years. But the federal government changed the formula to reference 35 years of work. Although earnings are indexed to inflation, workers nevertheless earn a lot less at the start of a career than they do at retirement. So including those early lower-income years in the calculation reduces the amount you receive.

It's a tricky way for the government to reduce Social Security benefits, and I bet you didn't notice that they changed the formula.

How the World's Largest Automobile Manufacturer Changed Retirement Plans Forever

The Studebaker family of South Bend, Indiana, started making wagons for farmers, miners and the military in 1852. Ten years after the first gasoline-powered car was tested in the United States, the Studebakers began manufacturing automobiles and became, at one point, the world's biggest carmaker. But by the 1960s the company was having financial difficulties, and the last Studebaker car rolled off the assembly line on March 16, 1966.

NON SEQUITUR   WILEY

One of Studebaker's problems was that its pension plan had so little money in it that the company couldn't afford to pay all its retirees the pensions they had been promised. So when the company went broke, the pensions ended as well, leaving thousands of employees and retirees with no pension or only a fraction of the amount they had been promised.

> Remember when I said that workers loved pensions because they paid nothing for them? Well, now you're beginning to realize how this hands-off approach came back to haunt them. By leaving all the details to their employers and merely assuming everything would be fine, millions of pensioners found themselves with no pension at retirement — and no savings, since they thought they didn't need to save. Big mistake.
>
> You can avoid this mistake easily: Don't believe that the promise of a pension alleviates you of the need to save for retirement.

Studebaker's collapse, along with similar events at other companies, caused Congress to create the Employee Retirement Income Security Act, signed into law by President Gerald Ford in 1974.

ERISA governs how pension plans operate, to help ensure that promises made to employees are honored by their employers. ERISA also created PBGC, the Pension Benefit Guaranty Corporation. Similar to the FDIC (Federal Deposit Insurance Corporation) for banks, PBGC restores some (not all) of the pension income that workers lose when a company goes out of business.

Chapter 2
How Retirement Plans Evolved from Defining *Benefits* to Defining *Contributions*

In 1981, Ted Benna, co-owner of a benefits consulting firm in Pennsylvania, noticed that the Revenue Act of 1978 added a paragraph to the tax code. This new text allowed a worker to set aside a portion of his paycheck into a separate account. The text was silent as to the tax treatment of this money, and everyone Benna asked told him the money couldn't be set aside on a pretax basis.

Unconvinced, Benna requested clarification from the Internal Revenue Service. The agency confirmed his suspicion: The new law did *not* require that taxes be paid on the contributions. So Benna created an account for his own company, and behold: The nation's first-ever retirement plan was established based on Section 401(k) of the Internal Revenue Code.

"You can be young without money, but you can't be old without it."

— Tennessee Williams

Thanks to Benna, employees could voluntarily set aside a portion of their pay into an investment account. Since they had not received the money they set aside, they weren't taxed on it. This reduced their taxable income. And since they hadn't received the profits that grew inside the account, the profits weren't taxed either (until withdrawn, that is).

For the first time, workers across America could save for their own retirement on a completely tax-sheltered basis.

The idea went viral (even without an Internet). Benna's plan was created in 1981, and by 1982 such major companies as Hughes Aircraft, Johnson & Johnson and PepsiCo had 401(k) plans in place. By 1983, nearly half of the Fortune 500 were either offering 401(k) plans or developing them.

At first, 401(k) plans were thought to be nothing more than a way for executives to provide themselves with additional income in retirement, as a supplement to their pensions. Indeed, only highly paid employees tended to participate in these plans. (Lower-income workers often felt they couldn't afford to contribute — and with pension plans in place, they often figured that they didn't need to.)

But then something happened.

Those same senior executives who were now happily deferring some of their income into 401(k) plans began to estimate the future value of their accounts and compared those future values to the income they expected to receive from their pension plans. They discovered that their 401(k)s would produce comparable future value.

And then those senior executives noticed something else.

The amount of money their companies were paying to create and maintain the new 401(k) plan was a tiny fraction of the money the companies were paying to fund their pension plans.

Shouts of "Aha!" were heard in corporate boardrooms around the country.

Instead of offering a 401(k) as a supplement to the pension plan, these companies used 401(k) plans to *replace* pension plans. This not only saved them a lot of money, but it also eliminated the very liability that killed Studebaker and dozens of other big companies.

You see, the pension plan promises you a monthly retirement income, but the cost to the company is unknown. By contrast, the company's cost to contribute to the 401(k) plan is fixed — and *you're* the one who doesn't know what the account will be worth in the future. Thus, with a 401(k) plan, the cost of the *contribution* is defined — not the *benefit*. Thus, 401(k) plans came to be known as *defined contribution* plans.

In other words, in one simple, crafty maneuver, companies shifted the burden of providing retirement security from themselves to their workers.

Today, only 11% of the Fortune 100 provide traditional pension plans to newly hired workers. That's an all-time low, according to Towers Watson. The other 89% offer 401(k) plans.

It's not just the elimination of the pension's promised income that has gone by the wayside. There is another massive difference between pension plans and 401(k) plans — and if you fail to understand this difference you could wind up retiring at the Poor Farm instead of Millionaire Acres.

In a pension plan, your employer contributes money to the plan and decides how the money is invested. You, as the employee, have no role in the management of the program.

But in a 401(k) plan, *you* contribute money to the plan (your employer also might), and *you* decide how the money is invested — not your employer.

> Originally, employers did make the investment decisions for employees, even though it was the employees' money. But after workers started suing their employers in the 1980s — either because the investments had lost money or failed to earn as much as employees wanted — employers turned the investment decision over to the employees.
>
> Now virtually all plans require employees to make their own investment decisions. That's great — provided you know how to invest. That's why I wrote this book and why you've decided to read it.

Assume Max started at a job years ago earning $20,000 and gets a 3% annual raise. By the time he retires in 30 years, he's earning $47,131. If his pension is equal to 70% of his highest pay, Max will get a pension of $32,992 each year. If Max lives 30 years after retiring, his company will pay a total of $989,758.

But if the company instead offers Max a 401(k) plan and contributes 5% of Max's salary to it each year, the company will pay a total of $47,575.

No wonder companies are abandoning pension plans in favor of 401(k)s!

Well, sort of. In truth, most defined benefit plans were not very generous to most workers. They were ideal if you were among your firm's highest paid employees and if you stayed with the same employer most of your career. But most didn't fit that description.

Unlike the hypothetical Max who stayed with his firm 30 years, the actual median job tenure for men over 55 peaked at 15.3 years in 1983 and is now less than 11 years, according to the Employee Benefits Research Institute.

The 401(k) plan, like most retirement plans, is a *qualified plan*. By meeting the requirements of Section 401 of the tax code, it *qualifies* for certain tax treatment, the most significant being that both employer and employee contributions are tax-deductible in the year they are made, and the employee pays income taxes only when money is withdrawn.

Although it didn't take long for 401(k) plans to become popular, a downside was immediately spotted: To enjoy the benefits of a 401(k), you had to work for a company that offered one. But what if you were self-employed or among the 50 million Americans who work for small employers that don't offer such benefits?

Congress fixed the problem in 1974 by creating the Individual Retirement Arrangement. Unlike 401(k) and related salary-reduction plans, IRAs are not run by employers. Instead, you create your own retirement account. At first, only employees without pensions were eligible, and the maximum annual contribution was $1,500. Today, IRAs are available to a wider group of people. The qualification rules are complicated, and we'll delve into the details in Chapter 16. For now, it's enough to say that IRAs have become a vital element of retirement planning.

Nearly 40% of Americans have one or more IRAs, totaling nearly $5 trillion. Worthy of note is the fact that much of that money started in 401(k)s or other workplace plans and was later transferred into IRAs.

That's why this book is devoting as much attention to IRAs as to workplace retirement plans. Odds are high that you have both or one day will (because you will shift money from one to the other). You need to know how to make such transfers and why it's important, and I'll explain it all for you.

For women over 55, median tenure is 10 years. That means few workers qualify for fat pensions.

Indeed, in 1975 only about one in five employees qualified for a pension, and the average check was $4,700 annually in 2011 dollars, according to the Investment Company Institute.

Thus, the idea that there was once a "golden age" of pensions is largely a myth, ICI says. Indeed, it probably can be said that old-style *defined benefit* plans were not so great after all, and the fact they've been replaced by new *defined contribution* plans has been mainly a good thing — for both employers and employees.

PEARLS BEFORE SWINE STEPHAN PASTIS

Chapter 3
Why You Need to Start Saving Now

There are two key elements to creating wealth, and they are inextricably linked:

They are *time* and *rate of return*.

To help you understand their importance, I'm going to offer you a series of examples. Let's start with a pool of water.

The Lily Pad in the Pond

There is a well-known story about a lily pad in a pond. The lily pad doubles in size every day, and after 10 days it has grown so big that it covers the entire surface of the pond. On what day does the lily pad cover half the pond?

Most people assume that half the pond is covered on Day 5. After all, if the entire pond is covered in 10 days, it seems logical that you'd be halfway done after half the time.

But that's linear thinking, and that's not how real growth occurs. Actually, growth occurs *exponentially*. Thus, half of the pond is covered not on Day 5, but on Day 9.

Think about it: If the lily pad doubles in coverage every day and the pond is fully covered on Day 10, then it must be 50% covered the

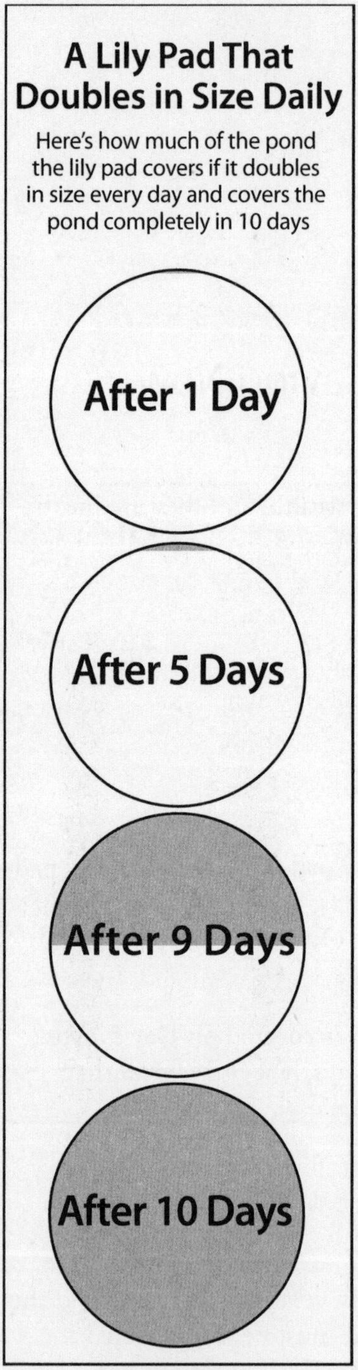

A Lily Pad That Doubles in Size Daily

Here's how much of the pond the lily pad covers if it doubles in size every day and covers the pond completely in 10 days

After 1 Day

After 5 Days

After 9 Days

After 10 Days

FIGURE 3.1

day before — so that the lily pad can double in size from Day 9 to Day 10.

Take a look at Figure 3.1. It shows how much of the pond is covered after Day 1, Day 5, Day 9 and Day 10. You'll probably be shocked to see how little is covered by the fifth day, when half the days are gone.

The Doubling Penny

Let's try another example.

Imagine you have a penny in your pocket and it doubles in value every day for 31 days. After one month, take a guess at how much money you will have.

Do you think you'll have more than $1,000?
❑ Yes   ❑ No

Do you think you'll have more than $10,000?
❑ Yes   ❑ No

Do you think you'll have more than $100,000?
❑ Yes   ❑ No

Do you think you'll have more than $1,000,000?
❑ Yes   ❑ No

Well, here are the results:

After Day 7   the penny is now worth 64 cents.

After Day 14   the penny is now worth $82.

After Day 21   the penny is now worth $10,500.

After Day 31   the penny is now worth $10.7 million.

Indeed, money doesn't grow linearly, as in Figure 3.2, but rather exponentially, as in Figure 3.3.

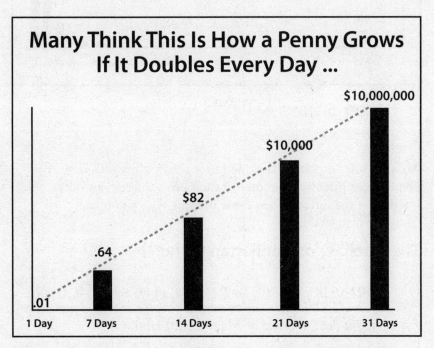

FIGURE 3.2

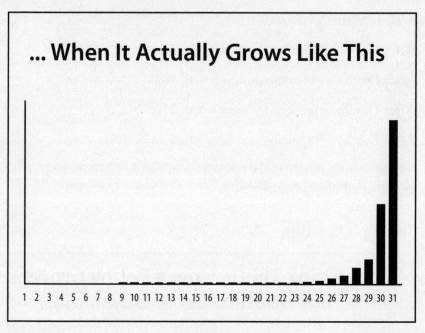

FIGURE 3.3

Money grows exponentially due to *the power of compounding*. A penny earns interest. The interest then earns interest, and the interest on the interest then earns interest. And so on.

The Purchase of Manhattan Island

I demonstrated the value of compounding in my book *The Truth About Money*. To illustrate the concept of compounding, I concocted a story about the 1626 sale of Manhattan Island.

Schoolkids know the colonists paid 60 guilders (the equivalent of $24) for the island. Suppose the Native Americans had invested that money and managed to earn 7.2% per year (in other words, doubling their money every 10 years).

How much money would they have had by the end of 2013?

The answer: $21.6 trillion!

But here's something even more fascinating: If the natives had actually invested $24 and earned 7.2% per year, they would have earned $1.73 in interest each year. And if they spent the $1.73 each year over the past 387 years, they would have earned and spent a total of $668.74 — and their account today would still be worth the $24 they started with.

The difference between $669 and $21.6 trillion is interest earning interest on interest. *Compounding is the key to wealth creation.*

Two Brilliant Men

Here are two real-life examples of people who illustrate the benefits you can obtain through compounding. The first one is a fellow who called my radio show one day. His name is John and he was calling from Manassas, Virginia. He said, "Ric, my wife just had a baby boy and I want to save some money for my new son."

I started talking about college planning, but John interrupted me. "I'm not talking about college," he said. "I want to save for my son's retirement."

I thought he was nuts.

No parent saves for a baby's retirement, I thought. *It's hard enough for you to save for your own retirement, let alone for a little kid's.*

But as I thought about it, I realized John is a genius. I pulled out my calculator and did some fast math while we were still on the air.

"John," I said, "let's assume you invest $5,000 and you earn 7.2% per year, and you let it grow for 18 years, using the money when your son goes to college."

At that rate of return, $5,000 would grow to about $17,000 — certainly not enough to pay for college in 18 years.

But I then changed the parameter to John's point. "Let's save this money for 65 years instead of 18 years," I said.

The ending value? You wind up with $450,000!

Yessir, John is a genius. Compounding money for 65 years instead of 18 can lead to incredible wealth at even more incredible ease. Compare these two scenarios:

A. You earn $50,000 and get a 2% annual pay raise. You put 6% of your pay into your 401(k) every year from age 40 to age 65, and you get a 50% employer match. Your account grows 8% per year. At age 65, you have about $464,000.

B. Or, your grandparents set aside $5,000 for you at birth, placing the money into an account that grows 8% per year. At age 65, the account is worth almost $744,000![3]

It's amazing: The results from a lifetime of sacrifice are dwarfed by a small and painless onetime deposit. Yep, John is a genius.

But there are three problems with implementing his idea:

1. Taxes (the 401(k) lets money grow tax-deferred, but an account your grandparents establish might not enjoy that feature).

2. Fees (I haven't debited any in my example, which could reduce the end values).

3. Access (when the grand-child turns 18, he might squander the money on a Corvette, so we need a way to make sure the money remains untouched until retirement).

Although you're probably lamenting that your grandparents didn't set aside $5,000 for your retirement, you can do so for your children and grandchildren. You can establish a RIC-E Trust® with a minimum investment of just $5,000, and you can learn more at RicEdelman.com or by calling 855-565-7249.

the
Retirement InCome -for- **Everyone**® trust

---

[3]The return shown is hypothetical and not meant to reflect any specific investment return.

At the time, there was no way to solve these problems. But John had intrigued me, so I went to work on a solution. It took two years and lots of lawyers, but I was able to introduce the Retirement InCome — for Everyone Trust,® garnering two U.S. process patents along the way. More than 5,000 children are now beneficiaries of RIC-E Trusts.®

John isn't the only person who realized the benefits of long-term savings. Another guy figured it out too.

His name was Benjamin Franklin.

Ben was the nation's first postmaster general. He founded the University of Pennsylvania and created the first public library and the first fire department. His inventions include the Franklin stove, bifocals, the lightning rod, the odometer and daylight saving time. And he was, of course, one of the most important statesmen in our nation's history.

When he died, he implemented perhaps his greatest innovation. Franklin's will bequeathed to Boston and Philadelphia 1,000 pounds sterling each (about $4,000 at the time). His instructions: The money had to be invested for 100 years, at which time half could be spent; the other half was to remain untouched for another 100 years.

Reprinted by permission of Randy Glasbergen

GLASBERGEN

"I found the problem. We earn money 5 days a week, but we spend money 7 days a week."

Franklin died in 1790. One hundred years later, in 1890, the Boston fund was worth $400,000. Two hundred years later, in 1990, it was worth $5 million. Look at Figure 3.4. See any resemblance to our exponential growth curve?

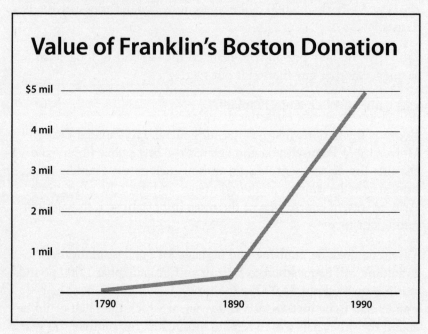

FIGURE 3.4

A 150,000 Dow

Now you understand why I've been predicting pretty regularly on my radio show that the Dow Jones Industrial Average is likely to be more than 100,000 by 2033. If I'm wrong, it will be 75,000, and if I'm *very* wrong (meaning if the Dow rises even more than I've suggested), it will be 150,000.

The basis for my prediction is simply the concept of compounding:

> » If it earns 7.2% per year, doubling every 10 years, the Dow (which is roughly 15,000 as I write this) will be 60,000 in 2033.

> » If the Dow earns 10% per year, which is its actual average annual rate of return since 1926, according to Ibbotson Associates, it will reach 100,000 in 2033.

> » If it grows 12% per year, the Dow will grow to 144,694.

Heck, if we get only 3.5% per year, the Dow will still *double* to 30,000.

People who find my prediction incomprehensible note that it took the Dow a century to reach 15,000. How can it grow another 85,000 points in one-fifth the time?

Those folks don't understand the concept of compounding.

What a Difference a Year Makes

Here's another example from *The Truth About Money*. It's my version of the children's story "Jack and Jill." My take is that Jack fell down and broke his crown — because Jill pushed him.

As a result of his head injury, Jack decided not to attend college. Instead he got a job at age 18. In his first year of employment, he contributed $5,000 to his retirement account, and he did so every year for eight years, from age 18 to age 26. We'll pretend that Jack earns 10% per year and that he leaves the money in his account until he retires at age 65.

MOTHER GOOSE AND GRIMM   MIKE PETERS

THE 401K FAIRY

MOTHER GOOSE&GRIMM ©2009 GRIMMY, INC. DISTRIBUTED BY KING FEATURES.

Thus, his first-year contribution is invested for 47 years, and it grows to about $450,000. He continues to invest $5,000 for the next seven years and then stops. By age 65, his eight contributions (which cost him a total of $40,000) have grown in value to $2.5 million.

Jack's sister, Jill, meanwhile, was so guilt-ridden by her brother's injuries that she devoted her life to medicine. She went to college, then to medical school and began her career at age 26. That's when she began contributing to her retirement account, saving the same $5,000 and earning the same 10% per year as Jack.

Thus, in the year that Jack stopped contributing to his account, Jill started. And she continued to contribute not just for eight years like Jack did but every year until she turned age 65. That means Jill contributed a total of $200,000 over 40 years.

And the total value of her account? Not $2.5 million like Jack's, but only $2.2 million.

Yes, even though she contributed five times more money than Jack and her account got the same rate of return, she ended up with about $300,000 less.

How is that possible?

You know the answer: Jack started sooner.

Indeed, the key to wealth creation is compounding, and the key to compounding is time. The earlier you start to invest, the more wealth you can attain.

Chapter 4
The Cost of *Not* Participating *Right Now* in Your Retirement Plan

If you have a retirement plan at work, you need to join it and contribute some of your pay.

If you already contribute to your plan at work, increase your contributions so that you are contributing the maximum permitted on a pretax basis.

That really is the order in which to save:

First, join your retirement plan at work. It's the easiest way to save, because money is automatically deducted from your paycheck — and you'll never miss what you never see. Also, you are probably allowed to contribute more to a plan at work than to an IRA.

Therefore, contribute to an IRA only if:

If you are already contributing the maximum and can afford to save even more, contribute to an IRA too.

And if you don't have a plan at work, then simply contribute to an IRA.

And you need to contribute *right now.*

The sooner you save, the less you need to save each month, the more wealth you will accumulate, and the sooner you can quit saving and start enjoying a life of leisure.

- **Your employer doesn't offer a retirement plan.**

- **Your employer does offer a plan but you're not allowed to participate.**

- **You are already contributing the pre-tax maximum to your plan at work and still can afford to save even more.**

If you are among those who ought to be contributing to an IRA, realize that there are several kinds, and you'll learn which one is best for you in Chapter 16.

Don't let anything stop you from saving — not even scary economic times. Consider the 2000s, for example. According to Fidelity (the nation's largest retirement plan provider), employees who had 401(k) plans in 1999 wound up 10 years later with account balances that were nearly 150% higher than when they started, even though the Dow Jones Industrial Average lost an average of nearly 1% per year during that time.

Even more astonishing: Fidelity found that the workers who continued to invest in their plans throughout the decade ending December 31, 2012, saw the size of their accounts *quadruple*. During the same period, the S&P 500 Stock Index rose only 62%.

The lesson: *You can grow your wealth no matter what the economy is doing.*

Here's another reason you need to save *right now*. Suppose you're 30 years old, and (for easy math) let's assume that for the next 35 years you contribute $5,000 a year (well below the maximum) and that you earn 8% per year. At age 65, your account will be worth $861,584.

But if you delay your participation just one year, starting instead at age 31, your account will be $68,451 less! And if your employer matches as little as 25 cents on the dollar, your total loss would be $85,563!

And if you were to contribute $1,000 a month and waited one year to start, your loss would be more than a quarter of a million dollars!

By now, you're probably kicking yourself for not having started saving sooner[4] and are feeling a chill from the cold realization that you've wasted years, perhaps decades, in your desire to create retirement assets.

You're also probably asking yourself a few questions.

Will I ever be able to retire?

If so, when?

and

How much money will I need?

You are about to receive the answers.

When Will You Be Able to Retire?

This is the most common question people ask my colleagues and me.

Our answer for most people: You will be able to retire 30 years after you begin saving.

People usually come to our financial planning firm in their 40s and 50s, saying, "I [or we]

Saving for retirement will give you peace of mind, lower your stress and improve your career. You'll be more likely to get promoted and make more money — which will boost your peace of mind and lower your stress even more!

Here's proof. In a 2012 survey of HR professionals by the Society of Human Resource Management, 83% said that money concerns were adversely affecting job performance of their company's workers. The HR executives said that, of their company's employees:

- 46% displayed stress at work;

- 26% had lower productivity;

- 24% had increased absenteeism and tardiness; and

- 26% had lower morale.

---

[4]"I wish I'd started 20 years ago!" is the most common statement people make after attending one of my seminars.

Another study, conducted by the research firm Financial Finesse, reported that "there appears to be a distinct correlation" between stress levels and personal financial management.

These two studies show that those who are in control of their personal finances enjoy less stress, better morale and greater confidence about their future. That leads to better job performance, resulting in raises, promotions and greater overall job satisfaction — a virtuous cycle.

don't seem to have saved a lot of money. Retirement by 67 seems impossible."

What these folks don't understand is the nature of exponentiality. They don't understand compounding. As a result, they look at their years of savings and the money they've accumulated, and they become despondent because their account values aren't higher.

What they need to do is look closely at my penny-a-day chart in Figure 3.3. It essentially condenses a 30-year career into four weeks. Notice how there's little apparent growth during the first three weeks, with an explosion in value during the fourth week.

Permission of Harley Schwadron.

Nobody wants to tolerate the drudgery of investing for three long weeks (75% of your career, in reality). What they want is the exciting result obtained by that fourth week (your last five to 10 years of employment).

Yep, people come to see us at age 55, saying, "I've been saving for 10, 20, 30 years. That's a lot of hard work and sacrifice, through all the ups and downs of the markets, and I don't have a lot to show for it. This doesn't seem to work. What should I do?"

Our answer, which surprises them: "Just keep doing what you're doing."

As financial planners, we know they've been growing that penny and are now approaching what we call *the knee of the curve* on an exponential growth chart. People in their 50s who are diligently saving a large amount of their income and who have been doing so for decades are about to experience increases in growth that are simply astonishing.

When can you afford to retire? Thirty years after you start saving.

Many people don't understand this, because it's not taught in school. Instead, the American education system provides people with knowledge and skills that they can use to get a career that provides a paycheck. People are thus trained only to believe that hard work, not investment, is the key to success.

Well, hard work might produce *career* success, but that alone won't produce *financial* success. The fact is that you need to work smart, not just hard. If you don't save at effective rates of return, it won't matter how much you save.

In other words, as is also explained in *The Truth About Money*, I have both good news and bad news for you. The bad news is that it is impossible for you to save enough money to meet your financial goals. The good news, though, is that you don't have to. All you have to do is invest the first penny and let that penny earn interest so that the interest can earn interest, and so on.

If you let your money do the work, you can achieve your goals. If you try to do all the work yourself, you will fail.

How Much Money Will You Need in Retirement?

Think for a moment about your annual income.

Will you need that amount of income after you retire? Or will you need more, or perhaps less?

Many people believe they will need less income in retirement. They will not have kids to support or college bills to pay. Perhaps the mortgage will be paid off, and they'll not have any more costs associated with work (such as commuting, wardrobe and lunch at work).

Don't fall for this false belief.

Although your expenses are sure to change after retirement, that doesn't mean you'll spend less. While you won't incur commuting expenses, you will find yourself with 10 hours a day of free time, and however you spend those hours, you're likely to spend money during them.

Avocations like gardening cost money. You'll have lunch with friends, go to the movies, travel and visit the grandkids. None of those activities is free. And I haven't even mentioned the cost of health care.

So instead of thinking your expenses will decline, it would be more accurate to say that your expenses will change.

Studies bear this out. McKinsey & Co. found that while 32% of workers say they'll lower their expenses in retirement, only 10% actually do. Another study, by the Employee Benefits Research

> *"So many roads.*
> *So many detours.*
> *So many choices.*
> *So many mistakes."*
>
> — **Sarah Jessica Parker,**
> as Carrie Bradshaw in *Sex and the City*

Institute, found that 55% of retirees spend as much as or more than they did when they were employed — and it's safe to say that the rest want to but don't simply because they don't have the money.

Add a Zero and Double It

If you want some idea of how much money you might want to have in your piggy bank by the time you retire, do this:

1. Imagine how much you want in annual income during retirement.

2. Add a zero to that number.

3. Now double it.

The result is the amount you need in total savings and investments when you begin retirement.

Say you want $100,000.

Add a zero to that amount. You now have the number $1,000,000. Next, double it. Your million is now $2 million.

Thus, $2 million is the total amount of savings and investments you'd need in order to generate an annual income of $100,000 per year for 30–40 years, enabling you to increase your income annually to offset the effect of inflation.

Want $250,000 in annual income? You'll need $5 million in savings and investments by the time you enter retirement.

Note that several factors could reduce the amount suggested by this quick arithmetic. For example, you might be OK accumulating less if:

» You will receive a pension or Social Security during retirement.

» You have a reasonable basis for expecting a significant inheritance.

» You don't wish or need to leave significant assets to heirs upon your death.

» You have a personal or family medical history that suggests you have a shorter life expectancy than actuarial tables suggest.

» You will work until you die (highly unlikely, due to eventual medical issues — yours or those of family members — or a change in attitudes — either yours or your employer's).

> **If you and your spouse retire at 65 and live to 85, you'll eat 43,800 meals in retirement! If each meal costs $8, you'll spend $350,400 on food.**
>
> **How much did you say you'd need to support yourself in retirement?**

Thus, my add-a-zero-and-double-it formula is fine for a book, but if you want a *real* answer that is more reflective of your personal situation, you should meet with a financial planner, who can conduct a thorough analysis of your circumstances for you.

Chapter 5
How to Save for Retirement When You Think You Can't Afford It

Your goal is to contribute *as much* of your pay to your retirement plan or IRA *as you are allowed* on a pre-tax basis.

> **Do not contribute after-tax money to a retirement plan or IRA. You're better off investing that money in a taxable account outside of your plan. The reason: taxes. Money in retirement plans is eventually taxed as ordinary income, while profits from taxable accounts pay capital gains taxes, which are usually lower.**

Yet only 9% of the nation's 60 million workers contribute the maximum, according to EBRI. And a survey by CouponCabin found that 73% of Americans age 18–34 don't invest for retirement at all.

There are lots of reasons why people don't contribute at all or don't contribute the maximum. If you're not contributing, you can state your own reason why. You don't need me to give you a list.

But I will anyway:

» You're simply procrastinating.

» You don't think you can afford to contribute.

» Your employer doesn't offer a plan or a match, or you're not eligible to participate.

» You fear you'll lose the money you contribute due to bad investments, theft (by your employer, the account custodian or administrator, or someone else) or government confiscation.

» You didn't think (until reading this book) that you needed to bother, or you thought you could wait until later to begin.

» You don't know how to participate — meaning you don't know how to sign up, how to decide how much to contribute or how to choose among the investment options offered by your plan.

» You've been following the awful advice provided by some newspaper, magazine, blog, radio and television blabbermouths on this topic.[5]

All of these reasons are absurd — including the one that you don't earn enough money. A study by the Commission of Thrift found that households earning less than $13,000 per year spend about 9% of their income on lottery tickets.

That's $100 per month *thrown away*. If those folks instead invested that money and earned 7.2% per year, they'd have $277,694 after 40 years. They'd think they'd won the lottery!

The reasons for not contributing are really nothing more than excuses. The fact is that you will either save for retirement or you won't. If you don't, you'll reach retirement age with no money — and the reasons won't matter.

If you are among those who are not saving for retirement, you'll later wish you did.

That's demonstrated by a 2012 survey of retirees by Bankers Life and Casualty. When asked to give younger people just one piece of advice, 39% said, "Save for the future."

---

[5]Except me, of course.

This answer was stated more often than "Be happy" and "Live life to the fullest" — presumably because you'll need money in order to achieve those two goals. In fact, "Save for the future" beat out every other answer, including finding work you enjoy, being responsible for your own life and continuing your education.

And when asked about the most important piece of *financial* advice they'd give, 93% said *start saving early* and 84% urged younger people to contribute to their workplace retirement plans.

Many of the respondents said they were shocked by the financial surprises they have encountered in retirement. The biggest surprise of all? Not having enough income to maintain their desired lifestyle for the remainder of their lives.

Clearly, many of these retirees are filled with regret — for not saving more during their working years.

Fortunately, you have a choice. Your future can be like theirs, filled with regret. Or your future can be like the one they wish they had.

It's your decision.

It should be obvious to you by now that failing to contribute the maximum to your retirement plan at work means you're not accumulating as much money as you will need.

But it's easy for me, sitting comfortably in my cozy den, to lambaste those who are not contributing the maximum. You're struggling to pay this month's electric bill, and I'm chastising you for not saving for a retirement that might be decades away.

You know you need to save for retirement, you do indeed want to save for retirement and you're not frivolously frittering your money away on lottery tickets. Still, you just can't figure out how to save, given the demands on your limited resources.

Read on for the solution to your dilemma.

In a perfect world, you'd be contributing the maximum to retirement plans and IRAs that the law allows. But life isn't always perfect. As much as you'd love to be setting aside big chunks of your paycheck for retirement, you might not be able to, due to all the bills you've got to pay every month.

OK, fine. I won't argue with you. I won't suggest that you cancel your cable TV subscription or take the bus instead of driving to work. Heck, you've probably already made those sacrifices. And still you're finding it impossible to save.

So here's what to do: Forget about contributing the maximum to your retirement plan at work.

Instead, just contribute 1% of your pay.

The average starting salary for college graduates in 2012, according to the National Association of Colleges and Employers, was $44,259. If you're paid twice a month, that's $1,844 per paycheck.

A 1% contribution would be $18.44.

"ONE IS FOR ME, AND ONE IS FOR MY 401(K)."

And even though you contribute $18.44, your *income* doesn't have to go down by that much. That's because your contribution lowers your *income taxes*. This means you can tell your employer to reduce the amount that gets withheld for taxes. The result: About $5 less can be withheld for taxes, meaning that your paycheck might drop by only about $13.

That's about a dollar a day.

You can afford that!

Not sure you agree? Here's an easy way you can find out. Just tell your employer to divert 1% of your pay to the retirement plan and to reduce your tax withholding accordingly.

Then wait for your next paycheck and see if you notice the cut in pay.

<u>If you do notice:</u>   Wait for your next paycheck and see if you still notice the reduction. I bet that after two or three pay periods, you won't notice anymore — meaning your contribution has become completely painless. It also means you're ready to go to the next paragraph.

<u>If you don't notice:</u>   You're not feeling any pain. The key to successful retirement (and the answer to the question *How much should I be saving for my future?*) is "Save until it hurts." If a 1% contribution hurts, stay at that level until it doesn't hurt anymore (that's the paragraph above). If it doesn't hurt (which is this paragraph), you're ready to increase your contribution by another 1%. Do that and then repeat — and keep repeating until you're saving the maximum.

> If even 1% sounds like too much money, then just make it $10.
> Then increase at $10 increments until it hurts.

Is the pain of contributing just 1% (or even ten bucks) too much for you to bear? OK, fine. I won't argue with you. Instead, just do this:

Do not contribute *any* of your current paycheck. Instead, wait for your next pay raise. When you get it, place half of that raise into the retirement plan. Your paycheck will still go up — because half of your raise will flow into it — and you'll find yourself contributing to the plan! Best of all, your contribution will be completely painless — because you'll be funding the plan with your pay raise! Since you never had that money before, there's no cut in pay — and no pain.

Then, at your next raise do the same. Eventually, thanks to future pay raises, you'll find yourself contributing the maximum to your plan!

Sure, the above strategy means that it could be years before you're contributing the maximum. That's OK. I mean, it's certainly not ideal, but it's far better than *never* contributing or *never* reaching the maximum.

And I am convinced that once you start to participate and you see your balance grow, you'll gain enthusiasm and confidence — and you'll work even harder to increase the amount of your contributions. At least that has been my experience in working with thousands of people just like you over the past 25 years.

And if you need some incentive to get you to hurry up and either start participating or start increasing your contributions, how's this? FREE MONEY!

Want some free money? It's yours for the taking. To see how to get it, keep reading.

JEFF MacNELLY'S SHOE   CHRIS CASSATT & GARY BROOKINS

SHOE: © 2002 MACNELLY. DISTRIBUTED BY KING FEATURES

Chapter 6
Free Money! Get Yours Now!

Most employers that offer retirement plans — including yours, probably — give you an incentive to contribute some of your pay to your plan: If you put some money into your plan, your employer will too!

Nearly 80% of employers add an amount equal to 3% of your pay, according to the Profit Plan Sponsor Council of America. Some require you to put in 3% of your pay to get their match, while others require that you contribute 6% to get the match.

Regardless of your employer's formula, one key fact is pertinent: Your employer is offering you free money!

To get this free money, all you have to do is divert some of your paycheck into the plan. The money you place there is still yours, so you're not losing anything or giving it away. And doing so means your employer will give you additional money!

If you contribute $100 of your pay, you get a tax deduction for your contribution, meaning it really only costs you about $75 (depending on your tax bracket). If your employer matches that $100 contribution, you now have $200 in the plan. In other words, your $75 has turned into $200 — and that's *before* your account grows in value!

This is quite possibly the greatest wealth-building opportunity you'll ever find!

And yet the Financial Industry Regulatory Authority says that only about 30% of workers are contributing enough to their plans at work to receive the full match that their employers are willing to provide.

FINRA said younger workers are the most likely to make this mistake, with 43% of employees age 20–29 failing to contribute enough to receive their employer's full match.

"Millions of workers, especially younger and lower-income workers who need it most, are leaving money — free money — on the table," FINRA said in a 2012 alert.

How can so many people be so foolish as to voluntarily miss out on free money? There can only be one answer: lack of awareness.

Watch Out! Don't Lose Your Employer's Match Accidentally

It's bad enough to see workers miss out on the free money their employers offer, but it's downright tragic when employees work hard to contribute the maximum to their plans — and then miss out on the match due to an administrative goof.

Indeed, we've seen cases where employees contribute 10% of pay into a plan that matches up to 6% of contributions — and the employee misses out on some of the match anyway. Make sure this doesn't happen to you.

Here's how the error occurs:

Some workers like to front-load their contributions in the early months of the year; they have *lots* of their pay withheld all at once instead of evenly throughout the year. That approach is understandable, because they know that the sooner you invest, the more money you usually make. They also like the idea of not having any pay withheld in December, when higher-than-usual bills occur due to the holiday season.

If a worker earns a lot of money, say $200,000 a year, he or she will bump into the rules governing contribution limits. In 2014, for example, the maximum that employees under age 50 can contribute is $17,500. If you are earning $200,000, you can't contribute a full 10% of pay — that'd be $20,000, an amount exceeding the limit. So, here's what would happen:

If your annual pay is $200,000, your monthly pay is $16,667. Contributing 10% to the plan means $1,667 is deducted from your pay each month — but only for 11 months. By the end of November you'd have contributed a total of $17,500 — the maximum allowed — and thus contributions from your paycheck would stop. You'll make no contribution in December.

But say your employer's policy is to match "50% of employee contributions, up to 6% per year." You'd expect to receive all 6% since you contributed far more than that.

But it might not work out that way. Some employers contribute 0.5% per month for 12 months — that's 6% for the year. But this requires that you contribute in each month. By completing your contributions in November, you won't get the December match.

You can lose a lot of free money this way.

To avoid this trap, find out how your employer implements its match. If your employer matches your contributions as you make them, then you're fine. But if your employer's contributions are made on a monthly basis, then you want to make sure your contributions occur evenly throughout the calendar year.[6]

> In addition to matching contributions, some employers make two other kinds of contributions. The first is called a "basic contribution." It's usually a percentage of your pay and is made whether you contribute or not.
>
> The second is a "profit-sharing contribution." It's additional money some companies voluntarily add to an employee's account based on that year's profits.

[6]Another way to avoid this trap is to review your plan's documents to see if the company offers a "true up" feature. If it does, any shortfall in the match is added to the employee's account.

Which Is Better: Getting a 50% Return on Your Money or a 100% Return?

It's a straightforward question. Which return on your money would you rather receive: 50% or 100%?

The answer seems obvious, but it's not. The problem is the question itself. It's highly misleading and even downright silly — and I wouldn't even be mentioning it, were it not for a couple of well-known radio and television "money gurus" who keep talking about it. But because they won't shut up, and because what they say is so harmful to the people listening to them, well, I have no choice but to correct their error.

Getting a 100% return on your money, in the context of their conversation, is *not* better than getting a 50% return.

Or stated another way, you'll create more wealth with a 50% return than you will with a 100% return.

Confused? You won't be in a moment.

The pundits — who aren't real financial advisors, by the way (they have no clients, counsel no individuals and manage no one's money) — offer this advice about retirement plans: "Contribute only up to the amount of your employer's match."

Let's use the example of a plan that offers a 5% match, and we'll pretend that you earn $50,000 per year. If you contribute up to the match, you'll put in $2,500 (5% of pay) and your employer will match it. You'll have a total of $5,000 in the plan — making your return 100%, even before the money gets invested.

But if you contribute 10% (or $5,000), your employer still adds only $2,500, meaning your return is just 50%.

Since 100% is better than 50%, they say, you should contribute only up to the amount of the match.

That, of course, is absurd.

The goal of investing is not to generate the highest percentage return from an arithmetic exercise but to produce the greatest amount of actual wealth.

If you follow their advice, you'll have $5,000 invested in the plan. But if you follow my advice, you'll have $7,500 invested. Guess which version will produce the greater wealth?

Remember: To create as much wealth as you can, contribute as much money as you can. Don't stop contributing merely because your employer stops matching.

> This is why it's important that you join your plan now and that you contribute at least enough so that you receive the entire match offered by your employer. Otherwise you're giving away free money![7]

Do You Need to Find a New Job?

If your employer doesn't offer matching contributions, I encourage you to find a job with an employer that does. According to Charles Schwab, 73% of employers that offer a retirement plan match employee contributions, so there's really no reason to work for an organization that doesn't.

This matters a lot. Consider this simple example: Say you contribute $5,000 per year for 40 years, earning 8% annually. You'll accumulate $1,295,283 by retirement. And if your employer adds 3% to your account yearly, the value of your account will be nearly $400,000 more!

Indeed, working at a job that doesn't provide a match could cost you hundreds of thousands of dollars. Are you sure that working at your

---

[7] And if you're one of those people who says you can't afford to participate, you're actually saying that you *must* contribute! Think about it: If you're rich, you can afford to decline the free money your employer is offering. But if you're not rich, you have no choice but to grab that money — and that means you *must* contribute to the plan!

matchless job is worth it, considering that thousands of other employers are willing to give you a match?

Too often, people think only about salary when considering a place of employment. It's important that you keep in mind *non-cash compensation* as well — not only matching contributions to a retirement plan but also paid time off, health insurance and other benefits. According to PayScale.com, noncash comp is worth up to 60% of base pay. If you're not receiving these benefits, you're giving away massive amounts of money.

You can fix that problem by choosing to work for an employer that provides a competitive salary and benefits.

*"Money isn't everything
... but it ranks right up
there with oxygen."*
— Rita Davenport

Chapter 7
Will You Participate by Accident?

Since 2006, employers have been permitted to automatically enroll employees in their retirement plans. So instead of telling your employer that you want to participate, you now must say no if you don't want to.

Thanks to the rule, 85% of employees now participate in their company 401(k) — up from 70% prior to 2006, according to Aon Hewitt and the Department of Labor. Never before has the participation rate been higher — and that means more workers than ever are saving for retirement. And studies have found that this is true for everyone — regardless of age, income, race and gender.

That's the good news. The bad news is that when a worker is auto-enrolled, the typical amount placed into the plan is only 3% of pay, according to EBRI. And the money is most often invested in a target-date fund (more on that later).

So, more people are participating than ever, and their money is getting at least some form of diversification. But according to *The Wall Street Journal*, 40% of those surveyed say they would have been saving even more had they not been auto-enrolled at the 3% level. The result: Millions of American workers are not accumulating as much money in their workplace retirement accounts as they otherwise might.

So don't allow the auto-enrollment feature to inadvertently reduce the amount of money you contribute to your retirement plan at work.

PART TWO

Fundamental Concepts You Must
Understand Before You Invest

Overview

Before you invest in your retirement plan, we need to make sure you understand the key issues so you can increase your ability to generate the most money in your plan by the time you retire.

Once you have this information, you'll be ready to begin investing the money in your retirement plan.

Chapter 8
Understanding Your Investment Options

You are solely responsible for deciding how the money in your retirement plan is invested.

Your employer will not make the decision for you. And under current rules governing workplace retirement plans, independent financial advisors are generally prohibited from giving you specific advice about that money too.

> **And if there's a stupider rule on this planet, I don't know of it.**
>
> **Our clients routinely have questions about how to invest the money in their workplace plans, and who better to ask than us? After all, we know everything about our clients — their goals, their attitude about investment risk, their income and expenses and much more — and we already give them investment advice about all their other money.**
>
> **But we can't provide specific advice about workplace retirement plans. Independent advisors can offer only general asset allocation advice; specific investment advice is prohibited. The situation is ridiculous and frustrating for everyone.**
>
> **When they make me king, this will be one of the first rules I'll change.**

While IRAs offer you virtually unlimited investment options (a topic we'll discuss further in Chapter 16), the typical workplace retirement plan offers 16 investment options from the three major asset classes:

» CASH

» LOANERSHIP

» OWNERSHIP

Here's a brief description:

Cash: This includes money market funds, a fixed account or even an account that literally holds cash (earning no interest). This category is best if you might need to withdraw or spend the money within three years, but it is sometimes (and incorrectly) used by people who are too scared to invest in the other two categories.

Loanership: With these investments, you are a lender: Buying a bond essentially means you're loaning money to the issuer of the bond. They pay you interest and you get your money back when the bond matures.

There are three primary risks of bonds: *interest rate risk* (as rates rise, bond values fall), *credit risk* (if the issuer's rating falls, so too can the value of the bond) and *default risk* (if an issuer goes broke, you might not get the interest that was promised, and you might never get your money back). Some bonds are riskier than others; short-term bonds have less interest rate risk than do long-term bonds, and issuers vary greatly in terms of their credit and default risks. This is why most retirement plans offer more than one bond fund — to give workers the opportunity to decide how much of each risk they wish to take.

Ownership: With these investments, you are an owner. When you buy stocks, real estate, gold or other assets, you profit when the price rises and you suffer losses when the price falls. Owners also sometimes receive income from their investments, such as stock dividends or rental income. It is generally viewed that owning is riskier than lending. (You don't really "own" bonds, since you are acting as a lender, not as an owner.)

Instead of letting you invest in individual stocks, bonds, real estate properties or whatnot, virtually all retirement plans offer mutual funds or annuities, which are "baskets" of those assets. A single fund might hold hundreds, even thousands, of stocks (or bonds or whatever).

By giving you multiple choices, you can choose the fund(s) you want, in any combination, taking as much or as little investment risk as desired.

This is great, assuming you understand the risks associated with each type of investment and are able to analyze each fund or annuity offered so that you can construct your own *asset allocation model* (meaning your mix of investments). But some investments that seem to be low in risk are actually high-risk choices, and making high-risk choices does not always mean you will earn high returns.

Recognizing that many (most?) workers are not skilled or experienced in investing, 70% of employers now offer target-date funds in their retirement plans, according to a study by the University of Pennsylvania's Wharton School. In fact, this is where your money will automatically be placed if you are auto-enrolled. While I'll explain more about target-date funds later (including my deep concerns about them), suffice it to say here that they are a mixture of all the other investments offered by the plan.

Chapter 9
The Importance of
Earning Effective Returns

Our look at the lily pad, the doubling penny, Jack and Jill, the sale of Manhattan, John from Manassas and Ben Franklin taught you the crucial role that compounding plays in your effort to create wealth.

Now, there's one final aspect to exponentiality that you need to learn.

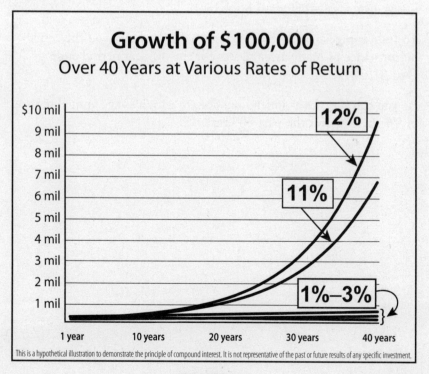

FIGURE 9.1

Look at Figure 9.1. It shows the results of investing $100,000 for 40 years. As you can see, there's virtually no "growth curve" when you earn only 1%, 2% or 3% per year. But there's a curve easily seen when you earn 11% or 12% annually.

The message embedded in Figure 9.1 should be obvious: In order for compounding to do its job, your gains must compound at an effective rate of return. Saving and investing for 40 years at 2% accomplishes little; to create true wealth, you need to compound your profits at high-single-digit or higher returns.

But be careful, because the message conveyed by Figure 9.1 is highly misleading. Of course you'd prefer to earn 12% instead of 3%! Everyone would! The problem is that Figure 9.1 isn't real. It's an illusion — crafted by me merely to demonstrate that compounding isn't effective unless you obtain higher rates of return.

If you fail to understand my point, you might ignore the real-world notion of investment risk and place all your money into products that claim to offer lofty returns. The result might be that you suffer losses instead of what you'd hoped for.

To fully appreciate this, look at Figure 9.2. It shows you the actual performance of many asset classes for the 40-year period ending Dec. 31, 2012.

As you can see, it was indeed possible to earn average annual returns of 9% to 12% over the past 40 years.

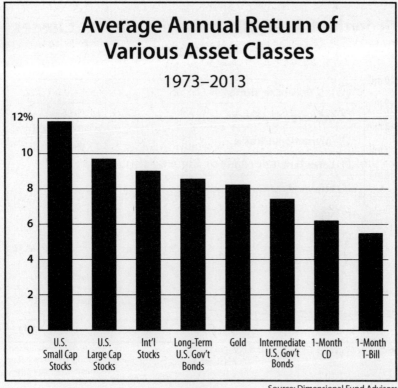

FIGURE 9.2

Source: Dimensional Fund Advisors

But wait! This chart is misleading too! Those higher-performing asset classes were very volatile during those 40 years — as demonstrated by Figure 9.3. Would you have been willing to tolerate the volatility that small cap stocks experienced? If not, you may well have lost money in that investment by selling during its sharp downturn!

Growth of $100,000 in Various Asset Classes
1973–2012

① U.S. Small Cap Stocks
② U.S. Large Cap Stocks
③ International Stocks
④ Long-Term Gov't Bonds
⑤ Intermediate Gov't Bonds
⑥ Gold
⑦ 1-Month CD
⑧ 1-Month U.S. Treasury Bills

FIGURE 9.3

Source: Dimensional Fund Advisors, National Association of Real Estate Investment Trusts, Bloomberg

Let's also keep in mind that the data in Figures 9.1, 9.2 and 9.3 do not reflect taxes or fees, even though you're likely to incur both.

Chapter 10
How Emotions Can Unravel Your Investment Strategy

You're an intelligent individual.[8]

Unfortunately, many people don't rely on their intelligence when making investment decisions. Instead, they act on their emotions. And too often, this causes them to incur massive financial losses.

Consider Tony. Listening to my radio show one weekend in late 2012, Tony heard my comments about the improving economy and stock market. That prompted him to send me this email:

> *What planet are you on? Get out in the real world. I lost my job, my house is underwater, my retirement funds are down 45% and I can't get even .02% interest on a savings account. I can't tell you how ridiculous you sound. It's like you are living in some other universe. If [blank] wins [in the upcoming presidential election], we're doomed. I sold all my investments before they become worthless and won't dare even look at another mutual fund.*

---

[8]This is proven by the fact that you're reading this book.

Tony's pain was real. But was he right?

Not at all. He was certainly suffering emotional distress, and his emotions colored his views of the economic situation. Psychologists in the field of behavioral finance could point to four types of mistakes Tony was making.

Psychological Mistake #1: Representative Bias

The first mistake is assuming that *your* observations are the *only* ones there are. Tony figures that, since he lost his job, so has everyone else. Since he owes more on his mortgage than his house is worth, everyone else must be experiencing the same thing. And since his investments have fallen 45%, all others have had similar fates.

What Tony failed to understand is that, at the time he wrote his email to me:

> » Of every 100 adult Americans, 92 still had their jobs, according to the Bureau of Labor Statistics.

> » Of the 132 million homes in America, only 10.4 million, or less than 8%, had mortgages in excess of the home's value, according to the Census Bureau and CoreLogic.

> » While Tony's investments were down, the S&P 500 Stock Index was actually up 58% for the past four years.

Indeed, as Tony demonstrated, "your" experience is not necessarily the same as "everyone's" experience. But believing it is could cause you to make bad investment decisions.

I think we'd all agree that if all Americans had lost their jobs and the equity in everyone's home had been wiped out, selling our investments might be a reasonable course of action. But that's not the case — and Tony doesn't understand that.

Psychologists would say that Tony was suffering from *small sample-size representative bias*. Tony took a small sample — his personal situation — and extrapolated it to reach a conclusion about the entire country.

Watch out for small sample-size representative bias. It could cause you to reach conclusions that are invalid, with adverse implications for your investment strategy.

Psychological Mistake #2: Recency Bias

Daily headlines and up-to-the-minute TV reports on the economy have nothing to do with your long-term financial situation.

Some people complain when their latest investment statements reflect a decline in value. But those statements show the results of only the past 30 days. I am always fascinated when people compare their current value to that of a month ago. Why not compare it to that of a year ago or 10 years ago?

There's a reason we don't. Psychologists call it *recency bias* — a natural tendency to ascribe greater weight to recent events than to longer-term results.

Tony was focusing on the loss of his investments from a short period instead of examining how his retirement account had done over the past couple of decades. By applying a recent event to the long-term future, you tend to make bad investment decisions.

So, the next time you catch yourself comparing your investment results to those of some prior date, ask yourself: To what date are you making the comparison, and is that comparison serving any useful purpose?

Thinking about it objectively makes you realize that any comparison is inherently random — and since you're investing for a retirement that is perhaps decades away, there's little value in any of these comparisons. So, avoid making them. Instead, stick with your long-term strategy.

Fidelity analyzed the 7.1 million retirement accounts it handles for the employees of thousands of companies. It discovered that only 117,000 participants (less than 2% of workers) sold all their holdings in stock mutual funds between October 2008 and March 2009 — the period of greatest volatility during the credit crisis. About half of those people hadn't reinvested as of July 1, 2011.

The accounts of those who had not returned to the stock market rose an average of 2%. But the accounts of those who maintained equities in their 401(k) plans saw their balances rise 50% on average.

Invest, and stay invested for the long term.

Psychological Mistake #3: Confirmation Bias

In an effort to determine whether the stock market is going to rise or fall (so you can decide whether to buy or sell), investors turn to economic data.

Unfortunately, there's an awful lot of data to peruse. Housing, manufacturing, automotive, energy, health care, interest rates, inflation, corporate profits and much more. To make it worse, some data tell us what has happened (*lagging indicators*), while others tell us what is happening (*coincident indicators*) vs. what will happen (*leading indicators*). Still other data are local or regional in nature vs. national or global. So it's no surprise that some data contradict other data.

Confirmation bias refers to a problem — not with the data but with the person reviewing it. You see, if you're like most people, you have an opinion, and you developed it before you reviewed the newest data. So when new information conflicts with your viewpoint, you tend to ignore or dispute it, but when you encounter information that supports your view, you use it to confirm your position.

Most of us suffer from confirmation bias. Here's an easy way to illustrate the point. Do you consider yourself to be a liberal, politically speaking? If you do, and if you ever tune in to any of the cable television news networks, you probably tune in to MSNBC. But if

On my Oct. 29, 2011, radio show, I cited the example of how one retiree's emotional response to short-term market volatility caused him to suffer a sudden and permanent loss in his retirement account.

My co-hosts and I noted that the stock market had gained 14% in October — the exact opposite of what it had done in August and September. Check out the Dow Jones Industrial Average during this period:

Aug. 1:   12,144

Sept. 30:   10,913 (a 10% drop in two months)

Oct. 28:   12,231

We noted that if you had left for a long vacation on Aug. 1, when the Dow was 12,144, and returned on Oct. 28 to see it at 12,231, you might have thought, "Gee, things sure were quiet." People who watched the market daily over that period, of course, saw wild fluctuations as the Dow fell 1,231 points and then regained 1,318 points — ending only slightly above where it had started.

The day before our show aired, a gentleman called to tell me his story. He had retired in May and transferred his 401(k) — about $300,000 — to an IRA, placing his money into stock mutual funds.

Then came August and September. The investor grew worried as prices fell, and by early October, he couldn't take it anymore. So, on Oct. 4, he sold all his investments at a loss and placed the remaining proceeds into a money market fund. By the end of October, the stock market recovered all its losses — but because he had sold at the bottom, his losses were locked in.

That's what can happen if you let emotions, sparked by current events, displace your long-term focus.

And if you think this anecdote is unusual, think again. From Jan. 1, 2007, through Dec. 31, 2012, investors withdrew $613 billion from stock mutual funds, according to the Investment Company Institute. It wasn't until 2013, after the Dow again reached a new all-time high, that net inflows to stock funds resumed.

In other words, millions of investors panicked at the sight of falling prices, sold after prices fell and then rebought what they had sold only after prices had recovered.

They bought high, sold low and then bought high again. And they wonder why they never seem to make any money in the stock market.

Avoid their mistake. Invest and stay invested, and don't let recency bias cause you harm.

you consider yourself to be politically conservative, you probably prefer Fox News. And if you regard yourself as neither, you watch … something else.

The reason is simple: Talk-show hosts and news anchors on MSNBC express views that liberals tend to support, while Fox's anchors and hosts tend to express the views of conservatives. Since we all prefer to be with people who agree with us, we tend to watch the network that agrees with our views — and since these on-air personalities say what we already believe, we regard their commentaries as confirming and reinforcing our beliefs.

Don't believe me? Go watch whichever of those networks you rarely view — and see how long it takes for you to regard their information as wrong.

Is what they're saying truly wrong, or is it merely information you choose not to believe?

This lesson is equally applicable to your investment strategy, for there are lots of pundits on financial news networks, in investor magazines, at financial seminars and, of course, pervading the Internet. If you have an opinion about the markets, you are likely to seek pundits who say what you already believe, and you might use their commentary as "proof" that you're right.

Beware of this trap, because all you might be proving are the dangers of confirmation bias.

Psychological Mistake #4: Catastrophisizing Bias

Did you notice that Tony sold his investments "before they become worthless"?

Behavioral finance psychologists call this *catastrophisizing*. This occurs when you draw an irrational conclusion from a current event. If it's been raining for several hours, a victim of this phenomenon might exclaim, "I bet it will never stop raining! There's going to be a huge flood!"

If you catch yourself growing despondent, check yourself. Are your dire predictions of a coming calamity truly realistic? You'll discover that they are not.

In times of fear, proper perspective is important. Maintain yours.

"I love money. I love everything about it. I bought some pretty good stuff. Got me a $300 pair of socks. Got a fur sink. An electric dog polisher. A gasoline-powered turtleneck sweater. And, of course, I bought some dumb stuff, too."

— **Steve Martin**

Chapter 11
How Media Hype Can Sabotage Your Retirement

Who do you think wields the most influence over the performance of the financial markets?

If you think it's one of the big Wall Street brokerage firms or giant hedge funds, guess again.

Is it the chairman of the Federal Reserve? Although Fed statements can cause a market reaction, that's not the right answer either.

What about the president, Congress or government agencies? They certainly affect the markets significantly too — but there's another entity with even more clout.

Indeed the biggest influence is the *media*. Although it has no official role, involvement or power, the media's army of reporters, broadcasters, columnists, pundits and bloggers exert a greater influence on investor behavior than does anyone or anything else.

It is hard to avoid getting swept away by the headlines of the day. In the United States today, there are approximately:

> » 13,000 newspapers (including 1,400 dailies)
>
> » 20,000 magazines
>
> » 15,000 radio stations
>
> » 1,800 full-power TV stations (and many more low-power ones)

The average household receives 119 TV channels, and news flows 24/7.

And let's not forget the Internet, which conveys news through email, web sites, blogs, pop-ups and social networks in staggering volume. There is simply no way to measure the number of news items — good and bad — that we are subjected to every day.

Sure, the Fed can change interest rates, or a brokerage firm can issue a stock projection. But that won't matter if the media buries the story — or doesn't report it at all. By contrast, if an insignificant item garners an emotion-grabbing headline on some home page, you can expect major market reaction.

The key term here is *emotion-grabbing*. Words are powerful tools, and members of the media are highly skilled at using them — for dramatic effect.

Two points are important here. First, you need to understand why they do that; and second, you need to know how to respond. I'll explain both.

Let's start by understanding that the media are engaged in a business enterprise. They must be financially successful to remain in business, and to be financially successful they must attract and retain an audience. That's you. They need your subscription fees and your eyes and ears so that they can attract advertisers.

So it all starts with you.

And the media know this. That's why they do their best to catch your attention. But boring topics delivered in a mundane manner won't grab you. Neither will good news. (Ever read about a liquor store that *wasn't* robbed?)

So what captures your attention? Bad news.

And the bigger, the better. If an event isn't newsworthy by itself, the media can make bad news seem bigger than it really is.

It's called exploitation. Another word for it is *hype* — short for *hyperbole*, which Webster's defines as *deliberate and obvious exaggeration used for effect, as in "I could eat a million of these."* Synonyms include *overstatement*, *overemphasis*, *magnification*, *inflation* and *embellishment*.

If you are exposed to the media — and who isn't? — you can't avoid hype.

The question is, how does media hype affect your thinking and actions? More specifically, how does media hype affect your investment behavior?

Your answer is crucial. If you tend to react to media hype — even subconsciously — you could make rash decisions that you may later regret.

Millions of investors fall prey to media hype every day, making financial decisions that do them harm. Read on, as I will help you separate media hype from sound investment strategy.

2011 — a Big Year for Media Hype

Let's begin with some examples of media hype. I draw your attention to Aug. 18, 2011. On that day, the Dow Jones Industrial Average fell from 11,410 to 10,990 — a drop of 420 points.

Here's how the media reported it that evening and the following morning:

One evening news anchor began his television broadcast by gushing, "Tonight the storm after the calm. Turmoil returns to the markets, and the Dow plunges more than 400 points!"

Early the next morning, the anchor of a network morning show announced "breaking news" by saying, "Markets plummeting again over those new fears about a possible recession!"

Not to be outdone, a competing morning-show anchor said, "Good morning. Fear and loathing: The Dow plunges more than 400 points over renewed fears about the economy. Are we headed toward another global recession?"

Meanwhile, a headline the following morning by one major news organization's web site stated, "Stocks get demolished!" Its lead sentence was "Wall Street got socked on Thursday."

Many investors panicked after reading or hearing these statements and sold their stocks and stock mutual funds. But those savvy enough to separate the hype from the truth didn't rush to judgment and unload their stocks while prices were low. They understood that, while 420 points is a large decline on a *point* basis, the decline was less significant on a *percentage* basis. In fact, daily market movements of 1% to 5% are quite normal — and the 420-point decline was well within that range.

The media didn't tell you that, however — maybe because a big *point* decline is news while a low *percentage* decline isn't.

Think of it another way: Is it news when the Dow falls just five points in a day? Hardly. Yet on Aug. 12, 1932, a five-point drop represented a whopping 8.4% decline in the market — the sixth largest daily percentage drop of all time — because the Dow itself stood at only 64 on that day. Five points is a very big deal when the Dow is at 64, but a 420-point drop is not so big when it's falling in 2011 from 11,410 on Aug. 17 to 10,990 on Aug. 18.

Likewise, consider Black Monday — Oct. 19, 1987 — which saw the biggest one-day percentage drop in stock market history (the Dow fell 23%). That decline was almost twice as big as the second-largest drop, which occurred when the market crashed on Oct. 28, 1929 (the Dow fell 12% that day, heralding the Great Depression). It fell another 11% the following day, Oct. 29, 1929. Declines of 23%, 12% and 11% were rightfully fearful.

But the Aug. 18, 2011, decline was a mere 4%. Yet the media used emotionally charged words like "plunge," "plummet," "demolished" and "socked" to describe the event.

Another headline on that Aug. 18 screamed, "Bloodbath for Tech Stocks!" The story said, "Tech shares plunged across the board Thursday following huge declines in global markets."

In fact, the Dow Jones U.S. Technology Index that day was down only 5% — just a tad more than the performance of the overall market — which is not surprising, given that technology stocks tend to be more volatile than does the overall market.

Knowing that, would you call a 5% decline in tech stocks a *bloodbath*?

It would be less annoying, perhaps, if the media were evenhanded. If they insist on exaggerating the negative, one would hope they'd put a positive spin on the positives. But they don't. Instead, they tend to bury positive news. Two examples:

A few days after the 420-point decline, the Dow rose 322 points. Certainly that seems worthy of mention, no? Apparently not. The lead stories that evening were the East Coast earthquake, Hurricane Irene and turmoil in Libya. But I'm not aware of a single TV newscast that reported on the Dow's turnaround.

When Fitch, one of the three major U.S. credit rating agencies, affirmed the nation's debt rating at AAA, major financial newspapers buried the story. One placed it deep inside the third section. But weeks earlier, that same newspaper had displayed the news of Standard & Poor's lowering the U.S. debt rating at the top of page 1.

It can be argued that one of the best times to invest is during a crisis. Since our nation and the rest of the world are always suffering a crisis of one kind or another, it's always a good time to invest!

As Figure 11.1 shows, markets consistently go up — whatever the crisis du jour. In fact, from 1945 through 2012, the market went up about 78% of the time — despite some very crucial events. Yet most investors dismiss this logic and instead act on emotion, which can result in investment disaster.

Was There Really a Debt Crisis in Greece?

Media hype on one particular topic triggered much of the market's volatility during 2011: Greece's difficulty in managing its debt.

Throughout that summer and fall, the media said Greece's debt "crisis" might have dire consequences for our nation. Greece might default on its debt, which, in turn, might lower the value of the euro and damage the dollar — which, in turn, might adversely impact the U.S. budget deficit, leading to higher taxes and lower stock prices.

Note that the word *might* appeared four times in the preceding paragraph. We could just as easily have said *might not*.

World Events Do Not Destroy Stocks

The S&P 500 Has Gone Down Only 15 Times Since 1945

Year	Event	S&P 500	Year	Event	S&P 500
1945	Roosevelt dies	+ 36.4%	1979	Inflation & oil prices skyrocket	+ 18.4%
1946	Labor strife	- 8.1	1980	American hostages in Iran	+ 32.4
1947	Cold War begins	+ 5.7	1981	High unemployment	- 5.0
1948	Berlin blockade	+ 5.5	1982	Worst recession in 40 years	+ 21.4
1949	Russia explodes A-bomb	+ 18.8	1983	Interest rates fluctuate	+ 22.5
1950	Korean Conflict begins	+ 31.7	1984	Deficit goes over $200 billion	+ 6.3
1951	Korean Conflict	+ 24.0	1985	Record number of S&Ls fail	+ 32.2
1952	Government seizes mills	+ 18.4	1986	Tax Reform Act 1986	+ 18.5
1953	Russia explodes H-bomb	- 1.0	1987	Stock market tumbles	+ 5.2
1954	McCarthy hearings	+ 52.6	1988	Fear of recession	+ 16.8
1955	Eisenhower falls ill	+ 31.6	1989	Invasion of Panama	+ 31.5
1956	Suez Canal crisis	+ 6.6	1990	Iraq invades Kuwait	- 3.2
1957	Russia launches *Sputnik*	- 10.8	1991	The Gulf War	+ 30.6
1958	Recession	+ 43.4	1992	Civil War in the Balkans	+ 7.7
1959	Castro seizes power	+ 12.0	1993	The Great Flood of 1993	+ 10.0
1960	Russia downs spy plane	+ 0.5	1994	Worst bond market ever	+ 1.3
1961	Berlin Wall erected	+ 26.9	1995	Oklahoma bombing	+ 37.4
1962	Cuban Missile Crisis	- 8.7	1996	Olympic Park bombing	+ 23.1
1963	Kennedy assassinated	+ 23.0	1997	Inspection crisis in Iraq	+ 33.4
1964	Golf of Tonkin	+ 16.5	1998	Asian currency collapse	+ 28.6
1965	Civil rights unrest	+ 12.5	1999	Y2K	+ 21.0
1966	Vietnam War	- 10.1	2000	Presidential election controversy	- 9.1
1967	Race riots	+ 24.0	2001	September 11 attack on America	- 11.9
1968	USS *Pueblo* seized	+ 11.1	2002	Threat of war with Iraq	- 22.1
1969	Japan is new economic power	- 8.5	2003	Invasion of Iraq	+ 28.7
1970	N. Vietnam invades Cambodia	+ 4.0	2004	Abu Ghraib prison scandal	+ 10.9
1971	Wage and price freeze	+ 14.3	2005	Hurricane Katrina	+ 4.9
1972	Record U.S. trade deficit	+ 19.0	2006	Gas prices hit record high	+ 15.8
1973	Mideast oil crisis — long gas lines	- 14.7	2007	Financial crisis begins	+ 5.5
1974	Deep recession in U.S. & Europe	- 26.5	2008	U.S. bank bailout	- 37.0
1975	Recession deepens	+ 37.2	2009	Swine flu pandemic	+ 26.5
1976	Gold prices plunge	+ 23.8	2010	Gulf oil disaster	+ 15.1
1977	Trade wars loom	- 7.2	2011	Greek debt crisis & tsunami in Japan	+ 2.1
1978	Interest rates surge	+ 6.6	2012	Fiscal cliff & Hurricane Sandy	+ 16.0

FIGURE 11.1

Media hype isn't limited to newspapers, magazines, television and radio. You'll find it ever more frequently on the Internet — and increasingly on social media sites. One example:

In December 2011, there were massive runs on two Swedish banks that do business in Latvia. More than 10,000 panicked depositors withdrew $29 million in a single day from the banks' ATMs. The reason? News that the banks were about to collapse.

The source of that "news"?

Twitter.

That's right: A 140-character message sent people racing to the two banks to withdraw their money.

The European news agency Reuters sent reporters to talk to people in the bank lines. One man said he'd heard the bank was about to go bust, and a woman said her son telephoned her to get there quickly and withdraw her funds. She didn't know why but was doing it anyway.

Executives at the two banks were left scratching their heads. There was nothing wrong at either bank.

The lesson: Be aware of the incredible power of social media and the dangers of reacting to news that you haven't verified.

As we pointed out to our clients at the time, Greece's economy is barely the size of Maryland's, and therefore its potential default was not much to worry about. And in the past 30 years, many European and Latin American countries defaulted on their debts, some repeatedly. The list includes Turkey in 1982, Mexico in 1994, Russia in 1998 and Argentina in 2001. Somehow, the world survived all of these.

Finally, in March 2012, Greece defaulted. But some bloggers and pundits said it wasn't so much a default as a "structured settlement" under which banks and other creditors wound up with much less than they were owed. And the story was buried by *The Wall Street Journal* and other major news outlets.

Why? Once investors knew that a Greek default was inevitable, securities were priced accordingly and everyone moved on. So when default occurred, there was no shock to the system and the world didn't come to an end.

Separating Hype from Reality

On the day Greece defaulted, the mainstream media began raising fears about the economies of Portugal, Italy and Spain.

Also, the media reported that growing tensions between Iran and Israel could lead to a conflict, which, in turn, might involve this country, adversely affecting our oil and gasoline supplies and prices. That hasn't happened. Or as some might say, that hasn't happened yet, and they'll wonder aloud if those headlines will ever prove true — making you scared just to be thinking about it.

We are certain that when those headlines die down, they will be replaced by others that are equally scary. After all, the media is in constant need of something to hype — and they are always on the hunt for a story that can rile investors and the markets.

So, you need to learn how to filter media hype from news that's real and meaningful. Here are three helpful ideas:

1. Recognize the 3 Types of Media

All members of the news media know how to use emotionally charged words to grab and hold their audiences. But not all media are the same. There are essentially three types, and understanding the difference between them is vital. They are:

Objective journalists. They aim to report facts and events with accuracy. They don't intentionally try to mislead, distort the truth or make errors; when they learn they've erred, they attempt to correct it.

Columnists, editorialists, opinion leaders and pundits. These folks are subjective — but they make it clear that they're giving you their opinions or viewpoints. So even if they're highly opinionated or downright biased, you are aware of it.

Charlatans. These people are the dangerous ones. They offer subjective views but in the guise of objective reporting, failing (often deliberately) to be clear that they're offering opinions or biased

If *The New York Times* published it, it must be accurate, right? After all, the *Times* is considered by many to be the nation's most reputable newspaper.

But even the newspaper itself notes that what it says ain't necessarily so. The *Times* published 3,500 corrections during 2011 — and another 3,500 online, because that is where the mistakes occurred. And the newspaper admitted that these were likely only a fraction of the errors it published.

The *Times* is frustrated by its own failings. But its imperfection is not isolated. Research into newspaper accuracy, conducted over the past 75 years, shows that news sources found an extraordinarily high rate of errors in newspaper articles. One study in 2005 found more than 60% of the articles in a group of 14 newspapers contained errors of various kinds.

Scott Maier, a co-author of that study (which did

statements and not facts. These people have an agenda, often hidden, and frequently are mere shills, offering the views of someone else or some organization.

When you read, watch or listen to the news, make a conscious decision as to which of the above categories applies. This will help you decide how to respond — or whether any response is needed at all.

2. Investigate — Look Beyond Page 1

When you read, see or hear something that makes you want to alter your investing strategy, take some time to investigate the matter further.

Don't immediately accept a negative or scary headline as truth or assume that it's correct. Instead, verify the story yourself by seeking confirmation elsewhere. And ask questions — including this one: "What did they *not* say that I'd want to know?"

3. Beware Books That Promote Fear

The daily news media aren't the only purveyors of financial fear. Authors who want to make a quick buck traffic in fear too.

They call out to you from bookstore shelves and Amazon.com's home page, promising to help protect you while the financial world comes to an end. Warning of crashes, collapses and meltdowns, they lure you in with their siren song, only to steer you into the rocks.

There are always mountains of newly published books predicting major market crashes and other economic calamities, especially in times of market volatility. At least 16 such books hit the market in just three years following the start of the 2008 credit crisis.

All were ridiculous. I've read hundreds of personal finance books and have discovered a pattern: When times are good, new books tout how you can earn huge profits. And when we experience a recession, new books predict the end of the world.

not include the *Times*), said follow-up investigation showed that only one in 10 of the news sources in the study ever reported the errors they found to the newspapers, and that less than 2% of all errors are ever corrected.

The lesson? If a news organization as heralded as *The New York Times* can't always get it right (and it tries hard every time), you can be sure that everything you read, watch and hear may contain errors. Even if media hype isn't the cause, the chance of simple human error means you must carefully examine what you read and carefully consider the content before you change your investment strategy.

Many of these make the bestseller lists for a short time, but quickly fade. The reason: The advice stinks. Their data are lacking, their premises flawed and their conclusions wrong. But the authors don't care because they're busy getting rich from the interview circuit.

Here are a few titles that came out in 2010 that you probably don't remember today:

> » *Aftershock: Protect Yourself and Profit in the Next Global Financial Meltdown*

» *Crisis Economics: A Crash Course in the Future of Finance*

» *The Dollar Meltdown: Surviving the Impending Currency Crisis with Gold, Oil, and Other Unconventional Investments*

» *How an Economy Grows and Why It Crashes*

» *Profiting from the World's Economic Crisis: Finding Investment Opportunities by Tracking Global Market Trends*

» *The Great Reflation: How Investors Can Profit from the New World of Money*

» *Freefall: America, Free Markets, and the Sinking of the World Economy*

Books like these have one purpose: to exploit your sense of greed or fear by fixating solely on recent events and telling you that this is the way it will always be. During boom times, they exploit your desire for profits, and in bad times they exploit your fear of losses.

Stay away from book hype. After all, if these authors were so busy getting rich doing whatever it was they were telling you to do, why would they bother trying to get rich by writing a book about it? The truth is that many of them don't follow their own advice — because they know they can make far more money selling advice to you than they'd earn following it themselves.

If you like to read books on financial issues, look for those (like this one) that teach you how money works rather than those that make predictions. Once you have the education and information you need, you'll be in a better position to make wise financial decisions that can truly help you reach your financial goals.

Chapter 12
Don't Mix Money and Politics

Five months before the 2012 presidential election, 90% of investors said they planned to change their investment strategy due to the election results, according to a survey by Phoenix Marketing International.

The election was cited by 39% of respondents as the "most significant" factor that would cause them to change their investments. Others said they planned to alter their strategy no matter who won, because they believed both parties would have no choice but to raise taxes and take other unpopular steps to improve the economy.

More people in the 35 to 44 age group (46%) and those over age 65 (45%) listed the presidential election as their chief motivating factor to make changes. Based on income groups, 96% of those making more than $100,000 a year said "election concerns" would lead them to change their investment strategy.

While investors correctly understand that political leaders do indeed have a huge impact on the *economy*, they fail to understand that politicians' policies tend to have a surprisingly small impact on the *financial markets*. As a result, tens of millions of investors make huge mistakes every election season by letting election results influence their investment outlook and strategy.

For starters, you need to remember that the president (*any* president) is not king. He may favor certain policies, but he cannot enact them on his own. Instead, he must win the support of Congress.

Nevertheless, you are certainly happy and probably optimistic about the future if your presidential candidate wins — and your emotional high could cause you to increase the amount of money you have in stocks or stock funds. As a result, you could expose yourself to excessive investment risk relative to your personal finance goals. And if your candidate loses, your disappointment and pessimism about the future could cause you to sell your stocks or stock funds. The result: You'd be likely to earn lower returns over the next several years.

So says a study published by the Social Science Research Network in February 2012. Written by economics professors at New Hampshire, Miami (of Ohio) and Brigham Young Universities, the study examined investment returns of investors who label themselves as either Republicans or Democrats and found that, when one party was in the White House, investors aligned with that party earned returns 2.7% higher than did investors of the other party. The result was the same during the presidencies of George H. W. Bush, Bill Clinton and George W. Bush — meaning it didn't matter whether there was a Republican or a Democrat in office. Either way, politically aligned investors allowed their political views to color their investment decisions. Optimism caused them to increase their risk, and pessimism caused them to suffer lower returns.

Want more proof? My colleagues and I examined investment returns since 1948, based on who controlled the White House, the House and the Senate. After dismissing three of the eight possible combinations as statistically immaterial (the nation never had a Democrat in the White House, Democrats controlling the House and Republicans controlling the Senate; a DRD alignment occurred only once and an RDR occurred only twice), we focused on the remaining five scenarios. Figure 12.1 shows the results.

Who's in Power? Doesn't Really Matter

Number of Years Occurred	President	House	Senate	Avg. Annual Return for the Period
4	Republican	Republican	Republican	15.1%
8	Republican	Republican	Democrat	18.5%
22	Republican	Democrat	Democrat	8.6%
20	Democrat	Democrat	Democrat	14.7%
7	Democrat	Republican	Republican	20.0%

FIGURE 12.1

As you can see, all five combinations produced terrific returns. And look closely at Figure 12.2, which shows the results when one party enjoyed a clean sweep of all three chambers.

Complete Sweep Is a Dead Heat

4	Republican	Republican	Republican	15.1%
20	Democrat	Democrat	Democrat	14.7%

FIGURE 12.2

As you can see, the returns are virtually identical. So much for fears that either party will destroy your investments.

Yes, we all need to be politically engaged. We need to encourage our elected officials to adopt policies that will benefit our nation and our communities. But that's very different from assuming that those policies will affect — either positively or negatively — your long-term investment results.

"Money is better than poverty, if only for financial reasons."

— **Woody Allen**

PART THREE

The Best Way to Handle the Money in Your Retirement Plans and IRAs

Overview

Now that you have an understanding of the fundamentals, you're ready to learn how to invest — and how not to invest — the money in your retirement plan and IRA.

This part will cover every aspect of saving for retirement, starting with the money you're depositing this month and ending with withdrawing your money in retirement — and everything in between.

So, let's begin.

Chapter 13
The Best Way to Invest the Money You're Depositing into Your Workplace Retirement Plan This Month

Every time you get a paycheck, a portion of your pay goes into the retirement plan. Most plans have a variety of investment options, ranging from low risk (money market funds) to high risk (stock funds), with lots of choices in between.

Let's see if you know the best way to invest. From the list below, you will invest your entire <u>new contribution</u> into which of the following?

a. cash (a fixed account, money market fund or the like)

b. bond funds

c. stock funds

d. the fund(s) with the highest returns over the past 10 years

e. a target-date fund (a diversified fund based on when you expect to retire)

f. your company's stock (if available)

g. an equal amount into all the choices offered by your plan

h. an appropriate mix of funds that balance your desire for growth and your tolerance for risk

i. whichever funds your co-workers or others suggest

The correct answer is ... at the bottom of page 84. No peeking until you pick an answer from the above list.[9]

Go ahead and look at the answer and then come back here. I'll wait.

...

Shocked? Well, keep reading, because people who invest correctly can amass hundreds of thousands of dollars more than people who invest incorrectly can.

Note the question I asked: What is the *best way* to invest? Clearly, the best way is to pick investments with the likelihood of generating the highest profit. And of all asset classes, the stock market has produced the highest returns in history.

Figure 13.1 shows the average annual rates of return since inception through 2012, according to Zephyr and Bloomberg.

---

[9]I don't want you to see the answer prematurely.

Average Annual Rates of Return from Inception Through 2012

Asset Class	Benchmark	Inception Date	Return
Government Bonds Short-Term	Barclays U.S. Treasury: 1–3 year	Jan. 1992	4.5%
Government Bonds Intermediate-Term	Barclays U.S. Treasury: 7–10 year	Jan. 1992	7.1%
Government Bonds Long-Term	Barclays U.S. Treasury: Long	Jan. 1974	9.7%
Corporate Bonds Short-Term	BofA Merrill Lynch 1–3 year Corp. USD Hedged	Jan. 1977	5.2%
Corporate Bonds Intermediate-Term	Barclays U.S. Intermediate Credit	Jan. 1973	8.2%
Corporate Bonds Long-Term	Barclays Long US Corp Total Return	Jan. 1974	9.0%
International Bonds	JPM Global Aggregate Bond USD	Jan. 1988	7.0%
U.S. Large Cap Value Stocks	Russell 1000 Value	Jan. 1979	12.0%
U.S. Large Cap Growth Stocks	Russell 1000 Growth	Jan. 1979	10.6%
U.S. Mid Cap Value Stocks	S&P MidCap 400 Value	July 1995	9.7%
U.S. Mid Cap Growth Stocks	S&P MidCap Growth	July 1995	13.0%
U.S. Small Cap Value Stocks	Russell 2000 Value	Jan. 1979	13.2%
U.S. Small Cap Growth Stocks	Russell 2000 Growth	Jan. 1979	9.2%
International Value Stocks	MSCI EAFE Large Value	June 1994	5.5%
International Growth Stocks	MSCI EAFE Large Growth	June 1994	3.9%
Emerging Markets Stocks	MSCI EM Emerging Markets	Jan. 1987	12.7%
Real Estate	MSCI U.S. REIT	Jan. 1995	10.9%
Natural Resources	S&P N. American Natural Resources Sector	Sept. 1996	9.1%

FIGURE 13.1

But wait, you're saying. *Stocks might have been the best-performing investment in the past, and maybe stocks will be the best-performing investment in the future, but stocks are also very risky. Just look at what happened in 2008! The Dow Jones Industrial Average fell 54% in just 18 months during that credit crisis, and I don't want to take that kind of risk or expose myself to losing that much money in such a short period.*

If this reflects a concern of yours, you are not alone.

You are also completely wrong.

It's important that you understand why, so that the experience of 2008 can help you become wealthy.

It's true that investing a large amount of cash into the stock market all at once is risky. After all, with your bad luck, you'll invest today and the stock market will crash tomorrow.

> **Hence the question all investors ask: Should I stay out and watch it go up, or should I get in and make it go down?**

But we're not talking about investing a single lump sum all at once. Instead, we're talking about investing a small amount of money from today's paycheck. In one, two or four weeks, you'll get another identical amount to invest.

And that makes all the difference. In fact, this is such an important difference that Wall Street gives it a name: dollar cost averaging. Let's explore it so you understand how it works.

The correct answer is c.

Understanding Dollar Cost Averaging

These days, just about all investors know that the best way to avoid losing all your money is to spread your money around. We call that *diversification*. If you buy one stock, you're gambling, but if you buy 500 stocks (think of the S&P 500 Stock Index), you lose less money if one loses money.

I once surveyed 5,000 ordinary Americans to find out how they became financially successful, and I discovered eight secrets they had in common. I revealed their secrets in 2000 in my book *Ordinary People, Extraordinary Wealth*.

One of the secrets was this: 96% of those still working participate in their employer's retirement plan, and of them:

- 87% contribute nothing to bond funds.

- 75% contribute nothing to fixed accounts.

- 73% contribute nothing to balanced funds.

- 90% contribute nothing to employer stock.

Where, then, are they placing their new contributions? Into U.S. and foreign stock funds. Kinda proves my point.

Taking that notion a step further, you can avoid the risk of losing money during a stock market crash by placing some of your money into bonds — and not just into a single bond but into dozens, hundreds or even thousands of bonds. Keep adding asset classes — real estate, gold, commodities, foreign securities and more — and you dramatically reduce your investment risks. The theory is that no single event will cause widespread, permanent losses.

You could be using this explanation, though, to support your contention that Answer C at the start of the chapter can't possibly be correct. *If diversification is so important, why is Ric telling me to place 100% of my contribution into stock funds?*

The reason for my advice is simple: You're not investing a lump sum all at once. Instead, you're adding money with each paycheck. In other words, making …

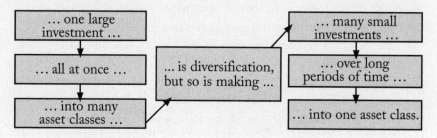

Indeed, both of the above are examples of diversification. But whereas the former is more familiar to you — it's diversification by *asset class* — the latter works too: It's diversification by *time*.

To help you understand this, consider the Dow during last decade's credit crisis. If you had invested at the high of Oct. 9, 2007, your account would have been down 54% at the low of March 9, 2009, and you wouldn't have returned to breakeven until March 5, 2013.

But if you were contributing to your retirement plan with every paycheck throughout that period, your experience would have been much better. Say you invested $1,000 with each month's paycheck (assuming you were paid once a month, placing your contribution into an investment replicating the Dow's performance). Your loss at the low of March 9, 2009, would have been about a third less than the Dow itself — and you would have recovered your losses by January 2011 — more than two years before the Dow itself recovered.

How could this have been possible? Simple: By investing every month, you would have gotten that month's price for that month's purchase of shares. As the stock market declined, each month's contribution would have purchased more shares than the prior month, as though you were buying during a sale![10]

Later, when prices rose, your shares would be worth more than before. Result: You suffered less of a loss as the stock market fell, and you enjoyed more of a profit when prices rose.

---

[10]Which is, of course, exactly what you were doing.

Figure 13.2 illustrates this. It shows what happens if you invest the same amount into an investment that falls in value and then recovers. As you can see, people who invest monthly actually get excited when prices decline — because they are *buying*, not selling! (And smart buyers know that the best time to buy is when prices are low, not high!)

Investing Regularly Can Produce Profits Even if Prices Decline

Month	Price per Share	Amt Invested	# of Shares Purchased
1	$10	$100	10.00
2	9	100	11.11
3	8	100	12.50
4	7	100	14.29
5	6	100	16.67
6	5	100	20.00
		Total: $600	84.57

This is a hypothetical illustration to demonstrate the principle of dollar cost averaging. It is not representative of the past or future results of any specific investment.

FIGURE 13.2

Decline in the price per share from the high: 50%

Value of account when the price per share is $5: $423, a loss of 30%

Value of account when the price per share returns to $10: $846, a gain of 41%

Price needed per share for your account to break even: $7.09

This is not just a theory. According to a Fidelity study of 1.1 million 401(k) plan participants, workers who stayed invested and continued contributing to the same 401(k) plan for the 10-year period ending

Dec. 31, 2012, saw the size of their accounts *quadruple* — despite considerable market volatility during that time.

And don't give the stock market too much credit for this result, because the S&P 500 rose only 62% during that period. Sure, a rising market helped, but participants benefited primarily from the fact that they kept investing when stock prices were falling. By buying cheap shares, they positioned themselves to reap the rewards when the stock market recovered.

> **The true glory of Dollar Cost Averaging is that it eliminates the need for you to be an expert market timer.**
>
> **We all know that the best time to invest is when prices are low. The problem is that we don't know when that is.**
>
> **DCA solves the dilemma. If you invest the same amount of money at the same interval — which is exactly what you do when you participate in your retirement plan at work — DCA takes care of the hard part.**
>
> **You see, if you invest $100 with this current paycheck, and stock prices are $10 per share, you'll automatically buy 10 shares.**
>
> **If prices are $5, then you'll automatically buy 20 shares.**
>
> **See? DCA says you'll buy more shares at low prices and fewer at high prices. The result: cost-effective accumulation of shares. And you get to do it without having to guess whether prices are high or low!**
>
> **Yes indeed: With DCA, everyone can be an investment genius![11]**

Are All Other Answers Incorrect?

We've devoted considerable attention to the value of Answer C. But does this mean that all the other answers are wrong?

Well, actually, yes.

---

[11] And in case you were wondering, yes, even you!

Here's why you shouldn't invest your <u>new contribution</u> in any of the other choices:

SAY NO to Cash

As covered in Chapter 9, you must earn an effective rate of return in order for compounding to perform its magic. You simply can't accomplish this if you select cash, a fixed account, a money market fund or the like.

Not only will cash fail to grow your money effectively, but it also will not even enable you to keep up with cost-of-living increases. Inflation rates are likely to be higher than the return you'll get from cash-type vehicles, which means you'll actually lose money, in real economic terms, by investing your retirement funds in this type of investment.

SAY NO to Bond Funds

These investments suffer similarly from inflation: Bonds are simply not designed to produce as high a return over long periods as stocks. The reason is simple: When you buy a stock, you become an owner of the company, and thus you share in the company's profits. But

" THE GOOD NEWS IS IT's NOT MAD COW DISEASE.
YOU'VE GOT BAD DOW DISEASE."

buying a bond makes you a lender; you get only a preset amount of interest, and the company's owners get to keep all of the profits. Naturally, the owners like this deal because they expect their profits to be far greater than the interest they have to pay you. No wonder that, from 1926 through 2012, according to Ibbotson Associates, $1 invested in stocks, as measured by the S&P 500 Stock Index, grew to $3,533. But that same dollar invested in bonds, as measured by the Long-Term Government Bond Index, grew to only $123.

SAY NO to the Fund(s) with the Highest Returns over the Past 10 Years

It's a canard. The mutual fund industry's advertisements often brag about track records of their funds, and outfits like *Morningstar* award those with the best performance "5 stars" or the like. All this deludes unsuspecting consumers into believing that the best way to invest is to buy the funds with the highest historical returns. But nothing could be further from the truth.

Mutual funds are not Hollywood films. You can watch a movie a dozen times, but its ending is always the same. Not so with mutual funds; how a fund performed in the past has nothing to do with how it will perform in the future.

Dozens of studies prove this, and I've written about many of them in my prior books. Here's one published in 2013: Researchers at Bryant University and John Carroll University found that the track records of the best mutual fund managers get worse over time rather than better.

That's right. *They get worse, not better.*

The study examined the performance records of every mutual fund manager who had been managing his or her fund for 10 years or more. That's 289 managers operating a total of 355 mutual funds. The study found that the top 50 managers produced average annual returns of 8.27% in their first three years, after which their performance fell to 5.96% annually.

In other words, above-average returns were followed by below-average returns. Thus, buying an investment after it *out*performs means you're probably buying just as it's about to *under*perform.

Don't invest in a fund merely because it has a good track record. In the world of investing, past performance does not guarantee future results.

SAY NO to a Target-Date Fund

I've hinted at my concerns about target-date funds, which are diversified funds whose holdings are based on when you expect to retire. And I'm going to continue to hint, because the real explanation comes in Chapter 15. For now, I'll just say this: Most target-date funds contain a mix of stocks, bonds and cash — and two of those three, as explained above, are not ideal for investing your new contribution.

It's possible (although highly unlikely, for reasons I'll explain in Chapter 15) that your retirement plan offers a target-date fund that doesn't invest in cash or bonds. But even if that's true, it's highly unlikely that you'll select it from among all the other target-date fund choices in your plan.

Best to just nix the idea.

And stay tuned for Chapter 15.[12]

SAY NO to Your Company's Stock

One word explains why you should never invest your retirement plan assets into shares of stock where you work.

Enron.

This widely admired corporation was ranked #7 on the Fortune 500 in 2000. A year later, it was bankrupt, its $64 billion in assets gone, its $90 stock price reduced to zero.

---

[12]Unless you've read my book *The Truth About Money*, in which case you already know what I'm about to say.

It's bad enough to lose your job. But can you imagine losing all the money in your retirement account at the same time?

That's exactly what happened to many of Enron's 21,000 employees, who had placed all their money in Enron's 401(k) plan into Enron stock.

If diversification matters, it's never truer than it is on this point: Don't put your time and your money in the same place.

Enron employees are not unique. Even today, after a decade of such debacles as Enron, WorldCom, Conseco, Global Crossing, United Airlines, US Airways, General Motors, Lehman Brothers and many more, employees still tend to place too much money into company stock.

In 2013, according to *Morningstar*, more than 70% of assets in the 401(k) of supermarket chain Publix was invested in company stock. Ditto for Sherwin-Williams. And the figure was over 50% for 19 other companies, including Colgate-Palmolive, Exxon Mobil, Dillard's, Chevron, McDonald's and Lowe's.

The problem is so extensive that the Financial Industry Regulatory Authority in 2011 issued an "Investor Alert" on the subject. "We are issuing this alert out of a concern that employees who have the opportunity to invest in company stock may be concentrating too much of their retirement savings in a single security. Of particular concern are those who have all or most of their 401(k) assets in their employer's stock. If the stock takes a beating, so does your retirement savings," FINRA wrote.

It's great to see that workers have faith in their employers. But it's one thing to have faith and quite another to gamble your financial future on it. Remember: Enron's employees had similar faith.

Do not include your company's stock in your retirement plan.

SAY NO to an Equal Amount into All the Choices Offered by Your Plan

Look, if you don't know how to invest, then just admit it, OK? Blindly checking every box on the new-account application is just silly, and your results — both in terms of how much risk you'll experience and how much you'll earn — will be completely random.

If you selected this answer, you're secretly saying that you have no idea how to invest. So instead of punting, get financial advice.

I do have to admit, however, that this choice isn't the worst choice you could have made. It's just a really bad choice — just like the next one.

SAY NO to an Appropriate Mix of Funds That Balance Your Desire for Growth and Your Tolerance for Risk

Betcha thought this was the correct answer — and it will be, just not here, just not yet. So don't be too angry with yourself.[13] The appropriate place for this answer will become clear soon.

SAY NO to Whichever Funds Your Co-workers or Others Suggest

I recall talking with a guy at a seminar who told me he just moved his money from one fund in his plan to another. I asked why and he said, "Because all the guys at work said that's what they were doing."

Psychologists call this the herd mentality bias. While they have a fancy way of explaining what this means, I'll just put it this way: People don't mind doing something stupid, provided they are not doing it alone.

If during the depths of 2008 you felt that everyone was selling their stock funds, then you probably felt it was OK to do so too — even

---

[13]Or with me.

though *buying* shares of those funds was the smarter course of action at the time.

Remember: If everyone were right, everyone would be rich. Whatever investment strategy you choose, you need a better reason than just "The guy in the cubicle next to me is doing it."

A Tax Strategy to Consider If You Own Company Stock

Although I advised you not to invest in your company's stock, you might own some shares anyway. Lots of people do. In fact, Fidelity says more than 15 million people own a combined $400 billion worth of company stock in the retirement plans it administers.

Ordinarily, if you withdraw money from your 401(k), you'll owe income taxes on the amount withdrawn. But if the money is in the form of company stock, you may enjoy lower capital gains tax rates — on part of it anyway. But to enjoy this tax benefit, you will have to move the money out of your retirement plan first.

Let's take a look to see how this works — so you can decide if the idea is worthwhile for you. (If you don't own any stock of your employer in your 401(k), this idea is of no value to you; stop reading and skip to the next section.)

This tax break refers to something called *net unrealized appreciation*. NUA is simply the difference between the price you paid for the stock (the *cost basis*) and what it's worth today. Thus, this strategy has potential value only if the company stock has appreciated significantly.

Say that, 15 years ago, you bought 100 shares of company stock at $25 a share — a total cost of $2,500. Let's say the shares are now worth $40, for a total value of $4,000. Your NUA is $1,500.

Let's further say that you leave the company (the reason doesn't matter). You have these options:

If company stock is the only asset in your 401(k)

You can do what people typically do when they leave a company: transfer the stock from your 401(k) to an IRA. The money will continue to grow tax-deferred, and when you make withdrawals in retirement you'll pay ordinary income taxes on the full amount of each withdrawal.

But instead of rolling your account to an IRA, transfer the stock to a taxable brokerage account (called an *in-kind transfer*). The amount equal to your cost basis is taxable this year (although you'll also pay a 10% penalty if you are under age 55), but the balance will be taxed at capital gains rates when you sell the shares in future years. Also, this account will not be subject to future required minimum distributions (see Chapter 21). Thus, the NUA rule can provide you with a huge tax savings.

> Note that the original NUA does **not** pass to heirs tax-free, as is usually the case with appreciated assets, although any appreciation from the original NUA does qualify for this so-called **step-up** in basis.

If you held both company stock and other investments (such as mutual funds) in your 401(k)

In this case, you can move the stock out of the retirement plan and roll over the remaining investment to an IRA. This way, your stock can enjoy NUA treatment while the rest of your money continues to grow tax-deferred inside the IRA.

If you instead cash out your entire account and roll none of it to an IRA, you'll owe ordinary taxes on everything except the company stock, plus a 10% IRS penalty if you are under age 55.[14]

To qualify for the NUA tax break, you must meet these four criteria:

1. You must distribute *all* the money in your 401(k) plan within one tax year;

2. You must distribute *all* the money in *all* "like-kind" qualified plans you have with your employer — even if only one of them contains company stock;

3. The company stock must be taken out as actual shares of stock; do not convert shares to cash first; and

4. You must have experienced at least *one* of these events:

   a) separation from the company (does not apply if you are self-employed)

   b) reached age 59½ (if the plan allows this)

   c) suffered total disability (if self-employed)

   d) death

Are the tax savings offered by NUA worth it?

To decide, you first need to know how your employer calculates the cost basis, since that determines that amount of NUA you can claim. You also must consider the difference in tax rates between your ordinary income tax rate and your capital gains tax rate (these figures vary depending on your circumstances); how much of your 401(k) balance consists of NUA; and — were it not for the NUA option — how long you would otherwise expect to leave the money in a tax-deferred account.

Keep in mind that if you don't sell the stock immediately after its distribution from the 401(k) plan, you might incur short-term gains,

---

[14]That's not a typo. The early-withdrawal penalty from 401(k) plans usually applies to people under 55; it's age 59½ for IRAs.

which will be taxed at a higher rate. Finally, taking advantage of NUA means you will miss out on the growth on the money that you use to pay taxes on the stock's gains. You'll also need cash from other sources so you can pay the taxes you'll owe — and this could be a large sum if you have a lot of stock in the plan.

Finally, remember that having a significant portion of your net worth in a single stock is the opposite of diversification. Our example of Enron, cited on page 91, should make you reconsider the idea of even buying, let alone retaining, stock in your employer.

As is so often the case, you should consult a tax or financial advisor before deciding.

Which Stock Funds to Choose

Now that you're convinced that placing all of your new contributions into stock funds is the best approach, you need to know which fund to select — and if you invest in more than one, you need to know how much to invest in each one.

My colleagues and I have been managing retirement assets for clients for more than 25 years. Our collective study of the financial markets throughout our careers has taught us that the best way to manage the money in your retirement account is to seek minimum risk *within* a maximum return strategy.

History tells us that stocks are the best-performing asset class. But history also tells us that individual stocks can become worthless at any time. Therefore, the solution is to invest your new contributions exclusively into the stock market and, in order to reduce the risk that any one stock will become worthless, invest in as many stocks as possible.[15]

---

[15]Financial geeks like us refer to this as *systematic risk* (the risk that an entire asset class might fall in value, as the entire stock market did in 2008) vs. *asystematic risk* (the risk that an individual security within an asset class might fall in value. Consider 2012: The S&P 500 Stock Index rose 13%, but Kodak filed for bankruptcy).

Putting your money into many investments is known, of course, as diversification, and the concept is particularly important when investing in a volatile asset class like stocks.[16]

But if you're not careful, you might inadvertently create a portfolio that is *redundant* rather than *diversified*.

For example, you would probably agree that owning two stocks is safer than owning just one. But if the two are Coca-Cola and Pepsi, or General Motors and Ford, or Marriott and Hyatt — well, owning any of these pairs might not produce as much safety as you intended.

By contrast, if you instead invested in Pepsi and Lockheed, or Hilton and Walmart, or IBM and Starbucks — well, now you might actually get the increased safety you're seeking while still enjoying the potential that these stocks can produce.

So it's important that you achieve true diversification and not merely create a portfolio filled with a bunch of stocks that are similar to each other.

But it's not as simple as pairing IBM with Starbucks. Although they are in different industries (known as *market sectors*, as we'll soon learn), they have other things in common. For example, both are very big companies, and both are based in the United States. So if we want to create a truly diversified portfolio — to reduce our risks while we strive for maximum return — we need to make sure we construct a portfolio that's truly filled with a genuine variety of stocks.

---

[16] After all, from the perspective of safety, would it really matter if you put your money into several bank CDs instead of into just one?

So let's take a look at the many ways in which Wall Street groups stocks together. With this information, you'll be able to see how a truly diversified portfolio gets created — and how you can do it yourself in your retirement plan.

There Are Indeed Many Types of Stocks ...

There are more than 6,000 stocks publicly traded on the New York Stock Exchange and NASDAQ. There are another 43,000 stocks traded on exchanges around the world.[17, 18]

Here are common ways all these securities get grouped together:

Style. Stocks are often described as either:

> » *Value.* These stocks are considered underpriced; the theory is that prices will rise as investors eventually discover their true value.

> » *Growth.* These stocks are expected to grow faster in price than the average stock.

Cap-weighting. "Cap" is shorthand for "capitalization," or the current value of a company.[19] Smaller companies are supposed to grow faster than bigger ones,[20] but they are also more likely to go bankrupt. Thus, some investors prefer to invest in small caps (due to the potential for higher returns) while others prefer large caps (which offer greater safety).

---

[17]There's another 27,000 *pink sheet* stocks, also known as penny stocks, that don't trade on an exchange. These are speculations, not investments, and not something you'll find offered in a retirement plan. Therefore this book ignores them — as should you. *Stay away from penny stocks and stocks listed on the pink sheets.*

[18]By the way, "pink sheet" refers to the time, long before computers, when penny stocks were listed in a book that was printed on pink sheets of paper. Municipal bond offerings were published on blue paper and corporate bonds on yellow paper. Even today there's still reference to the Beige Book (officially the "Summary of Commentary on Current Economic Conditions") published by the Federal Reserve Board. And you haven't seen a footnote to a footnote since you read *Discover the Wealth Within You*!

[19]It's determined by multiplying the share price by the number of shares outstanding.

[20]Because it's easier to turn $1 into $2 than it is to turn $10 billion into $20 billion.

<u>Sector</u>. Instead of choosing stocks based on size, some investors prefer to select them based on their industry or location. Sectors include:

» **Industrial**

- Agriculture
- Airline
- Communications
- Consumer
- Energy
- Entertainment
- Financial
- Health care
- Manufacturing
- Real estate
- Service
- Technology
- Utilities
- And many more

» **Geographic**

- U.S.
- Europe
- Far East
- Japan
- And many combinations, such as the rising economies of the BRIC nations (Brazil, Russia, India and China) or the falling ones of the PIIGS during the 2008 credit crisis (Portugal, Italy, Ireland, Greece and Spain)

Some employer plans allow workers to pick individual stocks. Reject that opportunity as too risky and stick to funds.

Sometimes employees are allowed to invest in the stock of their own employers. We already nixed that idea.

... and You'll Invest in Them Through Mutual Funds or ETFs

Rather than giving you a list of thousands of stocks to pick from, most employer-sponsored retirement plans package groups of stocks together, and you pick from these bundles. They're called mutual funds or exchange-traded funds.

Thus, you may find these types of fund choices in your plan:

Style-based funds:

> » growth fund   (it owns growth stocks)
>
> » value fund   (it owns value stocks)
>
> » blend fund   (it invests in both kinds of stocks)

Cap-weighted funds:

> » large-cap funds: S&P considers a fund to be large-cap if it invests in companies whose market caps are $4.4 billion or more.
>
> » mid-cap funds: These contain companies of $1 billion to $4.4 billion, according to S&P.
>
> » small-cap funds: These stocks, says S&P, are valued at less than $1 billion.

Sector funds:

> » a geographic region (such as Japan)
>
> » a specific industry (such as technology)
>
> » or both   (such as Japanese technology companies)

Go-anywhere funds: These invest in an eclectic mix of stocks, with no predictability and few restrictions.

Concentration vs. Diversification

It's important to note that most funds hold only some of the stocks in a given category rather than all of them. Consider the T. Rowe Price Science & Tech and Fidelity Select Technology funds. Both invest in technology stocks. But one of them has 60 stocks in its portfolio, while the other has 328.

So, which is better — a *concentrated fund* (meaning a fund that concentrates its money into just a handful of stocks) or one that's more diversified?

To help you decide, answer this question:

Which of the following would you rather receive?

A. Over long periods, the average return of the stock market

B. Over long periods, a better-than-average return

It's a silly question, of course — and that's the trap. After all, who wouldn't prefer to earn returns that are better than average?

The trap, of course, is that it's easy to get Answer A and difficult (some would say impossible) to get Answer B.

You see, to obtain Answer A, you simply buy a stock fund that replicates the S&P 500 Stock Index.[21] If you do that, your return will closely match the index.[22]

But to get the results of Answer B, you have to predict which stocks will do better than the rest. This is extremely difficult to do, and hundreds of studies have shown that the vast majority of funds that try to beat the market fail to do so.

"I never attempt to make money on the stock market. I buy on the assumption that they could close the market the next day and not reopen it for five years."

— **Warren Buffett**

---

[21]There are dozens of mutual funds that do this.
[22]Ignoring fees, which is a topic we'll cover below.

Here are two examples, one new and one old.

New: In 2012, 66% of actively managed domestic equity funds underperformed the S&P 500, according to the S&P Dow Jones SPIVA Scorecard.

Old: In August 1975, *Financial Analysts Journal* published a study revealing that actively managed funds underperformed the market in four separate time periods:

» for the ten years ending Dec. 31, 1974

» for the prior three market cycles (Sept. 30, 1962, to Dec. 31, 1974)

» for the prior two market cycles (Dec. 31, 1966, to Dec. 31, 1974)

» for the prior single market cycle (Sept. 30, 1970, to Dec. 31, 1974)

The study concluded that "costs are going up and the rewards are going down" — and studies have been saying this ever since. That's 40-plus years of studies proving that it is extremely difficult to find funds that beat the market.

And it's even harder to find a fund that *will* do well. The 2012 SPIVA Scorecard shows that, of the top 707 funds as of September 2010, only 10% of them were still top-ranked two years later. After five years, only 3% of them were still among the best. The rest faltered in their performance.

This might explain why the average tenure for fund managers is just 4.5 years, according to *Morningstar*. Turnover is high because managers who fail to beat their benchmarks get fired by their employers — like batters who can't hit a pitch.

One reason why fund managers have so much difficulty beating their benchmarks is that they are severely handicapped: Benchmark

If your fund owns 1,000 stocks, and one of those stocks becomes worthless, you still have 999 left. In other words (assuming each stock represents an equal portion of the fund),[23] one stock represents just 0.1% of your investment — meaning you still have 99.9% of your money after one stock goes broke.

But if your fund owns only 20 stocks, each one could represent 5% of your investment. That's 50 times more of your money. Obviously, in such a case, having one of 20 go broke would be far more costly than having one of 1,000 go broke. Indeed, there is "safety in numbers" — at least as far as investing is concerned.

On the other hand, a fund with just a few stocks is more likely to produce outsized returns than the fund that holds thousands. After all, you probably won't notice much change in your account value if one of 1,000 doubles, but you will if one of 20 does.

So, just as a concentrated fund might produce more losses than a diversified fund, it might produce more gains too.

[23]Which it won't. I'm just trying to explain a concept here. Work with me, people.

returns (being theoretical) don't incur expenses, while funds (operating in the real world) do.

For example, the S&P Composite 1500's annual return in 2012 was 16.17%. But only 34% of equity funds earned more than that; the others all earned less. That's because the index itself reflects the performance of 1,500 stocks; the funds themselves have to match that performance while also incurring annual expenses that, according to the Investment Company Institute, average 1.40%.

It's like running a 100-yard dash by starting 20 yards behind the starting line. No wonder funds aren't likely to beat their benchmark.

Active vs. Passive Funds

Funds that try to beat their index are called *actively managed*. They get this name because they hire fund managers who pick stocks they think will make the most money. But there's a separate group of funds that don't bother trying to win this unwinnable game. They

Quite frankly, the only people who claim that a certain concentrated fund will beat the market — and that you should therefore buy it — are the people who make a living telling you that.

An index is sometimes called a *benchmark*. The reference point is used to compare an investment's performance with its peers.

It's important, when making comparisons, that you use the right benchmark. Comparing stock returns to those of bank CDs is inappropriate because the risks are so different.

But it can be equally incorrect to make comparisons to the S&P 500 Stock Index. The S&P comprises the 500 largest stocks in the United States, so it might not be appropriate to compare its returns to those of a Japanese technology start-up.

You've heard of the S&P 500 and the Dow Jones Industrial Average (which

seek simply to replicate an index or benchmark, and they're known as *passively managed* funds.

Because these funds aren't trying to predict which stocks will do better than other stocks within a given index, they buy them all. This means they don't need to hire managers to pick stocks, and that makes them far cheaper to operate. As a result, these funds cost as little as 0.13% per year, or a tenth of the cost of the average actively managed fund.[24]

Thus, passively managed funds incur lower costs (by not having to hire a manager and by incurring less trading) and lower risk (by owning more stocks). As a result, they often produce higher returns. This is borne out by a 2012 *Morningstar* study of U.S. stock funds, which tried to figure out the best way to predict which funds would outperform all others.

Morningstar, famous for rating mutual funds, discovered that the best way to predict above-average performance is to look at fund expenses; the cheaper the fund, the better it is likely to do. In fact, the study found that the lowest-cost funds were more

---

[24]You'll read much more about fees in Chapter 17.

contains only 30 stocks), but you might not know that there are more than 20,000 indices, each of which can serve as a benchmark.

Want to know how the German aerospace industry did last year? There's an index for that, making it easy for you to analyze the performance of Lufthansa (or a fund that invests exclusively in German aerospace companies).

Ditto for Brazilian telecommunications.

And Singapore oil and gas.

And power utilities in the Republic of Srpska.

See the point?

than twice as likely to outperform the highest-cost funds. This single metric, *Morningstar* found, was actually more valuable in explaining a fund's success than the firm's own star-ratings system was.

Why would anyone bother to invest in actively managed funds?

How to Build a Stock Portfolio for Your Retirement Savings

By following our advice, you're going to place 100% of your new contributions in stock funds, and you want to own as many stocks as possible.

If none of the choices offered by your plan enables you to do this, you'll need to invest in several funds to obtain the diversification you want.

Here's a mix we commonly recommend to our clients:

TYPE OF FUND	PAYCHECK ALLOCATION
Growth Stock Fund	40%
Value Stock Fund	40%
Foreign Stock Fund	20%

Why Foreign Stock Funds?

In the period 1988–2012, the United States had the best-performing stock market in the world only once. We live in a global economy these days, and it's entirely appropriate that your investments reflect that reality.

Still, many people refuse to invest overseas. "I want to invest in American companies only," one person told me at a seminar. He's forgetting that the biggest U.S. firms generate much — and sometimes most — of their profits overseas.

> **For example, 57% of IBM's sales come from outside North America. So do 56% of Coke's sales and 68% of McDonald's.**

Foreign stocks offer legitimate profit opportunities, and diversifying with them helps lower your risks. However, foreign stocks have risks of their own, and for that reason we generally advise our clients to limit their investments in this asset class to 20% or less of their holdings. The two risks to note are:

> » *Currency risk.* You lose money when the U.S. dollar rises in value relative to another currency. So even if a foreign stock rises in price, a U.S. investor might still lose money if the dollar rises more against that nation's currency.[25]

> » *Political risk.* If a nation changes its laws or policies for its own purposes, investors could suffer.

Depending on the funds available in your plan, the previous 40-40-20 mix might be insufficient, and additional stock funds might need to be added or substituted. The goal is to invest in as broad a mix of stocks as you can, from small companies to large ones, from all over the world, representing every industrial sector you can.

---

[25] The knife cuts both ways: If the dollar moves favorably, your profits are enhanced accordingly.

Does Your Employer Offer a Roth 401(k)?

Some employers offer their workers both a 401(k) and a Roth 401(k). The plans are the same but the tax treatment is different, so you need to decide which is better for your situation.

Roth 401(k) accounts are similar to Roth IRAs, although there are a few differences. Refer to page 151 for a description of the Roth IRA, which will help you understand how the Roth 401(k) works. That information will help you decide if you should place your money at work into a 401(k) or a Roth 401(k).

Does Your Employer Offer a 403(b) or 457 Plan?

If you work for a nonprofit organization (such as a hospital or school) or municipal government, your plan might be based on Section 403(b) or 457 of the tax code. These plans are similar to 401(k) plans. Let's take a look.

403(b) vs. 403(b)(7)

The 403(b) plan is sometimes called a *tax-sheltered annuity* because participants were once allowed to invest in annuity products only. But in 1974, Section 403(b) was amended to give participants the ability to invest in mutual funds.

So, depending on your employer, 403(b) and 403(b)(7) plans allow you to invest in annuities, mutual funds or both. Most employers let you choose from a variety of vendors offering both types of products.

Which should you choose — annuities or mutual funds? To understand the answer, let's first make sure you know the differences.

An *annuity* is simply a stream of income, like that provided by Social Security or a pension. Annuity products consist of two steps. In the first step, your money earns a certain rate of return each year. In the second step, which is optional and presumably occurs in retirement, you convert your account balance into that monthly stream of income. (This is called *annuitization*.) You can choose to receive income for a fixed number of years or for the rest of your life.

This requires a balancing act: The longer you want to receive income, the less you'll get each month. So, which is more important to you: amount or time?

For example, say you're 65 years old and have accumulated $500,000 in your annuity. If you annuitize when interest rates are 2%, you can receive $4,600 per month for 10 years (after which the payments permanently stop), or you can receive $2,800 per month for as long as you live.

Which would you choose?

It's an important decision — made all the more dicey by the fact that your decision is irrevocable. Once payments begin, you cannot change your mind. Ever.

Like so many other personal finance issues, this decision needs to be made with the help of a financial advisor.

Every state has a guarantee fund to protect owners of insurance policies, should an insurance company fail and go into liquidation. State regulators will try to transfer policies to other insurance companies; if that effort doesn't succeed, the policy will be administered by the state guarantee fund. And there's no assurance the fund will provide you with 100% of what the failed insurance company had promised you. Coverage limitations are set by each state; New York's, for example, is $500,000.

Therefore, never believe any insurance agent or financial

Before you annuitize your annuity product, your money will be invested — perhaps for decades. But where? It depends on what kind of annuity product you choose. There are two kinds:

A *fixed annuity* offers a fixed rate of interest, operating much like a certificate of deposit. But instead of being offered by banks, fixed annuities are sold by insurance companies. That means your money is only as safe as the insurance company that issues it; if the company goes broke, your money could be lost.

advisor who claims that these state-run programs provide you with "guarantees" of any kind.

If you have any questions, contact your state insurance regulator.

Variable annuities often offer to provide you with two guarantees to ease your worry that the subaccounts might fall in value; to get these guarantees (called *riders*), you must pay additional annual fees of as much as 3%. While each insurance company has its own version of these benefits, here are a couple of general descriptions:

A *living benefit*. Here, the insurance company promises to return as much as 100% of your principal even if the subaccount drops in value, provided you make no withdrawals, often for at least 10 years. The living benefit, if paid, doesn't return your money to you all at once. Instead, you receive your money back over time — usually over your lifetime

A *variable annuity* does not offer a fixed rate of interest. Instead, you select from a variety of *subaccounts* — pools that are managed by mutual fund companies. If you choose a stock subaccount, for example, your money will rise or fall along with the value of the stocks held in the subaccount. Financial strength of the insurance company is not as important with variable annuities, because your money is invested in the subaccounts and not in the insurance company itself.

But don't take this to mean that your assets are necessarily safe in a variable annuity. After all, "safe" is a relative term. You can indeed lose money in a variable annuity if your subaccount loses money. Hence the name: Your return will vary with the performance of the financial markets.

From this description, it appears that the choices are innocuous enough. You could select:

A. a fixed annuity, which offers a predictable (but low) return;

B. a variable annuity, which offers the potential for higher returns (but might lose money); or

C. mutual funds (which have similar return characteristics of the variable annuity's subaccounts).

Which is the correct answer?

Without question, the correct answer is C. Our prior exercise reveals half the reason: Mutual funds give you the ability to create a highly diversified portfolio.

Sure, you're saying, you get that. But all that answer does is eliminate answer A — the fixed annuity, because its returns over many decades are simply too low. But if diversification is our goal, doesn't Answer B (variable annuity) work just as well as Answer C (mutual funds)?

From a diversification perspective, yes. But you've hit on only half the story. The other half matters just as much: fees.

A variable annuity is nothing more than a bunch of mutual funds with an insurance wrapper. Not only are you paying for the funds, but you're paying for the wrapper too. This explains why annuities feature far higher fees than mutual funds do. In fact, according to *Money* magazine and the Investment Company Institute, the average annual cost of variable annuities (including riders) is 3.61%, vs. 1.40% for mutual funds.

There is a solution to the annuity-cost problem: Some insurance

and often for a minimum of 14 years.

A *death benefit*. If you die, the insurer will give your beneficiaries the amount you invested (minus any withdrawals) or the value of the account as of your date of death, whichever is higher. This benefit doesn't "benefit" you, since you must die to receive it, but it can be of value to your spouse or children.

Even if you (or your heirs) eventually benefit from one of these guarantees or the other, the actual value of the benefits is reduced by the amount you paid for them. Say you invest $100,000 and pay an extra 1.5% per year for the living benefit. If 15 years later your account is $90,000 and you decide to execute your living benefit, the $10,000 you lost will be restored. But you'll have likely paid more than $20,000 for that right — and it could take you another 14 years to get all your money back. Doesn't strike me as much value to this benefit!

companies offer group annuities specifically designed for use in the workplace. Group annuities are often much less expensive than the individual annuity products sold by insurance agents and financial advisors to consumers.

> **But what about the living benefits and death benefits offered by annuities? You can't get those with mutual funds.**
>
> True, but that's OK. Why? Because those benefits offer little value. Remember that insurance companies charge you an extra fee for these benefits — typically 1.1% per year for the living benefit, for example.
>
> But all they're really doing is promising you that you'll be protected from something that is highly unlikely to happen anyway.
>
> Confused? Consider this: The living and death benefits pay off only if the stock market is lower in the future than it is now. But in U.S. history, the stock market has never ended any 15-year period lower than where it began. In other words, you're paying for a benefit you don't need!
>
> Even worse, many insurance companies are reneging on their promises, having discovered that they can't afford to honor them. In 2013, Hartford sent notices to customers requiring them to move at least 40% of their money into bond funds — or lose their guarantee (for which they might have paid 10% of their account value or more). Transamerica had already done the same thing to many of its policyholders, according to *The Wall Street Journal*. So had AXA, which asked policyholders to accept a onetime lump-sum payment so the insurer could cancel its guarantees. Prudential has canceled some of its promises too and made other changes to its contracts, such as restricting investment options and, like Hartford, forcing investors to change their investments. Meanwhile, other insurance companies, including ING and MetLife, have written off nearly $3 billion, and a report from Moody's says the insurance industry will lose billions of dollars more as it attempts to resolve this issue.
>
> Small wonder that many — including Hartford — have stopped selling variable annuities altogether.

Your goal is to get the opportunity to diversify at low cost. So do yourself a favor: Select mutual funds or group annuities for your 403(b) plan — not individual annuity products.

The 457 Plan

A 457 plan is offered mostly to state and local government workers, including police officers, firefighters and other civil servants. Employees of some state universities and school districts also can contribute to a 457 plan in addition to a 401(k) or 403(b) plan. (Some actually have access to all three — way cool!)

Depending on your employer, your 457 plan might offer you the options of fixed and variable annuities, mutual funds and/or bank instruments. Therefore, the points I made above about 403(b) investment options apply here as well.

And the 457 plan has higher contribution limits for those nearing retirement: If you are within three years of normal retirement age, you may qualify to contribute *twice* as much as younger workers.

No matter which kind of retirement plan your employer offers, if the plan is a good one, you'll have ample choices available that will enable you to construct a diversified portfolio. If your plan has limited choices, do the best you can and ask your employer to offer additional choices. Employers want their retirement plans to be popular, and many are willing to make changes suggested by employees.

Chapter 14
The Best Way to Invest Your Employer's Contributions

In most employer plans, your employer's matching contribution will be invested the same way as you invest your own contributions. That's fine.

So even if your plan lets you invest your employer's match differently, don't! Here's why.

Just as you're investing money with every paycheck, you're also investing your employer's matching contribution. So if you're going to invest your money entirely into stock funds, it makes sense to invest your employer's contributions that way too.

In fact, if you're hesitating to invest your new contributions entirely in stock funds, the existence of your employer's match should make your concerns go away.

Don't believe me? Consider this:

Say you contribute $100, and your employer matches a quarter of that, or $25. The first thing that happens is that you get a tax deduction on your contribution, meaning your $100 investment costs you only about $70 (assuming a 30% combined federal/state income tax rate).

Add the $25 from the match and you find that you have $125 invested. In other words, your investment could fall 44% in value and you'd still have all of your original investment! Even a 44% loss wouldn't cost you any money!

On the other hand, if the investment doubles in value (meaning a 100% gain), which, over time, it can eventually be expected to do,[26] the actual profit on the money you personally invested would be 330%!

Indeed, the combination of a tax deduction *and* an employer match gives you the best of both worlds: the reduced risk of losing money and the increased likelihood of generating profits.

That, in turn, means you can have a very high degree of confidence when investing all of your new contributions plus your employer's matching contribution exclusively into stock funds.

"The trouble with retirement is that you never get a day off."

— **Abe Lemons**

---

[26]Since 1926, the S&P 500 has doubled in value approximately every seven years. There's no reason to think it won't continue to do that for the next 85+ years.

Chapter 15
The Best Way to Invest the Money That's Already in the Plan

In Chapter 13, I offered you the question below about investing <u>new contributions</u>. Let's revisit the question, this time shifting to the <u>existing (or old) balance</u> of your account, meaning the money that's already there.

The money <u>already in your account</u> (the existing, or old, balance) should be invested in:

    a.   cash (a fixed account, money market fund or the like)

    b.   bond funds

    c.   stock funds

    d.   the fund(s) with the highest returns over the past 10 years

    e.   a target-date fund (a diversified fund based on when you expect to retire)

    f.   your company's stock (if available)

    g.   an equal amount into all the choices offered by your plan

    h.   an appropriate mix of funds that balance your desire for growth and your tolerance for risk

    i.   whichever funds your co-workers or others suggest

As I hinted in Chapter 13, the correct response in this scenario is H.

There is a simple reason for this: After receiving many paychecks over a period of time, you'll have made many investments into stock funds within your retirement plan. At some point, you'll notice that you have accumulated a significant amount of money in the plan.

Is it wise to keep 100% of that money exclusively in stock funds?

Sure! Go ahead and keep your money entirely invested in stock funds, *provided*:

> » you understand the risks of doing so; and

> » you plan to leave the money invested in stock funds for *at least* five years, preferably much longer.

These two criteria are crucial to your decision to leave the money invested in stock funds.

> **My concern is that you might have gotten spoiled by the success of Dollar Cost Averaging into stock funds, coupled with the tax deduction and employer match you've enjoyed. Your account might be worth many times more than the amount you've been contributing.**
>
> **Keep in mind that the tax deduction and employer match are both onetime benefits. Over time, their value erodes — and as your account balance increases, so does the amount of money that you can lose.**

If you ignore the risks of the stock market, you risk the fate of the gentleman I described in *The Truth About Money*. He had all the money in his retirement plan invested in stock funds throughout his entire career. He planned to retire in 2010 — which means he was two years from retirement when the 2008 recession hit. He lost his job at the same time his account fell 50% in value. Suddenly he wasn't going to retire in two years anymore.

Don't put yourself in a position where that could happen to you.

Leaving your money entirely in stock funds is fine if you are confident you won't need to withdraw any of it for many years because, as the 2000s showed us, the stock market can drop dramatically in a short period and then take years to return to prior levels. This doesn't sound like much of a problem if you're in your 30s, 40s or early 50s — but the story is very different if you're currently in your late 50s or 60s.

Even if you have the time to wait for the market to recover, you might not have the stomach. That is one reason why my colleagues and I say that, while you should continue to place 100% of new contributions into stock funds, *the best way to manage your existing account balance is to reallocate it into an appropriate mix of funds that blends your desire for growth with your tolerance for risk.*

No Catbelling Here

My favorite of Aesop's fables is the story of the mice who gather to find a way to avoid getting eaten by the cat. A young mouse suggests putting a bell around the cat's neck so the mice could hear him coming and run to safety. The group celebrates the wonderful solution until a wise old mouse asks a question:

Who is going to bell the cat?

The moral of the story is Aesop's famous line: *Easier said than done.*

And if you're a wise old mouse, you have two questions:

When, exactly, am I supposed to shift out of stocks? And how do I create "an appropriate mix of funds"?

Great questions. And lest I be accused of what I call "catbelling,"[27] allow me to answer both of them for you.

First, the *When*

The money in your plan is going initially into stock funds. As explained in Chapter 13, this will enable you to take advantage of Dollar Cost Averaging.

---

[27]I've always wanted to coin a phrase. Did I succeed here?

But DCA needs time to work. Markets tend to go through cycles — periods of rising prices followed by periods of falling prices, followed again by rising prices and so on, as shown in Figure 15.1 — and you need to invest through a complete cycle to maximize the value offered by DCA.

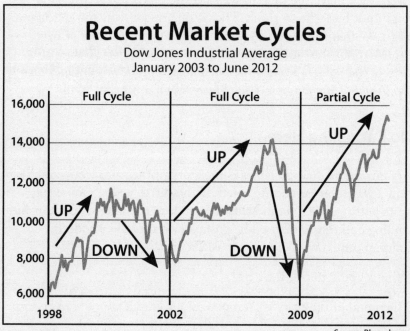

FIGURE 15.1

Since 1929, the typical market cycle has lasted six and a half years, according to Standard and Poor's, and cycles have been completed in as little as 34 months and as long as 12 years.

Therefore, we recommend that you invest 100% of your new contributions into stock funds (as explained in Chapter 13) and that you leave all that money invested in those funds until …

Until when?

That's the key question, and after devoting countless hours developing algorithms and strategies around this question, my colleagues and I at Edelman Financial Services have determined that, without a doubt, the best answer to the question "When should you diversify your account away from 100% in stocks?", is …

"It depends."

I'm sorry, but it does. It depends on how much money you have in the account, how much you have elsewhere and how that outside money is invested, how much you are currently contributing (both to the plan and to outside accounts), how long it will be before you begin to make withdrawals from the account, how much those withdrawals will need to be (relative to the amounts both in the account and in outside accounts) and — of course — how much volatility you are willing to tolerate from your investments. And let's remember to include in this evaluation all of your spouse/partner's accounts.

Thus, depending on your situation, you might need to continue investing strictly in stock funds for many years. Or you might realize that your need to shift out of stock funds is overdue!

Now or later, you will need to shift from stocks to other asset classes. So read on.

Second, the *How*

When the time comes for you to diversify beyond stock funds in your retirement plan, you'll find yourself facing the very conundrum vexing all investors: Which asset classes should you choose, and in what combination?

I don't know what investment choices you have in your plan, so I can't tell you specifically which choices to select. But I can tell you something almost as helpful: *Your goal is to own it all — all the time.*

In other words, you want to own every asset class that your plan offers. There are 20 or so major asset classes and market sectors, and the ideal retirement plan gives you access to all of them. But whether your plan offers you all 20 or just five (as in the case of the federal Thrift Savings Plan), invest in all that you can.

There's a simple reason for this. Just as no one can tell you *when* a given investment is going to rise or fall (because no one can predict the future), no one can tell you *which* investment is about to perform better than other investments.

Therefore, the best way to manage the money in your retirement plan is to invest your money in a highly diversified manner, holding as many asset classes and market sectors as possible at all times. This way, you'll enjoy the profits produced by that asset class or market sector whenever they happen to arrive.

If you follow my radio and television shows or read my books, you know I often use the words *diversification*, *diversify* and *diversified*. That's because, in the world of investing, they matter more than just about anything else.

The Worst System of All — Except for All the Others

Winston Churchill is widely credited with saying that democracy is the worst form of government, except for all the others that have been tried.

I believe that something similar can be said about diversification: It is the worst investment management strategy there is, except for all the others that have been tried.

You see, we all want the same thing from our investments: high returns, no risk, no fees, no taxes and ready access to our money whenever we want it.

Of course, no such investment exists.

Instead, investments vary in their amounts and types of return, risk, fees, taxes and liquidity. Some investments are best in one category or another, but no investment is ideal in every category. This forces investors to decide which category is of greatest concern to them and then to choose a strategy that maximizes the potential for winning in that category.

If all you care about is liquidity, you'll keep all your money in hundred-dollar bills under your mattress. It certainly will always be available to you that way![28] But money earning no interest will lose its value over time due to inflation. So while taxes and fees are avoided, so is growth.

If you want to avoid taxes, you might invest in tax-free municipal bonds. But bonds pay relatively low interest rates, and they can lose value if interest rates rise or if the issuer's credit rating is downgraded (see Chapter 8).

If you want to avoid fees, well, so does everyone. But there's no such thing as "free" in the financial services industry.[29]

If you want to avoid risk, you can find lots of investments that claim to provide this feature. The trade-off is that low-risk investments provide low returns — perhaps so low that you won't accumulate enough money to support yourself in retirement.

If you want high returns, you have to buy investments that promise to provide them. Unfortunately, these investments often lose money instead — sometimes lots of money.

Yes, picking investments can be quite frustrating. But if it seems complicated, I have good news for you: It's not complicated at all.

You see, you can either try to focus on one category — return, risk, fees, taxes or liquidity — and ignore all the others, or you can use an approach that combines them all. That approach is called *diversification*.

The concept was invented in 1952 by a graduate student at the University of Chicago named Harry Markowitz. His doctoral thesis suggested that you could lower your portfolio risks and increase your

---

[28]Even bank accounts won't do for people who insist they need constant liquidity — because banks aren't open 24 hours a day, and ATMs limit withdrawal capability.

[29]Please. Anyone who says you don't incur costs when buying or owning investments is a fool or (if the person is a financial-product salesman) a liar. Don't be naïve. The financial services industry is the most profitable in the world. Guess why?

returns simultaneously by owning a variety of investments at the same time. His radical idea was dismissed at the time — everyone in the 1940s and 1950s knew that investment success was achieved by picking a few good stocks, not by owning lots of them — but Markowitz was vindicated in 1990, when he received the Nobel Prize in Economics for what is now called Modern Portfolio Theory. Today, MPT is the basis for virtually all professional money management the world over.

The basic concept of MPT is simple: A portfolio that holds two investments is safer than a portfolio that holds only one. And if the two are very different — say, a stock and a bond, instead of two stocks — you get the safety of bonds and the return potential of stocks.

Modern Portfolio Theory turned Wall Street upside down. Instead of making money by trying to pick the best stocks, Markowitz showed that the key to investment success is in deciding how much of your portfolio to put into stocks in the first place — and by extension, how much to put into bonds, government securities, foreign investments, oil and gas, gold and other precious metals, commodities, and so on. The *asset allocation* decision became the most important decision — not what stock you buy or when you buy it.

Ric and Harry Markowitz outside Harry's office in San Diego, March 2008.

One reason why Harry's thesis was ignored in 1952 is that it was virtually impossible to implement it; few investors had the financial wherewithal to buy thousands of investments separately. But by the 1980s mutual funds were commonplace. A single fund can own hundreds, even thousands, of securities, and any investor can open an account with as little as $100 — giving almost every American the ability to create instant diversification.

Three Problems with Diversification

However, there are a few problems with diversification, and these sometimes cause people to reject the idea. Let's look at them.

Problem #1: Diversification Is Boring

Even if you earn 8% per year — which few manage to do year in and year out — you'd be earning 0.67% per month. That's 0.02% per day. In other words, $100,000 would earn about $20 a day. There's simply nothing exciting about that. If you love the thrill of watching your investments gyrate wildly, diversification will not satisfy your urge.

Problem #2: Diversification Trumps Personal Beliefs

Another reason why people veer from diversifying properly is that they buy investments that reflect their opinions or beliefs. For example, they may refuse to invest in companies that are involved with tobacco, firearms or nuclear energy. Indeed, the best-performing mutual fund in the second quarter of 2010, according to *The Wall Street Journal*, was Virtus (Latin for "virtue"), a socially responsible fund. It earned 8.4% in that three-month period. But the second-best fund was the Vice Fund (previously called the Sin Fund), which invests only in gambling, tobacco and alcohol stocks. And over the previous five years, Vice beat Virtue 3.4% to 3.3%. Instead of choosing between vicious and virtuous stocks, smart investors own both kinds.

Problem #3: Diversification Sounds Risky

A final reason why people dismiss diversification is because they erroneously think diversification is too risky for them. Put money into stocks, real estate, gold and commodities?

That sounds risky to the uninitiated. And that's a shame, because folks who think diversification is risky instead invest only in what they perceive to be "safe" investments. For example, annual investment income earned by retirees declined 34% from 2007 through 2012, according to the Department of Labor. That's because these folks invested only in bonds and bank CDs — and those devices paid low rates that kept getting lower. The result, DOL said, forced these people to withdraw principal to support themselves after their investments failed to generate sufficient interest income. Ironically, these retirees kept their money "safe" in CDs, money market funds and U.S. Treasuries — only to discover, too late, that lack of diversification caused them to suffer the very losses they wanted to avoid.

Being diversified offers no guarantees, of course. When a gentleman called my radio show to ask what return I could promise if he handed us $1 million to manage for him, I replied, "Over long periods, our goal is to provide you with a return that's comparable to the results produced by the global financial markets, minus our fee."

Can you rely on *Morningstar*'s ratings?

Uh, no.

In fact, *Morningstar* has acknowledged that its star ratings are not predictive. Rather, its rankings merely reflect past performance (which the organization defines as the past 36 months).

That's why, in 2012, *Morningstar* introduced a new system, one that it says is designed to predict a fund's performance over the next five years. The new system labels funds as gold, silver and bronze and as neutral or negative. We examined how many five-star funds won the gold medal when *Morningstar* introduced its new system and found that only 38% of them did! That means that *Morningstar* analysts believe that 62% of its five-star funds wouldn't be among the best performers in the coming five years.

If *Morningstar* doesn't believe its star ratings have any predictive value, you shouldn't either.

You don't need to achieve returns any better than that, and you shouldn't try to.

Do you really need to buy "everything"?

You might be wondering why you need to buy some of "everything" when you can instead just buy the best. Every personal finance magazine touts "hot" funds with "guaranteed" high returns in every issue. Why not just invest in those?

The reason is simple: Although it's easy to identify investments that have done well in the past three-, six- or 12-month period (or, for that matter, for the past one-, three-, five- or 10-year period), all studies done on the subject have shown that such investments never sustain their performance. As you've often heard, past performance does not guarantee future results.

Funds can't replicate their past performance because the environment keeps changing. Interest rates, inflation rates, corporate profits, employment levels, political and social issues and many other factors affect the economy, and as these factors change, so does investment performance.

"YOUR PORTFOLIO NEEDS A THEME SONG. HOW ABOUT 'IS THAT ALL THERE IS?'"

Permission of Harley Schwadron.

Neophyte investors don't understand this, so when they're unhappy with the return they've recently gotten from an investment, they tend to sell it and switch to some other investment — invariably one that has done well recently. After this new investment fails to maintain its prior good performance, the neophyte gets agitated again and sells that one too. Eventually, he gives up in frustration.

> I'm not just storytelling; this really happens — and it happens a lot. Dalbar's study of investor behavior shows that over the past 20 years, investors in U.S. stock mutual funds earned an average annual return of 4.25%, while the funds themselves returned 8.21% per year.
>
> How could the investors earn less than the funds they were in investing in? Easy: Data about fund performance assumes you invest on Jan. 1 and sell on Dec. 31. But investors don't do that; instead, they buy and sell at different times during the year — and they invariably buy when the funds' share prices are higher and sell when the prices are lower — often switching out of one fund that's doing poorly at the moment and into another that's been doing better recently. The result: They buy high and sell low — and they persist in this behavior.
>
> Dalbar's study clearly shows that, had investors merely kept their investments for years instead of shorter periods, they would have done twice as well as they actually did.

So, you need to buy everything for one reason: As soon as you decide *not* to buy everything, you have to decide what *not* to buy. And that places you in the position of having to make the right decisions at the right time: what to buy, what to sell — and when.

Nobody has ever demonstrated an ability to consistently make both decisions correctly. Oh, sure, you'll often hear that so-and-so made the right call at the right time, but no one has ever made a *series* of right calls. It can't be done, which is why it hasn't been done and never will be done.

Therefore, to protect yourself from making a mistake, own it all — all the time.

How to Own It All — All the Time

As you might imagine, telling you how to build a diversified portfolio featuring an array of asset classes and market sectors depends on two sets of factors: your situation and the choices offered by your retirement plan. Unfortunately, I can't address either of these issues in a book.

After all, your age, income and expenses, assets and debts, family situation, health, goals and risk tolerance all help financial planners like us determine the proper asset allocation for you. And the choices offered by your plan matter a lot too. (For example, if your plan doesn't offer a real estate fund, there's no point in telling you to invest in one.)

The Helpful Resources You Need

Since this book can't tell you how to construct the asset allocation that's best for you, let me tell you how to get the help and advice you need. Here are three resources for you:

Helpful Resource #1: Your Employer

Many employers (or the plan administrators they've hired) will provide you with education and information about your plan. Some will also provide specific advice to help you decide which funds to select from the choices available. *Your employer or plan administrator is the first place to turn to for advice.*

Helpful Resource #2: Edelman Online

If your employer or plan administrator doesn't (or can't) provide the help you need, turn to Edelman Online, where my Guide to Portfolio Selection will help you determine which portfolio is right for you.

The GPS was introduced in my book *The Lies About Money*, where 43 model portfolios were offered. Since then, we've updated and expanded the portfolios. Now you can access the GPS via Edelman Online. Just visit RicEdelman.com, and in less than two minutes, after answering a few questions, you'll receive our recommendation for your asset allocation.

Once you have your model allocation, you can easily apply it to your retirement plan, matching the choices in your plan against the asset classes and market sectors recommended for you by Edelman Online.

Helpful Resource #3: The Advisors of Edelman Financial Services

If you prefer not to go online but still want guidance, just call us or send us an email. My colleagues and I have helped thousands of people decide how to invest the money in their retirement accounts, and we can do the same for you.

After You Build It, You Must Occasionally Rebalance It

Let's say you've created a highly diversified investment portfolio, and you're committed to keeping your money in it for the long term.

You're not finished yet. There's one more step to complete, and it's vital (but often ignored): You must *maintain* the asset allocation model you've constructed. If you ignore your portfolio, it will soon become something different.

The reason: *portfolio drift.*

Over time, different investments perform differently. One asset class might rise faster than others, and some might even fall in value. This causes your portfolio's composition to morph, or drift, into something different than you had designed. If you don't make occasional adjustments, your portfolio over time will change into something very different — and possibly very dangerous, exposing you to higher risks and lower returns than you intended or desire.

Imagine your portfolio has only two assets, and you invest half your money into each, 50/50. As one rises faster than the other, your portfolio will drift … first to 60/40, then to 70/30, then to 80/20 and so on. Eventually, you no longer will be diversified.

You fix this problem by adjusting your portfolio, to compensate for the drift. This adjustment is called *rebalancing*. You do this by selling part of one asset and using the proceeds to buy the other.

The funny thing is, you don't sell what you're inclined to sell, and you don't buy what you're inclined to buy.

> *"A broker is a guy who tells you tomorrow why what he told you yesterday didn't happen today."*
>
> —**Anonymous**

For example, say you buy two investments equally — AA and BB. Later, you see that AA has doubled in price, while BB has dropped in half.

A lot of people would be very happy with AA and very unhappy with BB. Their inclination would be to sell BB and buy more AA — while wishing they had bought only AA in the first place.

After all, these people would think, AA is a much better investment than BB — so why bother keeping BB at all?

The reason, as we've seen, is that investments never perform in the future as they did in the past. But many investors don't understand this — so they sell BB and buy more of AA.

Rebalancing would have you do the opposite: You'd sell some of the winner (AA) and buy more of the loser (BB). That's the last thing most people would want to do.

Including you, probably.

So let me explain why it's so important that you do what rebalancing asks you to do. Let's again say you want to own equal amounts of AA and BB. That's a 50/50 portfolio. But as before, we'll say that AA rises and BB falls. When this happens, they will no longer comprise equal parts of your portfolio like they once did; because AA has performed better, the portfolio is now 60/40.

Since your goal is to have a 50/50 portfolio, you need to correct the drift that has occurred. You accomplish this by selling some of AA and buying some of BB. Thus, you've restored your portfolio to the original 50/50 allocation you wanted.

As you can see, rebalancing causes you to do the opposite of what you might have been inclined to do. Instead of selling BB, you bought some. Instead of buying AA, you sold some.

The advantages are huge. By buying assets that have fallen, you buy at low prices. By selling assets that have risen, you sell at a profit. Ever hear the phrase "Buy low, sell high"? That's what rebalancing helps you to do!

Just as there are benefits to rebalancing, there are huge dangers if you don't rebalance. If you don't fix the drift that occurs, that 50/50 portfolio that drifted to 60/40 might continue drifting to 70/30, then 80/20 and eventually to 90/10. You'll no longer be diversified! If that asset class then suffers a market crash, you could suffer severe and perhaps permanent financial losses. Your entire retirement could be jeopardized.

What happens if you take your hands off the steering wheel while driving your car on a highway?

The car begins to drift into another lane, and if you don't make a correction you could cause an accident.

But when the car starts to drift, you don't suddenly whip it back into position. Instead, you make a series of small adjustments that are imperceptible to your passengers but vital to them — and you.

Why Investors Don't Rebalance

There are three reasons why investors don't rebalance:

1. They don't know they need to.

2. They don't know how.

3. When it comes time to do so, they don't want to.

You now understand the importance of rebalancing. But you still might fail to act when the time comes.

Why?

Because your emotions might get in the way.

This notion is supported by a July 2012 study by Research Affiliates. The study found that when investors were faced with a rebalancing opportunity, they hesitated.

The reason was fear, according to the study. As the asset you should buy goes down in price, your tolerance for risk also goes down. Thus, if half your portfolio is invested in stocks, and they fall so that this part of your portfolio is now only 40% of your portfolio, it's likely that your overall tolerance for stocks also drops. That means you won't want to buy more stock — which is exactly what rebalancing would require you to do. The result: You don't rebalance.

In fact, you might even make the situation worse by selling some stock, cutting its portion of your portfolio even further, perhaps all the way to zero. Do you know anyone who got out of the stock market in 2008 — *after* the stock market fell 40% in value?

You must never allow emotion to interfere with the rebalancing process. Fear of falling prices or greed resulting from an asset's increase might prevent you from making the changes in your account that are needed — or cause you to do the opposite of what you should do.

The Two Ways to Rebalance

Rebalancing, when done correctly, is a systematic process. This means you don't "decide" when to rebalance; you simply rebalance when a trigger point occurs. Because there's no decision to make, there's no emotion involved — just like saying, "When it's dark, turn on the lights." You're not deciding whether it's dark; you simply act on the fact.

You can set a rebalancing policy in one of two ways. While both are good (and far better than doing nothing or guessing), one is clearly better than the other, albeit with some hassle. Let's explore both so you can decide which you prefer.

Approach #1: Calendar-Based Rebalancing

This approach is simple and easy. No surprise, then, that it's the more commonly used method of the two (among investors who rebalance, that is — which is a fairly small segment of investors).

Through calendar rebalancing, you simply rebalance your portfolio at some interval; four times a year is probably the most common, although some do it monthly, semiannually or annually.

Like I said, this is far better than doing nothing. But there is a big problem. When you rebalance on a preset schedule, two things can happen:

> » You may execute a rebalance when there's no benefit. Who says June 30 matters? Well, if you rebalance monthly, quarterly or semiannually, you'll rebalance on that date — and it might serve no useful purpose if the financial markets are quiet.

> » You may fail to rebalance when you should. Say something big happens on Aug. 19. If you're rebalancing monthly, quarterly or such, you miss this opportunity. This could prove costly.

Many employer-based retirement plans offer you the ability to automatically rebalance by calendar. When you create your account, you can stipulate how often you want the portfolio rebalanced — set it and forget it. It's very convenient — but efficient does not always mean effective. And that leads us to the next method.

Approach #2: Rebalancing by Percentage

This is the method we use for our clients, because it solves the problems described above.

Instead of declaring that you'll rebalance every three months regardless of what's going on with your investments, this method states that you will rebalance your portfolio only when necessary.

To make it work, you set a *drift parameter* for each of the investments in your portfolio. If an asset drifts beyond that parameter, you rebalance.

For example, say you place 10% of the money in your retirement plan into a certain asset class. You might decide to let its value rise to 12% of your total portfolio or fall to 8%. You'll do nothing if the asset's value stays within that 8%–12% range, but if it drifts outside this range, a rebalance will be due.

The benefit of this approach is obvious: You rebalance *only* when necessary, yet you *always* rebalance when necessary. There are no irrelevant moves and no missed opportunities.

But there is a challenge with percentage-based rebalancing: setting the right rules. Yep, you must make several decisions when designing this type of rebalance strategy. They are:

1. You must set the drift parameters. Should you limit the drift to be small (like 10%) or large (like 80%) or somewhere in between? If you set the drift parameters too wide, you'll miss opportunities; too narrow, and you'll rebalance too often, with little value each time.

2. You must decide if different investments require different drift parameters. Some asset classes fluctuate more

135

than others, so should they be given more room to move before a rebalance is triggered? You must make this decision.

3. <u>You must decide if your drift parameter(s) need(s) to be altered based on current market activity</u>. In periods of high volatility, such as 2008, setting wider parameters makes more sense than in periods when prices are more stable. This means you might need to change your parameters from time to time.

4. <u>You must decide the extent to which you will rebalance when a trigger is reached</u>. Say you targeted an investment to hold 10% of your portfolio, and you set a drift limit of 20%. If the asset rises on a volatile day to 25%, will you rebalance back to the 20% limit or all the way back to 10%?

5. <u>You must decide how extensively you will rebalance when a trigger occurs</u>. Say one investment has exceeded its limit. Will you rebalance just that asset, or will you rebalance the entire portfolio?

You might find these decisions daunting. We have answered all these questions for the portfolios we manage for our clients, so you're probably assuming I can provide you with that information here. Unfortunately, I can't[30] because I don't know what asset classes your portfolio holds.

In our firm's case, we typically provide our clients with as many as 18 asset classes and market sectors. But without knowing how many are in your portfolio or which ones and to what extent, it's impossible to give you this information here. Trust me, I'm as disappointed as you are.

So, you've got to get advice — see pages 129–30 — or decide on your own.

---

[30] Aaaaaaugh! Please, don't get mad.

And if that's not daunting enough, here's one more issue with percentage-based rebalancing that will probably cause you to forget the whole idea:

How will you know if a trigger point has been hit?

There's only one way to know, and that's to look at the portfolio and compare its current status to the allocation model you initially created. That means you must examine your portfolio every business day.

In other words, rebalancing by percentage is quite a chore — as if you didn't already have enough to do, now you've got to add this to your daily to-do list.

This is one reason why people hire us: They delegate that chore to us. We examine each client's accounts every day. Sure, it's drudgery. But it's also very effective, materially more so than calendar rebalancing.

So, my advice for you is to hire someone to rebalance by percentage or to rebalance by calendar yourself. But one way or another, you must rebalance.

Does percentage rebalancing really cause you to rebalance daily?

No, of course not. You *look* every day, but you execute a rebalance only when needed.

Does Rebalancing Conflict with Long-Term Investing?

It might appear that rebalancing conflicts with our strategy of investing for the long term because rebalancing involves periodic buying and selling of assets. So you'll be relieved to know that there is no conflict. In fact, rebalancing actually *reinforces* your efforts to stay focused on the long term.

Remember: You don't merely want to keep a portion of your money in a given asset class or market sector for decades; you want to keep a *specific portion* there.

If you don't rebalance, you'll wind up with too much or too little in that particular investment, interfering with your efforts.

Rebalancing indeed helps you sustain your long-term objective.

Why Not Just Use a Target-Date Fund?[31]

Target-date funds have become very popular in a very short time.

In 2006, 10% of plan participants had at least some of their money in these funds, according to Vanguard. That figure rose to 47% by 2011, and Vanguard predicts that 55% of all participants — and 75% of new participants — will have their *entire* retirement accounts invested in target-date funds by 2016.

Unfortunately, a trap lurks for unsuspecting investors. To avoid the dangers, you need to understand how target-date funds work so you can use them properly — and only when best suited for your situation.

> **Most people don't understand how target-date funds work. In a survey of investors sponsored by the SEC, 64% thought that target-date funds provide a guaranteed income in retirement. They don't.**

Target-date funds get their name from the fact that they provide diversified portfolios based on your anticipated retirement year — the "target." A 2040 portfolio, for instance, has an asset allocation designed for someone who plans to retire in 2040. On the theory that "the younger you are, the more risk you can take," a 2040 fund theoretically will, today, hold more of its assets in stocks than a 2030 fund but less than a 2050 fund.

---

[31]See? I told you we'd get to this!

Target-date funds were invented because those who create, manage and regulate retirement plans[32] agree on one point: American workers are terrible investors.

Yeah, I'm talking to you.

"Retirement is wonderful. It's doing nothing without worrying about getting caught at it."

— Gene Perret

Too many investors buy investments after they've risen in value and sell them after they've fallen. They choose investments that have good track records in the misguided belief that such investments will perform as well in the future, and they avoid funds they believe are too risky or purchase funds they believe are safe — only to discover after the fact (and too late) that the opposite is true.

Regardless of the reason, too many American workers reach retirement with far too little money. The solution? Give these employees a fund that provides diversification and that alters the investment mix over time, reducing risk as the worker approaches retirement age. In other words, a target-date fund might start out with all of its money in stocks, but by the time it reaches its "target year" it might have its money in lower-risk bonds and cash.

The idea is both admirable and sound, and today target-date funds are the default investment choice for employer-sponsored retirement plans nationwide.

Unfortunately, not all target-date funds are alike. Many are poorly constructed and badly operated, often charging excessive fees and exposing investors to too much risk. The result: Returns are often as dismal as the returns employees were obtaining on their own. The problem got so bad that target-date funds became the subject of hearings and investigations by the Securities and Exchange Commission, the Department of Labor and Congress.

---

[32]Read: fund companies, plan administrators and the Department of Labor.

I provided a detailed review of target-date funds in *The Truth About Money*, but let me provide the key information for you here.

Two Key Characteristics of Target-Date Funds

Target-date funds have two key characteristics: *asset allocation* and *glide path*. Both reflect the premise that you should shift from higher-risk investments (meaning stocks) to lower-risk ones (meaning bonds and cash) as you approach retirement.

But how much should your fund have in stocks in the first place? That's the asset allocation question: deciding how much to invest in stocks and how much to invest in bonds.

For example, should a 2040 fund have 60% or 90% of its assets in stocks? Or even 100%? Sure, you'd expect a 2040 fund to be invested very differently from a 2020 fund, but you might be shocked to discover that there are huge differences among 2040 funds themselves.

In fact, more than two hundred 2040 funds are available, and they range from having 95% to only 38% of their assets in stocks. That's a huge disparity.

And since your retirement plan probably offers only one 2040 fund, you're stuck with whatever allocation it offers even if that allocation isn't what you need.

Which brings up another decision each target-date fund must make: setting its glide path. This refers to the way the fund goes from owning 100% stocks (which it might do when the target date is decades away) to 0% stocks (when you're about to reach your target).

Funds execute their glide paths based on two criteria, and it's essential you understand them — because they are key to understanding how much risk your target-date fund is taking.

Criterion #1: Gradual or Cliff

Will your fund shift from stocks to bonds slowly over time, or will it make the shift all at once?

For example, a target-date fund that's 40 years from its target might reduce its stock holdings by 2% per year. By the time the fund reaches its target in 40 years, its stock exposure will have been cut by 80%. That's a *gradual* glide path — a slow, steady reduction in stocks.

Another fund, however, might leave its money entirely in stocks for decades — and then, three years before its target date, it suddenly cuts its stocks — all at once — by 80%. This is like falling off a cliff — hence the name: a *cliff* glide path.

Gradual paths reduce risk but also can reduce returns. Cliff paths increase risk but also can increase returns. Make sure you know which path your target-date fund uses so you can decide whether it's right for you.

Criterion #2: To or Through

It's the year 2039, and you own a 2040 fund. How much of that fund's assets do you think would be invested in stocks?

"To" or "through" matters a lot because many investors don't continue to hold their target-date funds after they retire. Fidelity's 2010 fund held $11.1 billion in assets on March 31, 2010, but only $5.9 billion on March 31, 2013, according to *Morningstar* — suggesting that nearly half the investors moved their money out of the fund.

If your target-date fund operates as a "through" fund and you sell at the "to" point, you could negate the benefits of owning the fund in the first place.

It might surprise you that the fund might be 80% in stocks — even though it's just one year away from reaching its target date.

That's exactly what millions of hapless investors discovered in 2008, when their 2010 target-date funds lost as much as 41% in value. The losses occurred because the funds had as much as 70% of their assets in stocks — even though the target date was only two years away.

How could this be? The answer resides in whether a target-date fund's glide path is set as *to* or *through*.

Some funds work on the assumption that, by the time the target is reached, the fund should have little to none of its money in stocks. After all, the logic goes, the investors have reached their target and are either retiring or soon will be. They'll need their money to support themselves, and that means the fund's assets should be in income-oriented, low-risk investments like bonds.

These funds set their glide paths "to" the target date.

But some target-date funds have a different view. They argue that reaching the target date is the beginning, not the end. A 65-year-old who's entering retirement has a life expectancy of 20 more years, and the glide path should be based on *that* date — not the retirement date. Therefore, with 20 years to go as of the target date, this fund will still have lots — perhaps even most — of its money in stocks.

Such funds have set their glide paths to go "through" the target date, all the way to the projected date of the investor's death.

Combined, the gradual/cliff and to/through methodologies conspire to radically alter the investment mix of target-date funds.

This is why one 2040 fund might have only half its money in stocks while another might have all its money there.

The Best Way to Handle Target-Date Funds

Now that you understand how target-date funds work, you're ready to decide if you want to use them in your retirement plan. Just follow these five easy steps:

Step #1: Review Your Plan's Target-Date Fund Offerings

Look at the target-date funds available in your plan, and become familiar with:

» the current asset allocation (stock/bond mix) of each fund

» the glide path

- gradual/cliff

- to/through

Step #2: Decide Which Target-Date Fund Most Closely Matches Your Retirement Date

Examine that fund's projected asset allocation mix at five intervals:

» now

» when you are one-quarter of the way to retirement from now

» when you are halfway to retirement from now

» when you are three-quarters of the way to retirement from now

» when you are at retirement

If the target-date fund that most closely matches your retirement date has a stock/bond mix that you believe fits your needs for each of these intervals, choose that fund.

If it doesn't, then choose a different target-date fund — even if that other fund's target date doesn't "match" your retirement date.

> **Even if you're planning to retire in 2030, you might find that you prefer the 2050 fund because of how the fund handles its asset allocation and glide path.**

Step #3: Be Willing to Skip Your Plan's Target-Date Funds

Don't settle for an asset allocation or glide path you don't like. There's nothing special about target-date funds — in many plans they are just a collection of the other funds offered in the plan. (The Thrift Savings Plan used by federal employees and members of the military, for example, has just five funds, and its target-date funds are merely combinations of the five. Indeed, a target-date fund often is nothing more than a fund of funds.)

Therefore, if you don't like your plan's target-date funds, you can simply construct your own. By investing your money into a variety of funds in your plan, you can create your own asset allocation. And by altering that mix over time, you can create your own glide path.

Admittedly, this is more work than some people are willing to perform. If that describes you, then just choose a target-date fund. But when you do, make sure you do it right, as explained next.

Step #4: If You Choose to Use a Target-Date Fund, Use It Exclusively

Many employees, not realizing that target-date funds consist of other funds, use them incorrectly — causing them to incur higher risks, lower returns or both.

Don't make this easily avoided mistake.

Remember that target-date funds were created for just one reason: to provide workers with a diversified portfolio, one whose asset allocation would be altered automatically — because workers don't know how to do it or won't devote the time and attention necessary to get it done.

So whether you agree with a target-date fund's asset allocation or not, you need to realize that its allocation was constructed after careful thought by the fund manager. For that allocation to work, you need to put all of your money into it.

But if you instead use a target-date fund in conjunction with other funds, you defeat the purpose of using a target-date fund in the first place. After all, putting half your money into a fund with a 25/75 stock/bond mix and the other half into a fund with a 75/25 mix means you'd actually have a 50/50 mix. Avoid this problem by selecting just one target-date fund — the one that's best for your situation.

Sadly, few workers get this right. According to the Thrift Savings Board, which oversees the TSP, more than half of federal workers who use the TSP's target-date funds are also using other funds the plan offers — and many employees have money in *every* fund the plan offers.

Private-sector employees are making the same mistake, according to Vanguard. It says that nearly two-thirds of employees in the plans it administers are using its target-date funds in addition to other funds.

Ironically, all these workers are making this error because they are trying to do what target-date funds are already doing for them: diversify. So many people have heard so often about diversification that they figure they just need to put their retirement contributions into a variety of funds instead of just one. They don't realize that target-date funds do this for them, and thus, with good intentions, they interfere with their own desire to achieve diversification.

Step #5: Don't Give Target-Date Funds More Glory Than They Deserve

A 2012 survey conducted for the SEC found that 65% of investors believed that some or all target-date funds provide a guaranteed income in retirement (like a pension). They don't.

In summary: Target-date funds are mostly similar to other funds. They:

> » are not free;

> » can lose money;

> » do not promise to generate any profits; and

> » do not offer to provide you with a guaranteed income stream in retirement.

That said, target-date funds are a good choice if you lack the knowledge, the time or the desire to manage the money in your retirement plan.

Or as my grandfather liked to say with a shrug, "You could do worse."

Chapter 16
The Best Way to Supplement Your Retirement Plan Savings: Open an IRA

Whether your employer offers a retirement plan or not, you need to contribute to a deductible or a Roth IRA if you are eligible to do so.

Unfortunately, relatively few do. In a 2012 survey by TIAA-CREF, 80% of respondents said they were not contributing to an IRA. Additionally, nearly half misunderstood the basics of investing in an IRA and two-thirds were not aware of the maximum contribution amounts. Worse, a full two-thirds said the reason they haven't opened an account was because they didn't know enough to do so.

So let's fix that.

There are several kinds of IRAs. Let's look at each of them.

Deductible IRA

The money you contribute is tax-deductible, and the money grows tax-deferred while it is in the account. Withdrawals are subject to income taxes. If you make a withdrawal prior to age 59½, you also may owe a 10% IRS penalty.

If you or your spouse is eligible to participate in a retirement plan at work (whether or not you do), you might also be allowed to contribute to a Deductible IRA. Figure 16.1 shows the 2014 deductible contribution limits for a variety of situations.

2014 IRA Contribution Limits

If You Are:	And Your Modified Adjusted Gross Income Is:	You Can Deduct:
Single or Head of Household	$60,000 or less	a contribution of up to 100% of your income, not to exceed $5,500, or $6,500 if you are over age 50
	more than $60,000 but less than $70,000	a portion of your contribution
	$70,000 or more	no deduction
Married filing jointly or qualified widow(er)	$96,000 or less	a contribution of up to 100% of your income, not to exceed $5,500, or $6,500 if you are over age 50
	more than $96,000 but less than $116,000	a portion of your contribution
	$116,000 or more	no deduction
Married filing separately	Less than $10,000	a portion of your contribution
	$10,000 or more	no deduction

If you file separately and did not live with your spouse at any time during the year, your IRA deduction is determined under the "single" filing status.

FIGURE 16.1

Source: Internal Revenue Service

If you file a joint tax return, you and your spouse can each make IRA contributions, even if only one of you has taxable earnings. It doesn't matter which spouse earned the money, but the amount of your combined contributions can't be more than your combined taxable compensation. If neither of you is eligible to participate in a retirement plan at work, all of your contributions (up to the overall limit on IRAs) are tax-deductible.

These limits change from time to time, so check with a tax or financial advisor instead of relying on these amounts.

Got Any Income from Self-Employment?

If you have any self-employment income, you may be able to create and contribute to one of several types of accounts. See Figure 16.2.

Self-Employed?

Consider These Types of Retirement Accounts

	Solo 401(k)	Simple IRA	Money Purchase Plan	Profit-Sharing Plan
As an *employee* of your small business, you can contribute	Up to $17,500, or $23,000 if you are age 50 or older	Up to $12,000, or $14,500 if you are age 50 or older	$0	$0
As the *owner* of your small business, you can also contribute	Up to 25% of compensation, subject to limits	An additional amount of up to $12,000, or $14,500 if you are age 50 or older	Up to 25% of compensation, subject to limits	Up to 25% of compensation, subject to limits

Source: Internal Revenue Service

FIGURE 16.2

Nondeductible IRA

Choose the nondeductible IRA if you are not eligible to contribute to a Deductible IRA. As this account's name implies, the money you contribute is not tax-deductible, but it does grow tax-deferred until withdrawal.

We don't recommend the nondeductible IRA (even if you're eligible) for two reasons: You can't deduct your annual contribution, and you must file IRS Form 8606 every year you add or withdraw money.

Bad things happen by not filing the form. First, you owe a $50 penalty for every year you fail to file it, and — if you don't maintain good records — you'll forget that you paid taxes (years earlier) on your contributions. Thus, you'll pay taxes *again* when you make withdrawals.

No matter how good your intentions are at keeping records, I doubt you'll succeed for 40 years. Even if you do, what will happen when you die? Your heirs might overpay the taxes you tried so hard to avoid.

Skip the nondeductible IRA. It just isn't worth the hassle.

> **Some people think Form 8606 is worth the hassle because they can withdraw their nondeductible IRA contributions tax-free at retirement. But they are wrong.**
>
> **Say you have $12,000 in IRAs, of which $2,000 was contributed on a nondeductible basis using Form 8606. You can't withdraw the nondeductible money first, tax-free; IRS rules state that each withdrawal from an IRA must be a pro rata distribution of deductible and nondeductible dollars. Thus, since one-sixth of your IRA ($2,000/$12,000) is nondeductible, only one-sixth of each withdrawal is tax-exempt.**
>
> **Clearly, nondeductible IRAs are not worth the hassle.**

Roth IRA

Tax treatment for the Roth IRA is the opposite of tax treatment for the deductible IRA: There is no deduction for contributions, but withdrawals are tax-free, provided you leave the money in the account for at least five years after making the first contribution and you reach age 59½ (with exceptions for death, disability, first-time home purchases, qualified higher education expenses and other more uncommon reasons like IRS levies, qualified reservist distributions and unreimbursed medical expenses that are more than a certain percentage of AGI).

You can contribute to a deductible or a Roth IRA even if you participate in a retirement plan at work, but the amount you can contribute and/or deduct might be limited (based on your income or marital situation). To wit:

» For 2014, the maximum you were able to contribute to all IRAs (whether deductible, Roth or a combination of the two) was the smaller of (a) $5,500 ($6,500 if you're age 50 or older), or (b) your taxable compensation for the year.

» If you were single and your modified Adjusted Gross Income was under $129,000, you could contribute to a Roth IRA.

» If you were married, filing jointly and your modified AGI was below $191,000, you could contribute to a Roth IRA (the amount depends on your modified AGI).

» If you were married, filing separately and you lived with your spouse, and your modified AGI was less than $10,000, you could contribute to a Roth IRA (the amount depends on your modified AGI).

» If you were married, filing separately and did not live with your spouse, the maximum contribution was $5,500.

Should You Contribute to the Deductible IRA or the Roth IRA?

You want to contribute to an IRA this year. Should you place that money into a Deductible IRA or a Roth IRA?

> There *is* a correct answer to this question. Let's see if you can guess it.

If you choose the deductible IRA, you get a tax deduction now, but you'll pay taxes on withdrawals later.

If you choose the Roth IRA, you get no tax deduction now, but future withdrawals[33] will be tax-free.

In other words, the deductible IRA lets you avoid taxes now on your small contribution, while the Roth IRA lets you avoid taxes in retirement on (by then, presumably) large withdrawals.

So, which would you prefer: a small tax break now or a big tax break later?

> All the information here comparing the IRA to the Roth IRA is also applicable when comparing a 401(k) to a Roth 401(k), unless otherwise noted.

You probably would choose the big break later. That means you choose the Roth IRA.

Sorry, but it was a trick question.[34]

You see, it's not a matter of choosing one over the other in terms of "which one saves more in taxes." The key to financial success is wealth creation — not tax avoidance.

Thus, the real question is, which type of IRA produces more wealth, net of taxes?

And the answer is … neither.

---

[33]Assuming you follow the rules mentioned earlier.
[34]C'mon. You knew that was coming.

Yep, that's right, folks. The deductible IRA and Roth IRA are wealth-neutral. Neither produces more wealth than the other.

Don't believe me?

Let's say you're in the 30% tax bracket, you earn $100 and you place it into a deductible IRA. You don't have to pay taxes on that $100. Thus, the entire $100 can be invested. Let's further say the account value doubles by the time you've retired. You now have $200. You withdraw the money, paying $60 in taxes. Result: You net $140 after taxes.

Now let's see what would have happened if you had invested in a Roth IRA instead. You are in the same 30% tax bracket[35] and you earn the same $100. But because you get no tax deduction for contributing to the Roth IRA, you must pay taxes on the $100, which costs you $30. You thus have only $70 left that you can place into the Roth IRA. By the time you retire, the account doubles in value[36] and it is therefore worth $140. You withdraw the money, and when you do, you owe no taxes because it is a Roth IRA. Result: You net $140 after taxes.

The Roth IRA Does Not Produce More Wealth Than the Deductible IRA

	Deductible IRA	Roth IRA
Earnings	$100	$100
Tax Rate	n/a	30%
Tax on Earnings	$0	($30)
Net Earnings	$100	$70
	BECOMES (Say the value doubles over time)	BECOMES
Future Value	$200	$140
Tax Rate	30%	n/a
Tax on Withdrawal	($60)	$0
Net Value	$140 ← NO DIFFERENCE →	$140

This is a hypothetical illustration. It is not representative of the past or future results of any specific investment.

FIGURE 16.3

[35]To keep the examples fair.
[36]Just as it did in the prior example.

As you can see, both types of IRAs produce the same amount of wealth after taxes. Sure, with the deductible IRA you paid $60 in taxes, while with the Roth IRA you incurred taxes of only half that much, but the deductible IRA compensated for that by allowing a larger account balance to enjoy growth through compounding.

Think my example is arithmetically flawed? Go ahead and change any of the numbers you wish — the amount you earn, your tax bracket, the time period and/or your rate of return. It won't matter; the results will always be the same. You produce the same after-tax wealth with the deductible IRA as you do with the Roth IRA.

But wait, you say. I'm assuming that your tax bracket in the future will be the same as it is today. If your future tax bracket will be higher, then surely the Roth IRA will be better!

True. But if your future tax bracket will be lower, then the deductible IRA will be better.[37]

The fact is that nobody[38] knows what tax rates will be in the future. We don't know what Congress will do even a year from now, let alone 30 years from now when you make IRA withdrawals in retirement. So don't kid yourself that you can predict what your future tax bracket will be.

> I highlight this because it's a common objection: Many people assume they will be in a higher tax bracket because of some cynical belief that Congress will keep raising taxes.
>
> I won't dispute that Congress will keep raising taxes. But I will dispute the notion that Congress will raise tax *rates*.
>
> Yes, there's a big difference there. We all know that the federal government collects more in taxes today than it did 30 years ago. But in 1980, the top marginal tax bracket was 70%; today it's just 39.6%. So who knows what tax rates will be in the future?
>
> For this reason, we have no choice but to assume — for planning purposes — that it will be *the same*.

---

[37]See? I can play this game too!
[38]Including you. Sorry.

> If that proves incorrect, we'll adjust our advice and strategy. But for now we don't pretend to know what future tax rates will be, and you shouldn't either.

Like I said earlier, there *is* a correct answer to the question of whether you should choose the deductible IRA or the Roth IRA. And the above exercise has led us to the answer: Because we can ignore the question of what *future* tax rates will be, we can focus on something far more important: *your personal, current* tax rate.

If you are in a low bracket — 15% or less — you should contribute to the Roth IRA. If you are in a higher tax bracket, you should contribute to the deductible IRA.

The reason is not because one produces greater wealth than the other, but because those in low tax brackets are (a) not getting much current tax savings via the deductible IRA and (b) are likely to be in a higher bracket due to increased income and wealth by the time they retire — meaning they will benefit more from the Roth IRA later than they benefit from the deductible IRA now.

Your personal circumstances could alter this scenario, and for that reason you should consult with a tax or financial advisor. But in our experience, the vast majority of people in low tax brackets are best served by contributing to a Roth IRA, and everyone else is best served by contributing to a deductible IRA.

Should You Convert Your Accounts to the Roth?

You may already have IRAs. And many employers now offer Roth versions of their retirement plans. Thus, many people wonder whether they should convert their accounts to Roth accounts.

If you don't convert, leaving the money as-is, you'll pay taxes when you make withdrawals in retirement. And you must start withdrawing money in your early 70s. But withdrawals from Roth accounts are tax-free, and you don't have to start making withdrawals until you want to.

But watch out! It's one thing to *contribute new money* to a Roth (see above section) and quite another to *convert existing accounts* to a Roth. Here's the harsh part: You must pay taxes *this year* on any money you convert from a current retirement account or IRA to a Roth.

So the choice is yours: You can leave the money where it is and pay taxes when you make withdrawals in retirement, or you can convert the money to a Roth account, paying taxes now on the current balance so that future withdrawals are tax-free.

Should you pay now or later?

As we have already seen, the Roth doesn't increase wealth *per se*. It just accelerates the tax liability. So if you believe that your future tax rate will be higher, then you will benefit by converting and paying taxes at today's lower rate.

Let's say you have $250,000 in retirement accounts and you decide to convert. You could owe $100,000 in taxes. Where will you get the money?

And you might need more money than you think, because the declaration of this taxable income could push *all* your income into a higher tax bracket — not just the dollars you're converting. And if you have to withdraw money from your retirement account to pay the taxes, you'll owe an additional 10% penalty if you're under age 59½. You might also have to file estimated tax payments, and failing to do so could cause you to incur interest and penalties.

And you won't even know what your tax liability actually is until the end of the year. So, you might owe more in taxes than you expected.

> **Pay attention to state income taxes too. If you currently live in a state that has an income tax but plan to retire in a state that doesn't (such as Florida, Texas or Nevada), converting now would force you to pay state taxes now, while not converting would let you withdraw the money in retirement from your new state that has no income tax.**

And is reaching retirement with nothing but tax-free income really so good? Before you say yes, consider this: If you are covered by Medicare, your Part B premium is based on your income. Converting increases that income (if only for a year or two), which could add hundreds of dollars to your monthly Medicare costs. Also, remember that the tax code offers a variety of tax deductions (including deductions for mortgage interest, real estate taxes and charitable contributions), but if all your income is tax-free, these deductions offer you no value. In other words, you might actually be better off financially by having *some* taxable income rather than having none.

What to Do If You Converted to the Roth — and You Now Regret It

Say you've rolled money from an IRA into a Roth IRA — and now you've decided that you wish you hadn't. Can you undo your conversion?

Maybe!

The IRS allows a process called *Roth recharacterization*. Through it, you simply reverse the conversion, usually by directing the trustee of the financial institution holding your Roth to transfer the money back to a traditional IRA.

But (and you knew a *but* was coming) recharacterizations must occur by Oct. 15 of the year after you convert. Thus, if you converted your IRA to a Roth in 2013, you'd have until Oct. 15, 2014, to undo it — even if you filed your 2013 return on or before April 15, 2014, and didn't seek a filing extension.

Thus, if you converted to the Roth a couple of years ago or more, it's too late to attempt a redo.[39] Also, note that you cannot recharacterize a Roth 401(k) conversion.

---

[39]Sorry if I got your hopes up.

Also, note that if you rolled money from an employer-sponsored retirement plan to a Roth IRA, you can't put those funds back into the employer's plan. Instead, you must move the money to a new or existing traditional IRA.

If you already filed your return and reported a conversion to the Roth but later recharacterized, you can file an amended return. This will allow you to recover the taxes you paid on the conversion. You must file Form 1040X within three years (including extensions) of filing your original return or two years after the date you paid the tax, whichever is later.

Want to undo your undo?

You can, and there might be a reason you'd want to.

Say you converted your IRA to the Roth and were surprised by how much the conversion caused your taxes to increase. So, you recharacterized, undoing the damage. But in a subsequent tax year, you discovered that converting didn't create much of a tax increase (perhaps because your income for the year was lower than it was in previous years), so you decided to convert all over again.

The IRA allows this, provided you don't reconvert previously recharacterized funds until the later of:

» 30 days after the recharacterization, or

» the year following the year of the rollover or conversion.

For more details about Roth recharacterizations, read IRS Publication 590. Better yet, hire a tax advisor.

Chapter 17
The Best Way to Handle Accounts Left with Previous Employers

In 2011, I was invited to be the keynote speaker at the annual convention of *Talkers* magazine — "The Bible of Talk Radio and the New Talk Media."

I found myself addressing hundreds of people in the radio business. Everyone knows that broadcasting careers are fleeting, so it was no surprise that a theme during the question-and-answer session was "What should I do with the money in old retirement accounts?"

Turns out that a lot of people in radio have had lots of jobs. And that means they have lots of retirement accounts — most of them dormant.

Actually, folks who work in radio aren't all that different from everyone else. If you're in your 40s, you've probably had lots of jobs too. According to the Bureau of Labor Statistics, people born between 1957 and 1964 held an average of 11 jobs by the time they were 44 years old. One in four Americans that age has had 15 jobs or more; only 12% have held four jobs or fewer.

Thus, if you're married or have a partner, the two of you could accumulate 20 or more retirement accounts by the time you both retire.

This happens because people who leave a job often leave money behind in that former employer's retirement plan. And it remains there, dormant. It's not at all uncommon for my colleagues and me to talk to clients who have old retirement accounts that have been sitting around for years — even decades.

It's understandable. Leaving an employer is a turbulent time. It's always stressful and emotional, regardless of the reason you left. If you quit for a position at another firm, you're excited and anxious about your new gig — and all your thoughts are on that. Even more so if the new job involves relocation. If you got laid off or fired, you're distraught, faced with telling the family — and wondering how you'll find a job. If you left due to injury or illness, your attention is focused right there.

So whether you leave for good reasons or bad, there's often little thought about what to do with the money in your retirement plan. Indeed, a 2011 Fidelity survey found that one in four respondents didn't do anything with his or her retirement plan when leaving an employer because he or she was preoccupied with the upheaval associated with leaving, lacked the time to deal with the old account or just didn't bother to take any action.

Many people "didn't bother" because they didn't know what to do. It was hard enough to sign up for the plan, contribute some of your pay and figure out how to invest the money. Now, in the midst of everything else going on, you're supposed to figure out what to do with that money?

Just leave it alone, the vast majority of people conclude. It's fine where it is. You don't know what else to do. And you have plenty of other things that need to get done.

Thus, inertia or procrastination takes over. Small wonder that, in Fidelity's survey, only 9% of those who have money in a former plan say they intend to move their money. The rest will just continue to leave it where it is. That's often a bad idea, so let me offer you an alternative.

The Four Choices for Handling Money in a Former Employer's Plan

Ironically, workers who do not decide what to do with the money in a former employer's retirement plan have, in fact, made a decision. They selected from a menu they might not have realized exists. So let's look at this menu and decide the best course of action.

When you leave an employer, you have four choices for the money in your retirement plan:

1. You can do nothing; the money will remain where it is.

2. You can move the money to your new employer's retirement plan (if the new employer permits this, and most do).

3. You can move the money to an IRA.

4. You can liquidate the account and spend the money.

Which is the best answer?

If you chose Answer #4, put this book down and go away.

> **Seriously.**

The Correct Answer Is #3 — and Here Are Six Reasons Why

For most people — including you, most likely — the best choice is Answer #3: Move the money in your dormant plan to an IRA. Here are the six reasons why:

Reason #1 for Moving Old Retirement Accounts to an IRA: More and Better Investment Choices

IRAs offer you virtually unlimited investment options, giving you the ability to diversify as broadly as you wish. Most employer retirement plans, by contrast, offer few investment choices — a study by Hewitt Associates, for example, found that more than half of employer plans offer only one bond fund![40]

Other plans have ridiculously few stock fund choices as well, reducing your ability to own a true cross-section of the global equities marketplace. Other asset classes, such as commodities, real estate, oil and gas, natural resources and precious metals, are also unavailable in many plans.

The result is that many plans force employees to choose expensive, higher-risk funds that produce lower returns than you might otherwise obtain in the broader marketplace. Moving your money to an IRA can solve this problem for you.

And this is a big problem — so big, in fact, that we need to stop for a moment and delve into this. This will be the longest sidebar of the book and probably the most important. Keep reading.

You want investments that will make money — but you can't predict or control how any investment will do.

But you *can* control something that will have a huge impact on your investment returns: fees. The more you pay in fees, the less profit you keep. So it's vitally important that you pay attention to fees and that you do everything you reasonably can to reduce the fees you pay for your investments.

In fact, there are two types of fees: those charged to your employer to operate the plan, and those charged to you when you participate in the plan.

Whoa, you're thinking. *I participate in my plan at work, but I don't pay any fees.*

Yes, you do. If you believe you don't, you're not alone. In fact, 71% of the people who participate in retirement plans said in a 2011 study by AARP that they believed they paid no fees to participate in their retirement plans at work.

---

[40]This is astonishing, considering that bonds vary greatly in terms of maturity dates, credit quality and issuers. Having only one bond fund to choose from is like going to a doctor who has only one drug to prescribe.

That's nonsense, of course. Seriously, do you think the mutual-fund industry and the nation's biggest banks, brokerage firms and insurance companies are all working *for free*?

Trust me on this. You're paying fees for the investments, plus record-keeping, custody and administration of your retirement plan.

Even many *employers* are clueless about plan fees, according to a 2012 report from the Government Accountability Office.

GAO found that employers didn't understand the fees they pay, including indirect fees paid to other companies. Half of employers in the study didn't know if they or their workers were paying management fees. Many claimed (incorrectly, it turns out) they weren't paying any management fees at all.

And we're not just talking about small-business owners, who have little sophistication or experience and even less time to tackle such issues. One CEO with 15,000 employees — and presumably a small army of HR executives, financial officers and lawyers — whose 401(k) plan held $100 million believed his firm's plan didn't pay any trading costs, such as commissions. Yet an independent review found the plan was actually paying more than $310,000 yearly in such fees.

The vast majority of retirement plans offer mutual funds, so that's probably what you're investing in — and I bet you have no idea how much your mutual funds are charging you. That's because you don't write a separate check to cover the fees. Instead, the fees are debited from your account — but don't appear on the statements they send you.[41] But to conclude that you pay no fees merely because the fees are not apparent is just silly.

---

[41]Most fees are listed in the fund's prospectus. You got a copy. Have fun reading it.

According to the Investment Company Institute, the average annual fee of all mutual funds is 1.4%. The impact of this fee is huge — as you well know, thanks to our earlier exercises involving lily pads and doubling pennies.

Just as you get wealthy through compounding, growth is equally hindered by the compounding effect of annual fees. Indeed, in 2010, the Department of Labor reported that every 1% you pay in annual fund fees reduces your future retirement plan balance by 28%.

And you could well be paying far more than 1% per year for the mutual funds offered in your retirement plan at work.[42]

Mutual funds have been available in the United States since 1924. Today, there is a better option available to you, but it's still quite rare to find this type of option offered in employer retirement plans.

I'm referring to exchange-traded funds.

Like mutual funds, ETFs offer extensive diversification. But they're much cheaper than mutual funds — as much as 90% cheaper — which explains why my firm recommends them for our clients and why the ETF industry is growing so rapidly while the traditional mutual fund industry is languishing.

Indeed, U.S. investors invested a record $183 billion in ETFs in 2012, surpassing the previous record of $178 billion set in 2008, according to State Street. At this writing, ETFs have $1.3 trillion in assets, spread among 1,194 funds. Invented in 1993, ETFs now account for nearly one-third of U.S. equity trading, according to *Barron's*, and are expected to replace as many as half of all mutual funds by 2015, predicts research and consulting firm Novarica.

The main reason for this is their low cost. If your mutual fund grows 8% but charges you the average 1.4%, your net return is 6.6%. But if your expenses are one-tenth as much, as is the case with many ETFs that invest identically to mutual funds, your net return is 7.9%.

_____

[42] And it's far worse if you are invested in annuities instead of mutual funds. Annuities can cost 3% or more per year — or triple the cost of mutual funds.

If you want to *look* hip, try sporting a cool pair of shades.

But if you really want to *be* hip — as well as wealthier, younger and better educated — try putting your money into ETFs. They're your ticket to join the "in" crowd.

That's the conclusion of a 2012 study by Cerulli Associates and the Investment Company Institute. Their research shows that the wealthier, younger, hipper and better-educated you are, the more likely you are to have bypassed ordinary retail mutual funds and instead own ETFs.

According to the report, the median age of the head of household for mutual fund investors is 50 vs. 46 for ETF investors. The median household income of mutual fund investors is $80,000 vs. $130,000 for ETF investors, and the median net worth of mutual fund investors is $200,000 vs. $300,000 for ETF investors.

ETF investors, 3. Mutual fund investors, 0. Game, set, match.

Eventually, workplace retirement plans will offer ETFs. Already, many plans offer low-cost mutual funds. If yours, though, limits you to higher-cost mutual funds and annuities, you can save yourself a lot of money by moving your account to an IRA when you leave your employer. That way, you can place your money in ETFs and low-cost mutual funds that you don't currently have access to.

Reason #2 for Moving Old Retirement Accounts to an IRA: More and Better Access to Advice

Do you feel overwhelmed by investment choices? You're not alone. A majority of working Americans feel the same, according to a 2012 survey by the MFS mutual-fund company.

It isn't that employers aren't providing information and advice. The problem is that the information is ineffective or limited.

Is it worth it to incur the fee charged by a financial advisor?

After all, you're already paying fees for your investments. Why pile on an additional fee from the advisor?

There's only one reason to pay an additional fee for an advisor: to get additional services. In our firm's case, for example, we provide our clients with complete financial planning services. That means our clients get advice about insurance, taxes, real estate, mortgages, employee benefits, estate planning, college planning, retirement planning, buying cars, paying for weddings — pretty much every issue in their lives that involves money.

And because we recommend low-cost investments to our clients, the money we can save them on their investment costs helps offset our fee — sometimes to the point of making our services virtually free compared to the total fees they were paying before becoming our clients. Many other financial advisors can tell a similar story.

According to the Plan Sponsor Council of America, about a third of employers offer guidance through third-party software, and 69% use newsletters or videos — but few provide the kind of specialized counseling you need to develop a properly diversified portfolio tailored to your situation. That's confirmed by another 2012 survey, this one from Charles Schwab, showing that 54% of CEOs and 62% of HR executives believe that participants fail to use the tools the company provides.[43]

The key, of course, is to provide workers with individual, direct advice. You might not be getting it from your employer, but you certainly can get it from an independent advisor when you move the money to an IRA.

Reason #3 for Moving Old Retirement Accounts to an IRA: No Cost for Doing So

You can move the money to an IRA without incurring

---

[43]Despite acknowledging that what they're doing isn't working, 93% of these same respondents said they would continue to offer the same tools. Really?

any taxes or IRS penalty and usually without incurring any transfer-related fees or expenses.

Reason #4 for Moving Old Retirement Accounts to an IRA: IRS Rules Are Friendlier for IRAs Than They Are for Employer Retirement Plans

When you reach age 70½, you must begin to make withdrawals (more on this in Chapter 21). You can satisfy this rule by withdrawing from one IRA (even if you have many), but you must make a separate withdrawal from each employer-based account. If you have many of them, you're burdened with a big administrative chore — and if you do it wrong you'll incur a 50%

But if all you're getting from your financial advisor is investment advice, and if those investments are expensive, then you're right to question the value of what you're paying for.

And if you're wondering whether a good advisor is worth his or her fee, consider these survey results from Schwab. In 2013, it asked more than a thousand 401(k) plan participants if they are confident about their ability to retire one day. Those who have a financial advisor were nearly twice as confident as those who don't have an advisor (61% vs. 32%).

You should get an advisor — and make sure you're getting the value from him or her that you need.

"In the long run, we shape our lives, and we shape ourselves. The process never ends until we die. And the choices we make are ultimately our own responsibility."

— Eleanor Roosevelt

One benefit of moving the money out of a former employer's plan is that you eliminate the risk that the employer might steal the money.

This problem is quite rare, so don't worry too much about it. It's occurred mostly at small companies; if business is bad and the boss needs cash to pay bills, he might "borrow" his workers' paycheck contributions. Even if he has good intentions (the alternative being layoffs) and intends to pay the money back, the act is illegal.

Could the money in your plan be at risk? Here are 10 warning signs, according to the Department of Labor:

1. Your 401(k) statement is consistently late or arrives at irregular intervals.

2. Your account balance does not appear to be accurate.

3. Your employer fails to deposit your paycheck contribution by the 15th business day of the month following the paycheck deduction.

4. A significant drop in your account balance cannot be explained by normal market fluctuations.

5. Your account statement doesn't show your paycheck contribution.

6. Investments listed on your statement are not the ones you authorized.

7. Former employees say they are having trouble getting their benefits paid timely or correctly.

8. Unusual transactions appear, such as loans to the employer, a corporate officer or a plan trustee.

9. There are frequent changes in investment managers, accountants or consultants.

10. Your employer has recently experienced severe financial difficulty.

If you suspect any problems, contact the Employee Benefits Security Administration at the U.S. Department of Labor at 866-444-3272 or visit askebsa.dol.gov.

IRS penalty on the account you missed, even if you withdrew enough from all the other accounts. This trap doesn't exist with IRAs.

Reason #5 for Moving Old Retirement Accounts to an IRA: Better Control

Moving to an IRA gives you complete control over your money. You'll never again have to deal with your former employer's HR department or its plan administrator.

Reason #6 for Moving Old Retirement Accounts to an IRA: More Convenient

Life is far more convenient when you have one IRA instead of a dozen or more old retirement plan accounts. Consolidating makes it easier to manage the money and reduces the risk you'll violate any tax rules.

In some cases, moving money from an employer plan to an IRA is not ideal. The common reason: creditor protection.

Some states don't let creditors go after money in retirement accounts but do let them go after money in IRAs. So if you have a high risk of getting sued (for example, 76% of OB-GYN physicians are sued at least once during their careers, according to the American Congress of Obstetricians and Gynecologists) and live in such a state, it might be smarter to leave the money in your employer plan. The same may be true, depending where you live, if you are having marital issues or if you work for an employer that requires you to keep money in the employer's plan in order to receive retiree health benefits.

Another reason not to move money from an employer plan to an IRA is the "age 55" rule. In some employer plans, you can start withdrawing money without penalty as early as age 55. But it's age 59½ for IRAs.

How — and *How Not* — to Move Dormant Accounts to an IRA

Now that you've decided to move your money that's lying in a dormant retirement account to an IRA, let me show you how to do it.

The simplest, easiest and quickest way is a *trustee-to-trustee transfer*. Simply instruct your old plan administrator to send your money directly to your new IRA custodian. That's all there is to it.

Transfers are easy — you simply sign a form. The process should take just a week or so — even less if your old plan administrator is willing to wire the money.

If the transfer isn't complete after 10 days, follow up with your administrator. We've seen cases where administrators have failed to act promptly — forgetting to process the paperwork or get the check issued. Might it be because they don't want to lose the assets and the revenues they're earning on the assets?[44]

There's another way to move money from a dormant plan to an IRA, but we don't recommend it. It's called a *direct rollover*. Through this method, you tell your plan administrator to liquidate your account, issue a check payable to you for the proceeds and mail the check to you.

When you get the check, you have to deposit it into your bank account, wait for it to clear, write a new check for the *exact amount* (don't round off!) payable to your IRA and, finally, mail it to your new IRA custodian. You must send the check within 60 days of receiving the money from the old account.[45]

This is not only a lot of work, but you also expose yourself to lots of issues when trying it. These include IRS limitations. To wit: You can

---

[44]Certainly not. Failing to complete the transfer as you've instructed is just human error. They weren't really trying to cause any delays. Honest.

[45]If you miss the deadline, you will owe taxes and, if you're under age 59½, a 10% penalty. The IRS rarely grants extensions to the deadline.

do a rollover only once every 12-month period per account. (If you have three IRAs and you want to roll two of them into the third, the 12-month clock on the first IRA does not affect the 12-month clock on the second IRA.) This is a big problem if you execute a partial rollover. (Say you have $10,000 in an IRA and you roll over $2,000 from it. The remaining $8,000 cannot be rolled over for 12 months.)

Also, the dormant plan's administrator will withhold 20% of the account for taxes. When money gets withheld, you can't roll it over, and money not rolled over is subject to taxes and a 10% penalty. Thus, the rollover method could cause you to incur taxes that are easily avoided by doing a transfer instead!

So, when moving money from an old plan or IRA to a new IRA, do it by trustee-to-trustee transfer.

By the way, as you've probably started to notice, there are many types of IRAs.

A *contributory* IRA is one where you contribute money. A *rollover* IRA receives money from other retirement accounts and IRAs. There is also the *spousal* IRA, which lets you contribute to an IRA even if you don't have any earned income — provided your spouse does. And an Inherited IRA (also called a Beneficiary IRA) holds money you received after someone who had an IRA died and named you the heir.

Some IRA custodians don't like to combine contributory IRAs with the others (and, in fact, you can't combine inherited IRAs with other IRAs), but from your perspective, there's no material difference between the two. Figure 17.1 shows which kind of IRAs and employer retirement plans can be combined with others.

Can You Do a Rollover?

	ROLL TO			
	Roth IRA	**Traditional IRA**	**SIMPLE IRA**	**SEP IRA**
Roth IRA	Yes	No	No	No
Traditional IRA	Yes,[3]	Yes	No	Yes
SIMPLE IRA	Yes,[3] after 2 years	Yes, after 2 years	Yes	Yes, after 2 years
SEP IRA	Yes[3]	Yes	No	Yes
457(b) Plan	Yes[3]	Yes	No	Yes
Qualified Plan[1] (pre-tax)	Yes[3]	Yes	No	Yes
403(b) Plan (pre-tax)	Yes[3]	Yes	No	Yes
Designated Roth Account [401(k), 403(b) or 457(b)[2]]	Yes	No	No	No

(Left vertical label: **ROLL FROM**)

[1]Qualified plans include, for example, profit-sharing, 401(k), money purchase, and defined benefit plans.
[2]Governmental 457(b) plans, after December 31, 2010.   [3]Must include in income.
[4]Must have separate accounts.   [5]Must be an in-plan rollover.

FIGURE 17.1

Can You Do a Rollover?

ROLL TO				
457(b) Plan	Qualified Plan[1] (pre-tax)	403(b) Plan (pre-tax)	Designated Roth Account [401(k), 403(b) or 457(b)[2]]	ROLL FROM
No	No	No	No	Roth IRA
Yes[4]	Yes	Yes	No	Traditional IRA
Yes,[4] after 2 years	Yes, after 2 years	Yes, after 2 years	No	SIMPLE IRA
Yes[4]	Yes	Yes	No	SEP IRA
Yes	Yes	Yes	Yes,[3,5] after 12/31/10	457(b) Plan
Yes[4]	Yes	Yes	Yes,[3,5] after 9/27/10	Qualified Plan[1] (pre-tax)
Yes[4]	Yes	Yes	Yes,[3,5] after 9/27/10	403(b) Plan (pre-tax)
No	No	No	Yes, if a direct trustee-to-trustee transfer	Designated Roth Account [401(k), 403(b) or 457(b)[2]]

[1]Qualified plans include, for example, profit-sharing, 401(k), money purchase, and defined benefit plans.
[2]Governmental 457(b) plans, after December 31, 2010. [3]Must include in income.
[4]Must have separate accounts. [5]Must be an in-plan rollover.

Source: Internal Revenue Service

FIGURE 17.1

Your Former Employer Could Close Your Old Account and Send You a Check

This is not a check that you should be happy to receive.

The IRS and the Department of Labor allow plan sponsors to force distributions if your account balance is less than $5,000.

If your account balance is between $1,000 and $5,000, your money might be moved automatically to an IRA. If the balance is less than $1,000, your former employer can simply close your account and send you the cash — forcing you to pay taxes and perhaps a 10% IRS penalty.

And watch out if part of your dormant account contains money that you had transferred from an IRA or a previous employer's plan. That amount doesn't have to be considered in determining whether your balance exceeds the $5,000 forced-distribution limit.

For example, say your dormant account balance is $14,000, which includes $9,500 that you had rolled over from a previous employer's plan. The employer can disregard the $9,500 — meaning your balance is only $4,500. That lets the employer distribute your entire $14,000 balance, giving you a massive tax bill. To make matters worse, your employer is required to withhold 20% for taxes on all distributions (even though your tax rate might be higher) and send it directly to the IRS. So even if you want to roll over the money into an IRA, you will have to come up with the amount that was withheld or you will have to pay taxes and an IRS penalty on the amount sent to the IRS!

The solution: Don't leave money behind when you leave an employer. Talk with a financial advisor who can help you manage the assets and avoid unnecessary taxes and IRS penalties.

Chapter 18
How to Move 401(k) Funds to an IRA While Still Employed

You might be able to move some or all of the money in your retirement plan to an IRA — even though you're still working for the same employer and still contributing to your current plan.

It's called an *in-service distribution*, and you can do this if you have reached a certain age (typically normal retirement age) and your employer's plan allows it. To see if you're eligible, just read your Summary Plan Description or contact your company's employee benefits department or plan administrator.

You might consider an in-service distribution if (a) you don't like the investment options in your plan or find them too limited to let you create the kind of diversification you need; (b) you can lower your fees by switching to investments that are not available in your plan; or (c) both.

Talk with a financial advisor to see if an in-service distribution is in your best interests.

Be Wary of Aggressive IRA Marketers

Even though moving dormant accounts to an IRA is the best strategy for most people, you need to exercise caution when dealing with some of the nation's largest IRA providers.

That's because the Government Accountability Office, the investigative arm of Congress, reported in 2013 that financial firms encouraged workers to move their employer retirement accounts into IRAs that might not be the best option for them. The advice workers were receiving was often too complex or too general, leaving them vulnerable to suffering higher fees, GAO said.

Seven of the 30 largest 401(k) service providers — names you know well — told undercover investigators that their firms' IRAs were "free" — without divulging that investment, transaction and other fees actually apply. Five of the 10 IRA web sites GAO examined made similar claims.

Ask yourself: Do you really believe that any of these big firms — or anyone on Wall Street for that matter — works for free? The word "free" alone should make you realize you're being hoodwinked.

So, when searching for a place to open an IRA, select an independent, objective, fee-based financial advisor for guidance.

Cool Investment   by Eric Perlin

Psst! Hey, bud! Wanna make some easy money? Just give me a few hundred bucks and I'll invest it fer ya in some top quality "Happy Days" memorabilia. You'll triple yer investment in no time!

I don't know. Frankly, this sounds like a Fonzie scheme.

www.funnytimes.com

Chapter 19
The Best Way to Destroy Your Retirement Plan's Savings

Once you begin to accumulate money in your retirement plan, you'll develop a sense of pride and satisfaction to see how the account balance has grown.

For some people, though, seeing that growth also triggers *temptation*.

Why not use some of that money to buy a house, a car, pay for a child's college education — even start a business?

Some workers view their employer retirement plans as a place to get a quick and easy loan. In most cases, there's no lengthy application process or credit check, and you can often get your cash in just a few days. Regulations give you five years to repay the loan, although you can pay it off faster if you wish, with no prepayment penalty. And the interest rate is not only low, but the interest you pay goes right into your own account, so it's like repaying yourself!

All this explains why so many people have borrowed money from their retirement plans at work.

In fact, more than one in four American workers have done this, using the money for mortgage payments, credit card bills and other expenses, according to HelloWallet. It reported that, of the $294 billion deposited into 401(k) plans by employers and employees in

2012–2013, about $70 billion — or 24% — was withdrawn for nonretirement purposes.

The percentage of people estimated to have outstanding loans against their 401(k) plans varies, depending on whom you ask. HelloWallet estimates it's about 14%; Schwab estimates about 16% of those in its retirement programs have such loans. Vanguard puts the figure at about 18%, while Fidelity reports a 22% outstanding loan rate.

Whoever's right, it's clear that far too many people are borrowing from their retirement plans.

But so what? You're just borrowing from yourself, so no harm done — right?

Wrong!

The best way to destroy your retirement planning effort is to borrow from your retirement plan. Here are 10 reasons why you must never do that:

Reason #1 to Never Borrow from Your Retirement Plan: You Defeat the Purpose of the Account

The money in your account is for your retirement — and nothing else. Period. No matter how demanding your current needs are, no matter how urgent your situation is or strong your desires might seem, nothing can match the crisis you will face if you find yourself at age 70 with no money. You simply must find another solution to your current dilemma and avoid tapping into your retirement account prior to retirement. Never touch the money in your retirement account until retirement.

Reason #2 to Never Borrow from Your Retirement Plan: Loss of Compounding

The loan is not really a loan; to provide the "loan," the money is actually withdrawn from your account. That means you're selling some of your investments. If those investments continue to rise in value, you won't enjoy the profits — because your shares will have been sold.

Reason #3 to Never Borrow from Your Retirement Plan: You're Forced to Sell Low and Buy High

When you repay the "loan," you rebuy the shares that had been previously sold — but at current (and likely, higher) prices. In effect, you'll have sold low and (re)bought high — eroding the benefits you learned about in Chapter 13 that you otherwise would have enjoyed.

Reason #4 to Never Borrow from Your Retirement Plan: You'll Pay Interest and Fees

Forget the nonsense that you're "paying yourself back" when you pay interest and fees. First of all, most plans charge an origination fee of $75 regardless of loan size, and this fee goes to your plan administrator — not to your account. (If you borrow $1,000, you lose 7.5% right away.) Second, although the interest you pay (which is based on prevailing rates; about 5% for many plans in 2013) does go into your account, it's money that you otherwise could have invested anyway, for possibly higher returns. In other words, paying interest — even to yourself — reduces the amount of wealth you otherwise would have been able to generate.

Reason #5 to Never Borrow from Your Retirement Plan: Ability to Contribute Could Be Suspended

Some plans prohibit you from contributing to your account until your loans are paid off. This means you can't add to your retirement savings — perhaps for years. And since contributions will have reduced your taxable income, your tax liability will rise until you pay off the loan.

Reason #6 to Never Borrow from Your Retirement Plan: Inflexible Terms, Less Take-Home Pay

Employers usually require that you start repaying the loan with your next pay period, via automatic paycheck deduction. This immediately lowers your take-home pay — perhaps by even more than the amount you had been contributing to the plan. But because this repayment isn't deductible, your taxes might rise, possibly further reducing your net pay.

Reason #7 to Never Borrow from Your Retirement Plan: Big Tax Risk If You Quit or Lose Your Job

If you leave your employer, you must repay the loan in full within 90 days. But you probably won't be able to pay it off, because you'll have already spent the money. (You needed the cash, remember? That's why you sought the loan in the first place.) If you don't repay it right away, the outstanding loan balance will be considered taxable income, and you'll owe income taxes (plus a 10% penalty if you're under age 59½). How will you pay the taxes? You won't have the cash! Now you'll owe the IRS instead of your employer — and that's a far more onerous lender to have.

Reason #8 to Never Borrow from Your Retirement Plan: Big Tax Risk If You Stay at Work but Fail to Repay the Loan by the Deadline

Most loans must be repaid within five years. If you fail to do so, your employer will treat the loan as a distribution, triggering the tax liability noted above. You also might be kicked out of your plan and prevented from contributing in the future.

Reason #9 to Never Borrow from Your Retirement Plan: Even Bigger Tax Risk If You Do Repay the Loan on Time

Watch out for a double-tax whammy: Loans cause you to pay taxes *twice* on the loan amount. Say you borrow $10,000. When you repay it, you do so with after-tax money. And later, when you withdraw the money in retirement, you'll pay tax on that money again — forcing you to pay taxes twice on the same money.

Reason #10 to Never Borrow from Your Retirement Plan: You'll Still Have Debt

If you use the loan to pay off other debts, all you'll have done is exchange one debt for another. Sure, you'll have changed whom you owe and maybe the interest rate you're paying, but considering all the disadvantages cited above, this does not justify taking the loan from your plan.

Need me to put dollars to all this? OK, consider this: A study by the mutual-fund company T. Rowe Price found that borrowing $10,000 from a retirement plan will reduce your account balance at retirement by $100,000.

Do yourself a favor: Never borrow from your retirement plan — because if you do borrow, you're likely to borrow again. According to a 2013 Fidelity study of 180,000 plan participants who have taken loans against their 401(k) plans in the past 12 years, two-thirds took out more than one loan, 25% borrowed three or four times, and 20% got loans five times or more. Fidelity calls these people "serial borrowers," and like alcoholics who are fine until they have "just one drink," these people were well on the way toward a successful retirement — until they got their first loan.

> Not all employers permit loans from their plans. If yours does, there's a limit to the amount you can borrow: usually the lesser of (a) $50,000 or (b) half of the value of your account.

Don't ever borrow from your plan, because if you do you might find yourself borrowing repeatedly — inflicting more and more damage to your retirement future every time you do.

Borrowing from Your Retirement Plan or IRA to Start a Business

It's a bad idea.

Yes, you can borrow the money from your 401(k) to start a business — the tax code refers to it by the acronym ROBS, or Rollovers as Business Start-Ups — but the process is fraught with so many problems that even IRS agents reportedly don't like it.

You start by hiring an attorney, who files an application with the IRS. The agency will grant you permission to proceed, but if you later violate any step, the IRS will *retroactively* assess penalties and taxes — meaning you won't really know until later whether you're in trouble with the taxman.

The effort involves forming a corporation structured in a particular way and transferring the IRA or 401(k) money to the corporation in a precise way. In its own study of the few taxpayers who have gone through this process, the IRS found that most violated one rule or another and ended up with tax problems. Even those who followed the rules didn't escape unharmed: The majority experienced business failures, with high rates of bankruptcy (business and personal), liens filed against them and corporate dissolutions. Not only did the taxpayers lose their businesses, but their 401(k)s and IRAs were wiped out as well, damaging and in some cases destroying the erstwhile entrepreneurs' retirement plans.

If you want to start a business, look elsewhere for the start-up money you need. Remember: Don't use the money in your retirement accounts for anything other than retirement.

Understanding Hardship Withdrawals

If you withdraw money from your IRA prior to age 59½, you usually have to pay both taxes and a 10% penalty, but you can avoid the penalty if you meet certain criteria *and* use the money for certain purposes.

You must meet one of these tests:

> » be totally disabled;

> » have medical expenses that are above 7.5% of your adjusted gross income;

> » be required by court order to give the money to your divorced spouse, a child or other dependent;

> » be separated from employment through permanent layoff, termination, quitting or taking early retirement in the year you turn 55 or later; or

> » be separated from employment and withdraw the money in substantially equal amounts over your lifetime (based on Section 72(t) of the Internal Revenue Code; more on this in Chapter 21).

In addition to meeting one of the above tests, you must use the money to pay for:

> » unreimbursed medical expenses for you, your spouse and other dependents;

> » preventing eviction from or mortgage foreclosure on, or repairing damage to, a principal residence;

> » college costs for you, your spouse or your children or dependents; or

> » funeral expenses.

Chapter 20
How to Handle a Division of Retirement Assets in a Divorce

It is an understatement to say that divorce is painful. Yet failing to handle your finances properly makes it even more so.

Retirement accounts are among the most frequently divided assets in divorce proceedings. That's not surprising. According to a study by Bowling Green State University, one in four divorces involves people age 50 or older, and retirement accounts make up the greatest portion of wealth for this age group.

If you're faced with the challenge of dividing assets that are in your (or your soon-to-be-ex's) retirement account, start with one question: Is the account covered by ERISA?

Dividing Funds in ERISA-Based Plans

ERISA plans are those that meet certain tests imposed by the Department of Labor, based on the Employee Retirement Income Security Act of 1974. These include most employer plans, including 401(k) and 403(b) plans as well as company pensions. IRAs *are not* ERISA plans; we'll cover those in the next section.

If the account to be divided is in an ERISA-based plan, do not execute any transaction until you receive a Qualified Domestic Relations Order, even if you and your ex agree on how to split the money in these accounts. This document gives an "alternate payee" (the spouse, former spouse, child or dependent) the right to receive some or all of the benefits that are otherwise due to the worker.

If the qualified account is yours, the QDRO (pronounced *quad-row*) protects you from being taxed or penalized for distributing funds from the account.

The party seeking the QDRO should hire an experienced attorney. The document must be approved by a court and then submitted to your plan administrator. Generally, you need a separate QDRO for each qualified account you own.

How to Handle the Money Granted to You by the QDRO

Let's say you obtain a QDRO that entitles you to money from your ex's retirement account. You must decide what to do with the cash, and you have four choices:

   a. Establish an account within your ex's retirement plan, and keep the funds there. (You have to confirm that the plan will permit you to do this.)

   b. Transfer the money to an IRA.

   c. Liquidate the entire amount.

   d. Liquidate some of the money and roll over the rest to an IRA.

Which is the best answer?

Answer B is best, although Answer A might be good too, depending on the investment options offered by the plan.

Answer C is deadly, because you're going to incur income taxes on the full amount (and a 10% penalty if you are under age 59½). If you are in genuine need of some money, consider Answer D instead, which allows you to receive some money (without any IRS penalty, even if you are under age 59½) while still letting you roll over the rest into an IRA.

If you're planning to receive money from your ex's retirement account, get a QDRO and submit it to your ex's retirement plan administrator as soon as possible.

This is particularly important if your ex's account is a pension plan, because many pensions don't permit lump-sum payments. Say you get a QDRO to split half of your ex's pension plan with you. Many pension plans don't allow for lump-sum payments and instead will give you only a monthly stream of income after you reach retirement age. If you were expecting to get money immediately from the pension, you could be in a lot of financial trouble. The sooner you discover this, the better — so you can negotiate for other assets instead.

But there's a downside to acting early too: Divorce negotiations often take a long time — and during this period the value of a retirement account can change dramatically. One of our clients was married to someone who filled his account with tech stock funds in 2000. When she finally got

Dividing Funds in Non-ERISA Plans

As noted above, IRAs are not covered by ERISA. Neither are military pensions, the federal Thrift Savings Plan or 457 plans. These therefore have their own rules governing asset division during divorce.

When done properly, transfers of money from nonqualified plans to a former spouse are tax-free. The name on the account is simply changed to the ex-spouse or, if the ex is due only a portion of the money, the custodian can be instructed to transfer the amount due to a new or existing IRA in the ex's name, pursuant to a divorce decree. The plan administrator or IRA custodian may require a copy of the divorce decree to process the request. (Remember: If the money is not transferred to an IRA, the ex will owe income taxes and, if under 59½, a 10% IRS penalty.)

her share of the account, she received only about half the amount she had expected — because the investments had fallen sharply in value. So, when negotiating for a share of your ex's retirement plan assets, consider specifying a minimum dollar amount and a percentage of the account.

For example, if the account is worth $400,000 and you're supposed to get half, you might have the agreement say that you will receive "$200,000 or 50% of the account, whichever is greater" — to protect you in case your ex mismanages the money between now and finalization of the divorce.

The rules governing retirement accounts and pensions during a divorce are complex. Rely on an experienced divorce attorney; some find QDROs so complicated they outsource this work to QDRO specialists. Consult your financial advisor as well, to make sure you stay on track toward a solid financial future after the divorce settlement.

WARNING!

DENSE CHAPTER AHEAD!

Skip this chapter and call an advisor instead!

Chapter 21
The Best Way to Handle the RMD Rules

So far, we've covered two of the three elements of retirement planning: putting money into retirement plans and investing that money. Now we get to the best part: taking the money out.

Yes indeed, all your years of hard work, dedication and sacrifice finally pay off — literally: You get to spend the money!

If you're not saying "Wahoo!" at this point, you really should. You deserve it! You've been aiming for this day for decades, and now it's here!

But let's not get *too* giddy, for there are two things you need to keep in mind: *why* and *how*.

The *why* is the easy part: remembering why you worked so hard to accumulate so much money in your retirement plans in the first place. You know the purpose of this money: to produce income for you so you can maintain your lifestyle for the rest of your life. The money is meant to provide you with financial security and to allow you, as you wish and at your option, the ability to help your children and grandchildren and the community at large.

While *giddy* might be a word for someone who finds himself or herself with a pot worth hundreds of thousands or millions of dollars, you certainly don't feel as though you've hit the lottery. Instead, you look at your account balance with a sound, sober view: You've spent decades accumulating this money, you need it for your future financial security and you won't get another chance to accumulate such a sum in your lifetime. Therefore, as you fully realize, you need to handle this money — and your spending of it — very, very carefully.

The second part is a bit more challenging for many: *how* to withdraw the money. While you'll strive to withdraw it in an ideal manner — meaning in an amount sufficient to meet your needs but not so much that you'll ever run out of money — you must contend with complicated tax rules that, if violated, could result in the IRS grabbing 90% of the money you spent your life accumulating.[46]

Let's tackle the second part first, because while you might have ideas or preferences about how and when and how much of your money you will withdraw from your retirement accounts, your preferences are trumped by the IRS. Yes, you must follow its rules — even if those rules conflict with your preferences.

> **Don't complain about the rules too much. Tax law gave you a tax deduction for your contributions and allowed your profits to grow without taxation for 40 years or so. Now it's time to pay the bill.**

The RMD Rules

You need to know the RMD rules because the RMD rules.[47]

The RMD rules get their name from the fact that the rules governing withdrawals from your retirement accounts are Really Mean and Dastardly.

---

[46]Yes, I said 90%. You'll soon learn how that could happen.
[47]Man, I love that sentence.

Well, not really — but you'll think so after reading this chapter.

Actually, tax law says that when you reach a certain point in your life (it depends on your age, your employment status and what type of retirement plan you have), you must begin to withdraw money from your retirement accounts. These withdrawals are called *distributions*, and the IRS stipulates the *minimum* amount that you are required to withdraw each year.

Thus, Required Minimum Distribution.

The rules are complicated — so much so that I sometimes think Congress and the IRS did it on purpose, just so you'll have to pay more in taxes and penalties than necessary. But that rant aside, the rules are what they are, and you must obey them.

So let's make sure you understand the rules.

First, let me set some ground rules of my own. We are going to assume that you have indeed retired. We are also going to assume that you have moved all the money that was in all those retirement plans at all those jobs you had over all those years into one or more IRAs.

I'm making these two assumptions for these reasons:

> » You shouldn't be withdrawing money from your retirement accounts until you are in retirement; and

> » Chapter 17 explained why you should move money from employer plans to IRAs. Re-read that chapter if needed. This chapter will show you the mess you'll create for yourself if you don't do as Chapter 17 says.

So, you're retired![48] Congratulations!

Here's a trick question for you: Ignoring the Roth IRA, at what age does tax law permit you to withdraw money from your retirement accounts?

---

[48]If you're not, come back to this chapter when you are.

The information on these pages does *not* refer to the Roth IRA but *does* pertain to the Roth 401(k). Withdrawals from the Roth IRA are subject to a completely different set of rules. For Roth IRAs, a qualified distribution is any payment or distribution that is made after the five-year period beginning with the first taxable year for which a contribution was made to a Roth IRA set up for your benefit, *and* the payment or distribution is made:

- on or after the date you reach age 59½;

- because you are disabled;

- to a beneficiary or to your estate after your death; or

- for the purpose of purchasing a first home (subject to IRS limits).

If you receive a distribution that is not qualified, you may have to pay a 10% penalty.

Make sure you consult a tax advisor if you plan to withdraw money from a Roth IRA prematurely.

If you said 59½, you're wrong.

If you said 70½, you're wrong.

The correct answer is: Tax law lets you withdraw money whenever you want, at any age.[49]

The IRS doesn't care when you withdraw the money. It's your money, after all; you can do with it as you please. Tax law merely describes the taxes and penalties you'll owe when you do, and those taxes and penalties are based mostly on your age at the time you take the distribution.[50] Whenever you take money from a retirement account, you will owe federal and state income taxes.

---

[49] I told you it was a trick question.

[50] Note that some employer-sponsored retirement plans restrict your ability to withdraw money while you are working for the employer. In many cases, the only way to get the money out of such workplace plans is via a loan or hardship withdrawal (if offered; see Chapter 19) or to quit — because separation of service makes the entire account available to you (see my trick question on page 191).

Note that you owe *income taxes,* not *capital gains taxes.* Most people pay higher tax rates on ordinary income than for capital gains — much higher. For 2014, the top tax rate on income is 39.6%, vs. 20% for capital gains.

And because withdrawals are considered income, they affect your entire tax situation. For example, they might push you into a higher tax bracket. That, in turn, might affect your Medicare costs, cause your Social Security benefits to be taxed or reduce your ability to qualify for certain tax deductions, further raising your taxes. This is why the decision to withdraw money from retirement accounts — including the amount and timing — should be done with the help of a tax or financial advisor.

If you are under age 59½ when you take a distribution, you may also owe a 10% IRS penalty. (Chapter 19 mentioned the exceptions that let you avoid this penalty.) If the ability to let profits grow tax-deferred for decades is the carrot, the penalty is the stick. "Go ahead and save for retirement," Congress is saying, "and we won't tax the profits along the way. But if you pull the money out prior to retirement, we will not only tax you, but we will also penalize you." Seems fair enough to me.

In some cases, depending on the plan and your employment or participation status, penalty-free withdrawals are permitted as early as age 55.

The Best Way to Avoid the 10% Penalty

Don't make any withdrawals from your IRA and other retirement accounts prematurely. (In most plans that means prior to age 59½.) That way, you'll avoid the penalty.

Well, duh. That's obvious.

Actually, it's not so obvious — which is why I'm highlighting it for you.

You know you'll incur a 10% penalty if you make a withdrawal at age 58, and you know there is no penalty if you make a withdrawal at age 60. But what about age 59?

Watch out for this trap! It's not good enough that you make the withdrawal in the year you turn 59; the actual withdrawal must occur after you are six months past that birthday.

Say your birthday is Feb. 9. You must wait until Aug. 9 of the year you turn 59 before you make a withdrawal. If you make the withdrawal in, say, May, you'll incur the 10% penalty.

So take that above sentence literally: Don't make any withdrawals from your IRA and other retirement accounts prior to age 59½.

The Best Way to Avoid the 10% Penalty When Taking Money Prior to Age 59½

You might find yourself retired prior to age 59½ and needing income from your retirement accounts. But if you make withdrawals, you'll incur that 10% penalty. Recognizing this dilemma, Congress added Section 72(t) to the tax code.

This law allows you to withdraw money from retirement accounts without penalty even though you have not yet reached age 59½. (Important note: Income taxes are still due.) But you must handle the withdrawals in a specific manner to qualify.

The law says you must make withdrawals in the form of *substantially equal periodic payments*. In other words, you can't just take some money from the account. Instead, you must take the money at regular intervals — monthly, quarterly, semiannually or annually (*periodic*) — and the amount of each withdrawal must be the same as the others (*substantially equal*).

But here's the Killer Part, Part 1: *You* don't get to decide the amount of each payment; the IRS does. The amount is based on your life expectancy. For example, if you are 50 years old with $300,000 in your retirement account, IRS tables say you are required to withdraw at least $731 per month.[51]

And here's the Killer Part, Part 2: Once you start to receive these payments, you cannot stop taking them for five years or until you reach age 59½, whichever is later. If you stop or alter the amount you receive, or if you move the money from one IRA to another, you will owe that IRS penalty — retroactively, on *all* of the income you've taken from the account to date.

> **Do not change IRA custodians while receiving payments either. If you do, the IRS may contend that you have broken the SEPP rules and hit you with that 10% penalty.**

If you're 50 years old, it's really hard to say with certainty that you won't ever want to withdraw a lump sum from your IRA — and yet you've got to make that promise to yourself. If you break that promise, you'll hit yourself with a big IRS bill.[52]

Let's go back to that example of a moment ago: A $300,000 account for a 50-year-old produces $731 income per month. You might feel that this amount is less than you expected, wanted or needed — so much so that it might cause you to just forget the whole idea. Lots of people would agree with you.

On the other hand, you might decide that this amount is more than you need. I had a case once where a client wanted to buy a new car and simply wanted to withdraw enough from her retirement account to cover the monthly car payment. She needed only $400 a month — not the $1,200 that the IRS tables said she'd have to withdraw.

---

[51]I say "at least" because the IRS actually offers three formulas: the RMD method, the fixed amortization method and the fixed annuitization method. The amount you must withdraw depends on which formula you use; choosing between them (and correctly calculating them) is complicated, so you should rely on a tax or financial advisor for help.
[52]And where will you get the cash to pay that penalty? By making yet another withdrawal from the account — exacerbating the problem!

Here's how we solved the problem for her: Reverse-engineering the tax tables, we determined the account balance needed to permit $400 in monthly withdrawals. We then moved this amount to a separate IRA and began SEPP withdrawals from that account. Her original account retains the rest of her money, and it remains untouched and ready for use whenever she wants.

And because she was 57 when she started, she got a five-year loan, and when the car was paid off at age 62 we stopped the withdrawals, in accordance with IRS rules. Result: no tax penalty.

So if you are under age 59½ and want to start receiving income from your IRA, consider Section 72(t). Let a financial or tax advisor help you reverse-engineer the calculations so you don't have to lock up any more of your money than is necessary to produce the income you need (and that is allowable under IRS rules).

The Best Way to Handle Your First RMD

Now that we've explored the issues associated with taking money from your IRA and other retirement accounts *before* age 59½, you're ready to examine the idea of making withdrawals *after* that age.

You probably think you must take your first RMD when you reach age 70½.

Wrong.[53]

You must take your first RMD by April 1 in the year following the year you turn 70½.[54]

Who's the clown on Capitol Hill who wrote that rule?

The absurd and unnecessary complexity of this rule serves no useful purpose. Why didn't Congress just say "Dec. 31 in the year you turn 70" and make life easier for all Americans?

---

[53] And I didn't even bother making a trick question out of it, because I didn't want to annoy you any further than I already have.

[54] A different RMD deadline may apply for pre-1987 contributions to 403(b) plans. I'm not elaborating because I bet you didn't make any contributions to a 403(b) plan prior to 1987. If you did, send me a nasty email.

Say you'll reach age 70 in 2015, and your birthday is Sept. 12. That means you will be 70½ on March 12, 2016. Technically, your RMD is due to be taken by Dec. 31, 2016 (and every year thereafter), but the law lets you delay your first RMD until April 1, 2017. That's nearly a year and a half after you turned 70!

Note: If you choose to delay your first RMD to April 1, 2017, be aware that you'll have to take two RMDs that year — one for 2016 (which was technically your first RMD year) and one for 2017. The RMD for your first year must be taken by April 1, 2017, and the second by Dec. 31, 2017.[55]

So which is better:

taking one withdrawal this year and one next year

or

two next year?

It might seem obvious that the better option is to delay your first RMD until April of next year, so you can delay the tax bill to next year. But this is often not the better approach.

Indeed, here are the best ways to handle your first RMD:

> » <u>If you need the money you'd get from the RMD and have no other resource to produce that cash:</u> Take that first RMD this year. But if you have other sources, use them instead of your IRAs and retirement accounts.

> » <u>If you don't need the cash you'd get from the RMD</u> (meaning you're making the withdrawal only because IRS rules demand that you do so): You need to do some tax calculations to determine whether you should take the RMD in this tax year or delay to the next tax year. The reason: If you take two RMDs in a single year, you might pay more in taxes than if you had taken one RMD per year over the two years. The analysis can be complex, depending on your income needs and tax

---

[55]You following all this?

situation. For example, bundling two RMDs into one year could increase your Medicare costs, increase the taxes you pay on Social Security income or reduce the tax deductions you'd otherwise receive for medical expenses. The list of potential implications is vast, so talk with a tax or financial advisor for help.

The Best Way to Handle All Subsequent RMDs

For every year following your first RMD distribution, you must take the RMD by Dec. 31. You must do this until you die or until your IRAs and retirement accounts are empty.

That's an important point, actually: The IRS stipulates the minimum amount you must withdraw, not the maximum. In fact, there is no maximum. Therefore, you are free to withdraw any amount at any time — including amounts that exceed the RMD.

But if you do withdraw more than the minimum that's required, you can't count any excess toward next year's RMD.

The Worst Way to Handle Your RMDs

After devoting an entire working career to amassing money in your IRAs and retirement accounts, the very worst thing you could do is fail to take your RMD every year.

If you fail, you could wind up losing 90% of all the money in your accounts to federal and state tax collectors.

Remember that the purpose of the RMD is to let the government tax the money you withdraw. But failing to make the withdrawal won't avoid the tax; they'll tax it anyway. And then you'll get slapped with a 50% penalty — applied to the entire amount that you were supposed to withdraw.

Say you are in the 40% combined federal/state income tax bracket. Further say you are required to withdraw $20,000 from your IRA this year. That would produce a federal/state tax bill of $8,000.

But say you fail to make that withdrawal. You'll still owe the $8,000 in taxes. And now you'll also owe a 50% penalty on the $20,000 — an *additional* $10,000. Thus, you'll lose a total of $18,000 of that $20,000, losing in effect 90% to federal tax collectors. Even more for state income taxes!

Can the 50% penalty be waived? Yes, if you can prove that your failure to follow the RMD rules was due to reasonable error and that you are taking reasonable steps to remedy the situation. File Form 5329 and attach a letter of explanation containing a darn good reason why you failed to meet your obligation.

By the way, blaming it on a tax, legal or financial advisor probably won't help. If the IRS hits you with a penalty and you appeal to the Tax Court, you'll have to pass a three-pronged test: You must show that your advisor was a competent professional who had sufficient expertise to justify your reliance on him or her; that you provided all the necessary and accurate information to the advisor, and that you actually relied in good faith on the advisor's judgment. Merely having a CPA prepare your tax return is insufficient for purposes of meeting these tests, according to court rulings.

FRANK & ERNEST   BOB THAVES

WE HAVE MANDATORY RETIREMENT AT MY HOUSE, TOO. THEY MAKE ME GO TO BED BY EIGHT-THIRTY.

The worst part about the RMD rules is that they can easily trap innocent taxpayers who are sincerely trying to do their duty. So when you become subject to the RMD rules, make sure you follow them accurately, completely and timely.

The Best Advice for Complying with the RMD Rules

The best advice I can give you is this: Don't try to manage your own RMD compliance program. Instead, hire a tax or financial advisor to do it for you. This approach offers you three benefits:

1. Your advisor is a trained professional who is up-to-date on the latest RMD rules, with years of experience in performing the calculations dozens, perhaps hundreds, of times. He or she is far more likely to perform the task correctly.

2. You avoid hours of stress-filled work by delegating the task to a professional.

3. If an error is made that causes you to violate the rules, your advisor should pay for any interest and penalties you incur — including that massive 50% penalty.

Relying on a professional offers you a win-win scenario: If the RMD is handled properly, you incur no effort, and if it's handled improperly you incur no cost.

Don't try this at home. Turn to a professional tax or financial advisor.[56]

If You Insist on Calculating Your RMD Yourself

OK, here goes. Don't say I didn't warn you.

---

[56]Note the word *professional*. Do not rely on a family member or friend to do the calculations for you, because he or she won't stand behind his or her work if an error occurs. Make sure you hire a professional tax advisor who promises, in writing and up front, to reimburse you for any interest and penalties you incur due to his or her mistakes. All true professionals will give you this guarantee.

The RMD is based on the value of your account, your age, your beneficiary's relationship to you and your beneficiary's age.

Life expectancies are found in IRS Publication 590. Figure 21.1 can help you determine which life expectancy table to use:

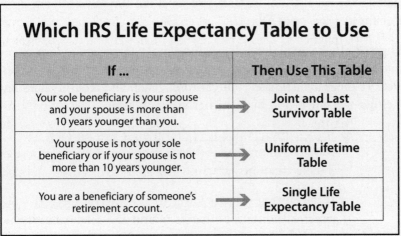

Which IRS Life Expectancy Table to Use

If ...	Then Use This Table
Your sole beneficiary is your spouse and your spouse is more than 10 years younger than you.	Joint and Last Survivor Table
Your spouse is not your sole beneficiary or if your spouse is not more than 10 years younger.	Uniform Lifetime Table
You are a beneficiary of someone's retirement account.	Single Life Expectancy Table

Source: Bloomberg and DFA

FIGURE 21.1

Once you've determined the factor from the correct table, divide your account value by that number. The result is the amount of money you must withdraw from your account this year. You'll report that withdrawal on your tax return and pay taxes on it accordingly. It's that simple.

And if you think it really is that simple, I have a really neat bridge and some really cool swampland to sell you.

In fact, the simple arithmetic hides the fact that the calculation is actually laden with traps. Fall into any of them, and you could find yourself paying far more in taxes than necessary or, worse, incurring that dreaded 50% IRS penalty.

Let's take a look at the three RMD calculation traps so you can try to avoid them.[57]

RMD Calculation Trap #1: The Account Value

You must not use the value of your account as of the date you are making the calculation. Instead, you must use the value of your account *as of the prior Dec. 31.*

This seemingly small detail has caused many taxpayers to lose huge amounts of money to the IRS. Using the current date instead of last Dec. 31 means you'll base your calculations on an account value that is either too low or too high. Either way, you lose:

> » <u>If the current value is higher than it was on Dec. 31</u>, you'll withdraw more than is required — paying more in taxes than necessary.

> » <u>If the current value is lower than it was on Dec. 31</u>, you'll withdraw less than is required — incurring the dreaded 50% penalty.

So, make sure you base your calculations on the proper account value.

RMD Calculation Trap #2: Your Life Expectancy

Sorry to break the news to you, but next year, your life expectancy will be shorter than it is today.[58] Therefore, you must determine anew your life expectancy factor and use it to recalculate the amount you must withdraw, and you must do this every year. Otherwise, you'll withdraw too little and again incur that dreaded 50% IRS penalty.

---

[57]Good luck with that.
[58]Advances in medical technology might change that, but until the IRS updates its tables, that doesn't matter.

RMD Calculation Trap #3: Mismanaging Multiple Retirement Accounts

As we noted in Chapter 17, it would not be unusual if you participated in a dozen or more retirement plans over the course of your career. If you ignored my advice to consolidate them all into a single IRA, you are about to suffer the consequences.

Ready? Here goes: You must determine the RMD for each retirement account and IRA (except for any Roth accounts; you can exclude those). If each account has a different value, and if your beneficiary designations vary from account to account, your RMD for each will vary as well.

Here are the details for:

> » IRAs: Once you know the sum of all your IRAs' RMDs, you can withdraw that amount from the IRAs however you wish. For example, you can take the entire RMD from just one IRA, or you can take a portion of the RMD from several of them in any combination. Just make sure the total withdrawn from all the IRAs satisfies the RMD.

> » 403(b) plans: Handle the same way you handle the IRAs above.

> » 401(k) plans, 457 plans and the Thrift Savings Plan: You must take the RMD separately from each of these accounts. Taking money from just one, or from an IRA or 403(b) above, does not satisfy the RMD rules for these types of retirement accounts. Also note that this applies to Roth 401(k) accounts too; although the RMD rule doesn't apply to Roth IRAs, it does apply to Roth 401(k) plans.

It'll be a sad day if you discover that you owe a 50% penalty not because you failed to withdraw the proper amount, but simply because you withdrew it from the wrong account.

And although this happens often, it is easily avoided: Simply consolidate all your retirement accounts into IRAs (and better yet, a single IRA[59]), and *voila!* You won't incur this costly error.

The Best Way to Handle RMDs When the Money Wasn't Originally Yours

This chapter is focused on helping you handle the RMD of your IRAs and retirement accounts. But you could find yourself managing accounts that weren't initially yours.

This happens when someone who dies had named you the beneficiary of his or her retirement account or IRA. Your choices — and obligations — under the RMD rules depend on your relationship to the deceased. Figure 21.2 shows your options and their implications.

The Best Way to Handle RMDs When You Don't Need the Money

Everything we've covered in this chapter deals with how you comply with the RMD rules. But for many people, quite possibly including you, the net effect of the RMD rules is that you are forced to withdraw money that you don't want right now from your IRAs and retirement accounts. This means that, after paying taxes, you'll have money left over from the distribution.

What should you do with it?

Simply reinvest it. If you were happy with where the money was invested before you withdrew it, simply reinvest it right back into the same investment. If you weren't happy, then choose new investments as prescribed in this book.

---

[59]Exception: Don't combine IRAs and Roth IRAs; keep them separate.

Required Minimum Distributions for IRA Beneficiaries

	Designated Beneficiary		
	Spouse	Nonspouse	No designated beneficiary (including an estate, charity, and some trusts)
If IRA owner dies on or after Required Beginning Date	• Spouse may treat as his/her own, or • Distribute over spouse's life using Table 1* • Use spouse's current age each year, or • Distribute based on owner's age using Table 1* • Use owner's age as of birthday in year of death • Reduce beginning life expectancy by 1 for each subsequent year • Can take owner's RMD for year of death	• Distribute using Table 1* • Use younger of (1) beneficiary's age or (2) owner's age at birthday in year of death • Determine beneficiary's age at year-end following year of owner's death • Use oldest age of multiple beneficiaries • Reduce beginning life expectancy by 1 for each subsequent year • Can take owner's RMD for year of death	• Table 1* • Use owner's age as of birthday in year of death • Reduce beginning life expectancy by 1 for each subsequent year • Can take owner's RMD for year of death
If IRA owner dies before Required Beginning Date	• Spouse may treat as his/her own, or • Take entire balance by end of 5th year following year of death, or • Distribute based on Table 1* • Use spouse's current age each year • Distributions do not have to begin until owner would have turned 70 ½	• Take entire balance by end of 5th year following year of death, or • Distribute based on Table 1* • Use beneficiary's age at year-end following year of owner's death • Reduce beginning life expectancy by 1 for each subsequent year	• Take entire balance by end of 5th year following year of death

*Table 1 - Single Life Expectancy, Appendix C, Publication 590, *Individual Retirement Arrangements (IRAs)*.

Source: Internal Revenue Service

FIGURE 21.2

An important point, however: You cannot put the money back into the retirement plan or IRA it came from — or into any retirement plan or IRA, for that matter. Instead, you'll need to move it to a taxable investment or bank account (or create one if you don't already have one). Thus, all future profits from this newly invested money will be subject to annual taxes; there will be no more tax-deferred growth provided by the account (although the investment itself might provide tax deferral or other tax advantages, as many do).

For a more complete conversation on managing the money once you do want to spend the income available from your IRAs and retirement accounts, proceed to the next chapter.

Chapter 22
The Best Way to Prepare Yourself So You Can Generate Income for Life from Your Accounts in Retirement

The previous chapter explained how to withdraw money from your retirement plans and IRAs when you're required to do so by tax law. But what about withdrawing money when you *choose* to do so?

It seems easy: Just withdraw whatever amount you want to withdraw. Give a portion of the withdrawal to the taxman and spend the rest. *Ta-da!*

If only it were actually that simple.

Unfortunately, it's not. There are realities you must acknowledge, preferences you must establish, decisions you must make and external factors you must consider. Let's explore them in detail, for this is a vital step in preparing you to manage your retirement accounts and IRAs in the best possible way, so that you can generate the income you want and need for the rest of your life.

The Six Realities You Must Acknowledge

With apologies to Milton Bradley, life is not a board game, and we rarely get the opportunity for do-overs. If you fail to acknowledge the fundamental facts associated with retirement, you run the risk of living your final decades in poverty and despair.

I'd prefer to state these issues in a friendlier, more subtle way, but the harshness of these realities does not permit such pleasantries. So, let's take a sober look at the realities you face in retirement.

Reality to Acknowledge #1: You have a finite amount of money in your retirement accounts — and it's a lot less than you think.

If you're at or near retirement age, you have probably amassed a substantial amount of money. But no matter how much it is, that's all there is — for once you stop working, you lose your ability to make further contributions.

Worse, the account value is perhaps 40% less than you think it is. That's because of taxes: If you are in the 35% federal and 6% state income tax brackets, you actually have about 40% less to spend than your account value would suggest.[60]

> I remember meeting a new client once who was proud that his retirement accounts were worth $1 million. He was crestfallen when I explained that his accounts were really worth about $600,000.

Reality to Acknowledge #2: For the first time in your life, the money you have when you start retirement is perhaps the most money you will ever have.

Depending on the amount you withdraw and the rate of return you earn on the remaining money, the day you make your first withdrawal from your retirement accounts could be the wealthiest day of your life. From then on, you get poorer every day.

---

[60]If you own Roth accounts, your current balance is the actual value, because you will pay no taxes when you make withdrawals. But don't get too excited: Your current balance is already 40% less than what it would have been, because you've already paid the taxes that those in non-Roth accounts have yet to pay. See Figure 16.3 on page 153 for more on this.

You've been poor before, but not with this same implication. Back in your 30s, losing or spending money wasn't that big a deal because you knew you'd have 30 years or so to replace the money you lost or spent.

But spending or losing money in your 60s is a totally different experience. Knowing that the money that's gone may never be replaced[61] can produce that sinking feeling no one likes.

For this reason, you have no choice but to be a careful steward of what is now most likely the most money you will ever have for the rest of your life.

"If we take a late retirement and an early death, we'll just squeak by."

---

[61]Outside of inheritances, life insurance or lottery winnings — all of which (or rather, two of which) need to be factored into your retirement spending plan.

Reality to Acknowledge #3: You will probably live a very long time in retirement.

The above point wouldn't be so important if it weren't for the high probability that you are going to live for a very long time. Those IRS actuarial tables we talked about in Chapter 21 say a 65-year-old will live to age 86. Those same tables say that if you're married or have a partner and you're both 65, one of you can expect to live to at least age 91.

And these assumptions ignore advances in medical technology and health care. Futurists are now widely predicting that many of today's 65-year-olds will live to 110 or 120. Whether they are right or wrong, you need to assume that *your money* needs to last a long time, because *you* will.[62]

And that is why our next two items are so important.

Reality to Acknowledge #4: Your expenses won't go down in retirement.

Someone somewhere once said something absurd, and somehow it caught on and is repeated frequently — as though it were one of the laws of physics or carved into the stone tablets Moses brought down from Mount Sinai.

I'm referring to the silly idea that you will spend only 70% of your pre-retirement income in retirement.

My experience in working with thousands of retirees, along with data from dozens of surveys and research studies, shows that the only reason people spend less in retirement than they did while working is that they are forced to, due to insufficient retirement savings.

---

[62]The easiest way to make sure you don't run out of money is to shorten your life expectancy. But I've yet to have a client regard this as a good option.

But if you have the ability to sustain your pre-retirement income in retirement, you will. This means you should assume that your expenses will *not* go down in retirement.

Oh, sure, your expenses will change. But that doesn't mean you'll spend less. You'll stop spending money on that awful commute, you won't need a workplace wardrobe anymore, and you won't be contributing to Social Security or your retirement plan.

But while at work you weren't able to spend money — because you were, you know, working.[63] Now that you're retired, though, you have 8–10 hours a day at your disposal, and no matter what you do with that time you're likely to spend money doing it.

One of the things you'll spend money on is health care. Of the more than $3 trillion Americans spent on health care in 2010, 37% of it was spent by those over age 65 — even though they represent less than 15% of the population.

The average annual cost for a one-bedroom unit in an assisted living facility in 2013 was $41,400, according to Genworth, the largest seller of long-term care insurance. It says the average cost for a home health aide was $19 per hour and the average cost of a private room in a nursing home was $83,950 per year. Since the Department of Health and Human Services says the average stay is two and a half years, you may find yourself spending $210,000 for your care or for care for your spouse/partner (and maybe for your parents, or your spouse's/partner's parents).

For all these reasons, you should assume that you'll spend as much in retirement as you were spending prior to retirement.

Reality to Acknowledge #5: Inflation will cause you to spend more than you anticipate.

Whatever you spend money on is going to cost you a lot more than it used to cost. Since 1926, the average annual rate of inflation has

---

[63]Unless you're one of the 16% of American workers who spend more than two hours a day shopping online during working hours, says software monitoring firm Ipswitch.

been 3%, according to Ibbotson Associates. A measly little 3% doesn't sound like much — a $10 movie ticket rises to $10.30 a year from now — but over time, the compounding effect can be devastating (as our study of lily pads showed).

So the question is not whether you can afford your lifestyle today, but whether you will be able to do so in the future. If you are spending $100,000 per year at age 65, you'll need $143,000 in income at age 77 and $200,000 in income at age 89, assuming a 3% annual inflation rate.

Put another way, if your principal never grows and you're withdrawing 4% from your portfolio at age 65 to produce the income you need, you'd need to withdraw 6% at age 77 and 8% at age 88. At an 8% withdrawal rate, you could be broke by age 78. What happens if you live to 79?

And these figures refer to the average rate of inflation. Health care costs have been growing much faster — an average of 12% rate — since 2003, according to the Commonwealth Fund.

Pay attention to the future cost of living, not just the current cost.

Reality to Acknowledge #6: The financial markets generate only limited rates of return.

The obvious way to counteract the impact of inflation, of course, is to earn a rate of return that's higher than the rate of inflation. Unfortunately, the financial markets do not make this easy.

So-called safe investments, such as bank accounts, certificates of deposit, U.S. Treasuries and money market funds, all produce returns that are below the rate of inflation — especially when you consider their returns net of taxes. Figure 22.1 compares the returns of these vehicles to inflation rates for the past one, five, 10 and 25 years.

All of these "safe" investments have lost money in real economic terms throughout all of these time periods, and since the people who buy these products tend to be focused on safety, it is accurate to say that these people are going broke safely.

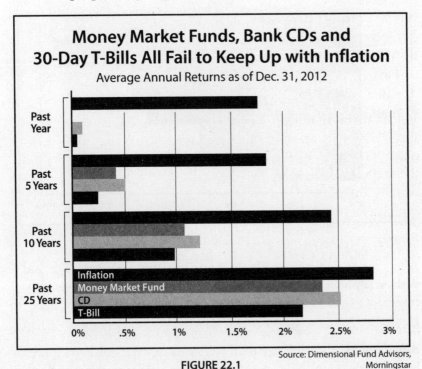

Money Market Funds, Bank CDs and 30-Day T-Bills All Fail to Keep Up with Inflation
Average Annual Returns as of Dec. 31, 2012

FIGURE 22.1

Source: Dimensional Fund Advisors, Morningstar

And don't consider stocks, bonds, real estate, gold, or oil and gas to be a panacea. Those investments have historically delivered returns that exceed inflation — as Figure 22.2 shows — but there have been periods when their returns were sharply negative instead, making you wish that all you did was underperform inflation a little bit.

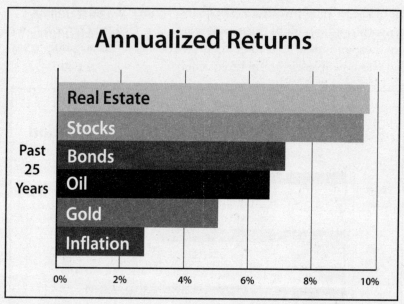

FIGURE 22.2

Source: Zephyr Associates

Allow me to summarize. Despite your intentions, expectations and desires, you will likely retire one day. You'll need more money in retirement than you need now, and your investments are not likely to generate returns as high as you might hope.

So … you have less money than you think, it's the most you'll ever have, you're going to live a long time, your expenses won't go down, inflation will cause you to increase your spending and the financial markets will provide only some help as you try to deal with all this.

Fun, eh?

The Two Preferences You Must Establish

With the above realities in mind, it's time for you to establish two important preferences. Your choices will impact the decisions you'll make next. So, let's consider these issues.

Preference You Must Establish #1: Do you want to leave a specific amount of money to children and grandchildren?

Some people regard themselves as sentries, guarding the money they've saved for the primary purpose of leaving it to their children and grandchildren. Some of our clients have told us that they feel this is an obligation because that's what their parents did for them (or because that's exactly what their parents *didn't* do for them).

Whatever your motivation, the desire to leave a substantial amount of money for heirs reduces the amount of money that's available to you — with important implications for how you manage the accounts.

For example, if you enter retirement with $500,000 in retirement assets and want to make sure that your kids (or grandkids) get at least $100,000 (combined), you've reduced your income potential by 20%. Perhaps you don't care about that, either because you can still enjoy the lifestyle you want or because you're willing to reduce your lifestyle to accommodate this preference. But you need to acknowledge your attitude about this topic.

And don't feel bad if you have no such predilection. An equal number of our clients have stated quite bluntly that they don't care if, when they die, their kids ever get a cent. These folks have lots of reasons to feel this way: They've already given their kids a good home and education, they've already scrimped and sacrificed for decades to do it, their kids are doing well financially on their own, and, gosh darn it, it's time for them to live a little, guilt-free! Besides, these clients tell us, their kids wouldn't have it any other way.[64]

> More than 20% of people with $10 million or more worry they will not have enough money in retirement, according to U.S. Trust.

So, choose whichever approach you like. But choose.

---

[64]And they're usually right about that.

Preference You Must Establish #2: Are you willing to spend principal during your retirement, or do you want your principal to remain intact when you die?

I often joke that many retirees believe in the 11th Commandment: *Thou shalt not spend thy principal.* These folks have no problem spending all the interest and dividends they earn, but that is all they will spend. And if the interest and dividends are not enough, then so be it: They will simply have to make do.

Others have a different point of view. This group has no problem spending freely — and if they go broke on the day they die, that's perfectly fine with them.

I suspect you're somewhere in the middle: You're willing to spend principal, but you want to make sure you don't spend it too fast because you don't want to find yourself old and penniless. Better to spend less so that ample reserves exist in case a major unforeseen expense arises, goes this thinking.

Decide how you feel about this issue because, like the prior one, it will color the decisions that follow.

The Two Decisions You Must Make

The above information can help as you now contemplate important decisions that you need to make. They are:

Decision #1: How soon will you start to withdraw money?

The sooner you plan to start making withdrawals, the sooner your money must be invested in a manner designed to produce income for you. And the sooner you plan to start, the longer the IRAs and retirement accounts must be able to sustain their ability to produce income for you.

If your answer isn't "now," then when? Try to provide as specific an answer as possible. "In about five years" is much better than a vague "maybe in a few years — who knows?"

Decision #2: How much money will you withdraw annually?

Equally important is deciding how much you'll want or need to withdraw each year. And it's OK (normal, actually) for your withdrawals to vary over time.

For example, say you retire prior to being eligible for a pension or Social Security. In that case, you might choose to receive more money from your retirement accounts until those income streams begin, at which point you would then reduce your withdrawals.

Likewise, you might assume that you'll spend more money in your early years of retirement, due to travel expenses you don't plan to incur in your 80s, to help support children or pay for college for grandchildren — expenses that, again, you expect to evaporate over time. Therefore, in these scenarios, you might plan to spend more now and reduce your withdrawals in future years or decades.

But there's more than just the timing of withdrawals and amounts that you'll need. There are five external factors that might affect you, so let's look at those.

The Five External Factors That Might Affect the Handling of Your Retirement Accounts

As important as your IRAs and retirement accounts are, they are not necessarily the only resources you have at your disposal. As a financial advisor, I remind you that proper retirement income planning takes into consideration your entire financial situation, not just the money you have in IRAs and retirement accounts. To wit:

External Factor #1: Will you ever again earn an income?

Just because you need income of, say, $80,000 after you retire doesn't mean you have to obtain that money entirely from your retirement accounts. One place you might get some or all of the money you need is from … yourself.

Or rather, your continued gainful employment. As I wrote in *The Truth About Money* in 1997, retirement was a 20th century invention; it didn't exist in the 19th century and wouldn't, I predicted, exist in the 21st century. Early indications suggest that I'm right.

When my grandfather retired at 62 in 1960, he was old. His life expectancy at the time was 13 years more, and his health was already suggesting it. But today's 62-year-olds are far healthier, thanks to major improvements in public health and medicine. Not only is longevity increasing, but morbidity[65] also is decreasing. In 1975, the oldest runner in the New York City Marathon was 68 years old. In 2011, there were 376 runners older than that.

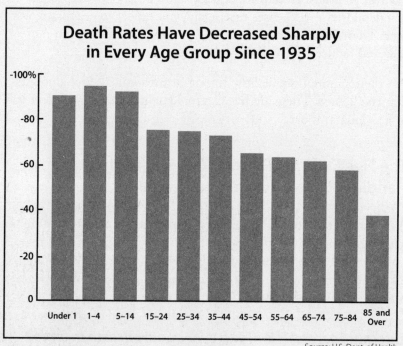

FIGURE 22.3

Source: U.S. Dept. of Health and Human Services

---

[65] The state of being diseased or unhealthy.

Aging expert Ken Dychtwald likes to illustrate the difference by referencing two famous women, shown on this page. When Whistler painted his mother's portrait in 1871, she was 67 years old; when Sophia Loren posed for the photo below in 2004, she was 70.

You are not going to experience your mother's retirement. You will be healthier and feel younger at later ages than people of prior generations ever did.

That not only means you'll stay active, but it also means you might well want to continue earning an income. I'm not saying you'll want to sustain or return to the 50-hour rat race. I'm simply saying you might want to engage in an activity for a few hours a week that isn't entirely extracurricular in nature. You might certainly spend a lot of time with family, travel or volunteer — but you might also enjoy getting involved in a completely new career or engaging in your old career in new ways (such as speaking, mentoring, blogging or inventing). And an avocation might become a vocation — with earned income as one of the results.

Extra income — even just $10,000 — from such activities can sharply reduce the need to spend money currently in your IRAs and retirement accounts. So give this notion some thought: Might you generate any earned income after you "retire"?

Sophia Loren, 2004, age 70.

Anna McNeill Whistler, 1871, age 67; painting by her son, James.

External Factor #2: Will you receive pension or Social Security income?

Just as you might generate income yourself, you might receive a significant monthly income from a pension or Social Security. These amounts, which can be easily projected (just ask your employer or the Social Security Administration), can significantly reduce the need for you to spend money from your IRAs and retirement accounts.

External Factor #3: Do you have any other savings or investments?

I sure hope the answer to this question is yes, because most Americans fail to amass enough money in retirement plans to meet all of their income needs in retirement.

The existence of money in other accounts is not only important to help you enjoy a financially secure retirement, but it also creates an important question for tax and income planning: From which accounts should you withdraw money?

The question matters because there are potentially huge tax implications. If you take the money from your retirement accounts, you create tax liabilities this year. Taking the money from taxable accounts instead might lower this year's tax cost — but possibly causing higher taxes in the future.

It all depends on how much money you have in taxable accounts, the type of investments in those accounts, your overall net worth and your estate planning preferences (such as those we considered earlier). This topic is beyond this book's purview and requires the attention of a professional financial advisor.

External Factor #4: Will you receive an inheritance?

Obviously, receiving a substantial inheritance reduces the need to rely on withdrawals from IRAs and retirement accounts.

But don't be so quick to say yes to this question. In a study of baby boomers ages 47 to 66, Allianz Life found that nearly 70% expected an inheritance — but only 41% of older Americans say they plan to leave one. If your parents have money, they are likely to spend it. And if they don't, you might have to wait decades to receive it (thanks to ever-longer life expectancies),[66] and once you do, you'll have to split it with other heirs — and possibly the IRS as well.

Before you lie back in your easy chair, comfortable in the knowledge that your elders will provide for you, I suggest you ask them. Blame me for the indiscreet nature of your question.[67]

External Factor #5: What is your and your family's medical history?

We've been discussing the fact that you are likely going to live into your 90s and beyond — perhaps way beyond.

But I'm talking about the population in general. While the average American might live that long, that doesn't mean *you* will. If you have certain medical conditions, or if members of your family have certain medical histories, you may be able to say with some degree of reliability that your life expectancy is different from what we've been assuming.

It's important that you apply your actual situation to this analysis. If you don't know your medical situation, get a complete medical examination from a physician soon.

All the information we've collected about your realities, preferences, decisions and external factors have prepared you to determine how to invest the money in your IRAs and retirement accounts so that you can generate the income you want and need for as long as you live.

Ready? Let's get to it — and get ready for a surprise.

---

[66]Which, by the way, further increases the likelihood they'll spend it.

[67]If you don't want to ask, then I suggest you assume that you will get no inheritance. Better to omit it and receive it than to plan for it and not get it.

Chapter 23
The Best Way to Invest Your Retirement Accounts and IRAs During Retirement So You Can Generate the Income You Want and Need

In Chapter 21, you learned how to determine the amount you must withdraw from your IRAs and retirement accounts in order to satisfy the RMD rules. Now you're going to learn how to generate the income you actually want and need and how to make sure you can sustain that income for the rest of your life.

And the last chapter prepared us for this by reviewing all those realities, preferences, decisions and external factors — so the information can help you design the investment strategy that's best for you.

So, to begin, take all that information you gathered from the previous chapter — all the realities, preferences, decisions and external factors — and throw it all away.[68]

Now, before you audibly express your annoyance,[69] let me explain.

We are certainly going to use the information you've collected, just not yet. The reason: Instead of trying to insert all that data into our

---

[68] *Surprise!*
[69] Too late?

calculations, I'm going to show you a much easier and more effective way to figure out how to generate retirement income.

We're going to reverse-engineer the process.

The Best Way to Invest When You Have All the Money You Need

It's really quite easy to invest money when you have lots of it: Just put it all in T-bills. I mean, if Bill Gates did that, he'd still be able to withdraw whatever amount he wanted to support himself and never run out of money.

If you are wealthy too, you can invest as you wish. Then withdraw as you wish. Give a portion of the withdrawal to the taxman and spend the rest. *Ta-da!*

And if this sounds familiar, that's because it is: You read it in Chapter 22. When you read it last time, I cynically added that it couldn't be that easy. Well, maybe it is — if you are truly wealthy relative to your income needs.

For example, if you have $5 million in your accounts and you want only $100,000 in annual income from them — a 2% withdrawal rate — you'll never run out of money. Even if you never earn a nickel in interest, the money will last 50 years. If you earn just 1%, it will last 70 years. If you earn 2%, it will last forever, and if you earn more than 2%, you will die richer than you are today.

In fact, it's not uncommon for us to meet people who have this very type of circumstance. They've done a great job at saving and investing money throughout their lives, and they live comfortably but not lavishly. Their savings are more than ample to allow them to live forever in financial comfort and security.

If this describes you, then you have my hearty congratulations! You can invest as conservatively as you choose.

Certainly, that will not prove to be the most profitable strategy; a diversified approach is virtually certain to generate higher returns over time. But so what? Too often, investors focus on the potential return on their money when they should really be focusing on getting the return *of* their money.

Consider this: If you have that $5 million and need only $100,000 in income, what good will it do you to double your money? You're not going to buy a bigger house or fancier car — meaning the increased net worth won't improve your lifestyle. But any attempt to double your money forces you to take investment risks that could result in the opposite: cutting your net worth in half. And while your $100,000 income is secure when coming from a $5 million nest egg, that security diminishes if your nest egg drops to $2 million.

In other words, the upside reward is dwarfed by the downside risk. Stated yet another way, the best investment management approach is the one that is most likely to help you achieve your goals — not the one that might produce the highest returns.

So like I said, congratulations to you if you have more money than you're likely to ever spend. But if you don't think you live in that wonderland, keep reading.

The Best Way to Invest When You *Don't* Live on Easy Street

It's more likely that you are entering retirement with substantial but not endless assets. That means we must take great care in the management of those assets.

Proper management is a challenge because you must accomplish two goals, not just one: You must generate current income *and* you must secure your ability to generate that income in the future — perhaps decades into the future — and that future income must be increased to adjust for inflation.

It's relatively easy to achieve one goal or the other; the challenge is to accomplish both. And you master this challenge by investing your money correctly. But be warned: If you earn too little, you might run out of money. And if you seek too high a return, you might lose money in risky investments.

So let's proceed with your challenging assignment. This is where our reverse-engineering strategy comes into play, so get ready to use the data you collected in Chapter 22.

Reverse-Engineering Your Way to the Best Investment Strategy, Part 1

We begin with a question: How much in annual income do you need right now?

These were Decisions #1 and #2 that you made earlier. (You remember what you said, don't you? You'll need this information to continue.)

Now that you know how much money you want annually, let's figure out where to get it. *Let's say you want or need $75,000 in annual pre-tax income.* (This is shown in Figure 23.1.)

Annual Income Needed	$75,000

FIGURE 23.1

Don't assume that you'll turn to your retirement accounts for this money (at least not yet). That's because you might still be earning some income (External Factor #1). *Let's say you earn $12,000 a year from a part-time activity.* If so, subtract it from your income need, as shown in Figure 23.2.

Annual Income Needed	$75,000
Minus Earned Income	- 12,000
Remaining Income Needed	$63,000

FIGURE 23.2

Next, how much income will you receive (or are you receiving) from External Factor #2 — pensions and Social Security? *Let's say you receive $24,000 from such sources.* Subtract those amounts from your need, as in Figure 23.3.

Annual Income Needed	**$75,000**
Minus Earned Income	**- 12,000**
Minus Pensions/Social Security	**- 24,000**
Remaining Income Needed	**$39,000**

FIGURE 23.3

It's now time to consider External Factor #3 — money you can access from other savings and investments. This item is a bit more complicated, because the amount you can access from such resources depends on several factors, including:

1. the amount of money you have in non-retirement accounts;

2. the return you're earning on that money, compared to the returns available in your retirement accounts;

3. the accessibility of that money;[70] and

4. your need to maintain cash reserves.

It's therefore difficult to state here how much income you can draw from any nonretirement assets, and comprehensive financial planning is beyond the goal of this book. Suffice it to say that if you have other assets and want to determine how much of those assets you can and should use toward generating current income (which could range from 0% to 100% of your income need), you should talk with a financial advisor. *Let's say you complete that planning exercise and determine that you can apply $10,000 from other assets toward your current retirement income needs.* See Figure 23.4.

---

[70]You might have millions in other investments, but sometimes those investments cannot be sold or incur substantial fees or other penalties to do so. Also, there might be adverse tax consequences involved, reducing the desirability of accessing these assets (either now or ever).

Annual Income Needed	$75,000
Minus Earned Income	- 12,000
Minus Pensions/Social Security	- 24,000
Minus Income from other Assets	- 10,000
Remaining Income Needed	$29,000

FIGURE 23.4

Next, let's consider income you might generate from External Factor #4: inheritances. If you get a lump sum of a material amount, you can invest it to produce income — similar to the way you manage other assets you own. But unless you have that inheritance in hand already, you'll need to ignore it for now. *Let's assume that you will not receive any inheritance for the foreseeable future.* Figure 23.5 reflects this.

Annual Income Needed	$75,000
Minus Earned Income	- 12,000
Minus Pensions/Social Security	- 24,000
Minus Income from other Assets	- 10,000
Minus Income from Inheritance	- 0
Remaining Income Needed	$29,000

FIGURE 23.5

This example demonstrates that you might not need to withdraw as much from your retirement accounts as you might have anticipated — at least not right away. While our hypothetical retirees want $75,000 in income, their retirement accounts need to produce only $29,000 of it. That's a huge difference. In fact, it might make all the difference in their — and similarly, your — ability to enjoy a financially rewarding retirement.

Reverse-Engineering Your Way to the Best Investment Strategy, Part 2

Now that you know how much income you must generate from your retirement accounts, you might think you're ready to construct an investment portfolio designed to produce that income. But not yet.[71] We have a few more items to consider.

First, recognize that some of the items you noted so far might be temporary conditions. For example, you might be currently generating some part-time income (External Factor #1), but you shouldn't assume you'll do that forever. Depending on the amount of money you have in other investments (External Factor #3) and that you received from inheritances (External Factor #4), income from them might also not last indefinitely.

Permission of Harley Schwadron.

SCHWADRON

"JEROME IS RETIRED, BUT HE STILL WORKS IN ORDER TO AFFORD BEING RETIRED."

---

[71]Sorry.

The opposite might be true as well. It's possible you don't currently have other employment income, pension or Social Security income (External Factor #2), or nonretirement investments or inheritances but that you will in the future. It's not uncommon for people to truly retire only for a few years, after which time (often from boredom) they return to gainful employment. Or you might not qualify for (or you choose to delay) pension or Social Security benefits for a number of years. And you may realize that inheritances will be coming later based on the age and health of your benefactor.

For all these reasons, it is entirely possible that you might need to assume that you need one amount from your retirement accounts this year but different amounts in future years. You need to make estimates that are as accurate as possible, because the question of how long the money will last is largely determined by the amounts you expect to withdraw each year between now and your death (or the death of your spouse/partner, whichever comes later).[72]

"Have you given much thought to what kind
of job you want after you retire?"

---

[72] And if you are taking into consideration the income needs of a spouse/partner, you also need to consider the implications on the survivor when one of you dies: Often, pension and Social Security benefits are reduced upon the first death. Therefore, don't assume that current pension and Social Security benefits will never change.

Finally, as you project your income needs year by year for your life expectancy,[73] you need to include Reality #4 (your expenses won't go down) and, even more important, Reality #5 (due to inflation, your expenses will actually rise). So as you adjust the amount of money you think you'll need to withdraw from your retirement accounts annually, you should probably increase those amounts by some rate of inflation.

You should also assume, unless your personal health or family medical history suggests otherwise (External Factor #5), that you will live to age 95 or longer (Reality #3). The longer you live, the harder it is to sustain your assets — and that's all because of Realities #1 and #2 (the money you have is less than you think and more than you'll ever have again). Thus, diligent planning is vital.

Now you're ready for our third and final step.

Reverse-Engineering Your Way to the Best Investment Strategy, Part 3

You now know how much of your retirement plan and IRA assets you need to withdraw each year. What you need to do is convert that dollar amount into a percentage of the accounts' total value.

In our hypothetical case, we determined that $29,000 was needed in Year One of retirement. Let's assume that our make-believe retiree couple has $500,000 in retirement assets. Simple arithmetic produces the answer:

$$\$29,000 \div \$500,000 = 5.8\%$$

Faced with this equation, many readers might assume that they must produce a 5.8% rate of return from their investments. But that's not necessarily true. In fact, depending on your point of view, earning less could be quite sufficient — or you might need to earn far more.

---

[73]Don't worry if you get it wrong. You can make adjustments annually as needed. That's why financial planning is a process (something you engage in regularly) and not a product (something you get once).

The answer to the riddle is found in your answer to our two preference questions. Preference #1 asked if you want to leave the bulk of your money to your kids and grandkids, and Preference #2, which is related, asked whether you want to leave your principal intact vs. allowing the account value to decline over time.

Your attitude matters to a huge degree. If you don't care about leaving any money to heirs and are willing to spend principal as needed, you need to produce only a 4.6% rate of return.[74] This return will produce less than the amount you'll withdraw annually, forcing you to spend some of your principal each year. And because you'll be increasing your withdrawals annually to compensate for inflation, your rate of principal erosion will accelerate over time — eventually leaving you penniless by the time you die after our projected 35 years from now.

But you don't care — you said so above. And this plan is quite likely to succeed, because history shows that producing a 4.6% rate of return has not been terribly difficult to do.

On the other hand, if you *do* care about leaving money to heirs or if you fret that you might live longer than we are currently projecting, then we need to adjust something — either the amount you're withdrawing from your portfolio each year or the rate of return you're earning on your portfolio.[75]

If your preference is to leave the principal untouched, you'll need to earn more than the 5.8% suggested by our earlier arithmetic. If we increase your annual income need by 3% per year — meaning your income in Year Two is $29,870 and $30,766 in Year Three and so on — you'll need to earn 8% annually so your income can increase while also keeping your principal value intact.

---

[74]Here's how I arrived at this figure for our hypothetical retirees: I assumed $500,000 in retirement accounts, $29,000 in annual withdrawal needs increased 3% annually for inflation and a life expectancy of 35 more years.

[75]You could also adjust your life expectancy — by making it shorter — but like I said before, no one likes to do that. Stick with the other two choices.

And that returns us to Reality #6: The financial markets produce limited returns. It is simply not prudent to assume that you will be able to produce an annual return of 8% every year for the rest of your life.

So the realities, preferences, decisions and external factors you've considered all join together to help us determine the rate of return you need to earn on your investments in retirement. And knowing that target return is how we go about creating your investment portfolio.

Do you see the value of our reverse-engineering exercise? Instead of buying some investment based on how much income it will supposedly produce and hoping that the income will be enough, we've taken a far better approach. You know now what rate of return you need to achieve, and this knowledge allows you to create a portfolio designed to generate that return.

This is truly the best way to invest the money in your retirement accounts. By using this approach, you have become goals-based. The alternative is to be products-based — and sadly, that is what most retirees do. They bounce from investment to investment, succumbing to sales pitch after sales pitch, often attending free-lunch seminars where they hear about "income oriented" investments that are designed to provide "high yield" with "no risk" and the like. High-yield bonds, Master Limited Partnerships investing in oil and gas, nontraded Real Estate Investment Trusts, life settlements, hedge funds, bonus annuities and other products are often aggressively sold to unsuspecting retirees who think they must earn high returns. They haven't accurately determined their true income needs, and they haven't considered the situation they're in.

These unhappy retirees know they can't succeed if they keep their money in low-yield bank CDs, and they're miffed by the yields offered by U.S. Treasuries, so they turn to esoteric products without understanding the risks. The all-too-common results: They fail to get the interest they were promised, and they can't get their money back at any price or can get it only after paying substantial fees and penalties. Soon their dreams of a financially secure retirement are replaced by a nightmare of reduced wealth, limited income — and no hope for a do-over. You probably have friends or family members who have suffered this fate.

By being goals-based, you are not concerned with earning the highest returns possible, and this saves you from investing in equally high-risk investments. Instead, to produce the returns you need, you can turn to a far more effective, proven and indeed *familiar* approach to investment management. It's an approach you already know well because we studied it closely in the earlier pages of this book.

I'm talking about *diversification*.

The Importance of Being Diversified After You've Retired

If diversification was important to use throughout your career, it's doubly important once you're in retirement.

The reason is simple logic: The opposite of diversification is concentration. We talked about it in Chapter 13, but it's worth revisiting the topic now that you're retired.

If you think the idea of buying many types of investments (diversifying) is a bad idea, your only alternative is to concentrate your money into a single type of investment. Let's assume you do indeed dismiss the idea of diversifying. That means you have to pick one type of investment as the alternative. Which type will you pick?

To help frame the question, let me offer you two choices that are extreme opposites:

your mattress   vs.   lottery tickets

Assuming you have only these two choices available, which would you select for the money in your IRAs and retirement plans?

I have yet to meet anyone who would choose the lottery for their life's savings, and I highly doubt you'd select that option either. Sure, you can win lots of money in the lottery, but it's far more likely that you'll lose all your money. Since my question requires you to pick only one or the other, you're forced to choose the mattress. You won't earn any interest with that choice, but at least your money will be safe.

And *safe* is the key word here. Given the choice, retirees typically choose safety over growth — and for good reason. While you would love it if your money was to grow in value, you know that you can't let this desire take priority over the goal of preservation of your money.

This is why so many retirees — believing that safety is paramount — select *only* safety-oriented investments for their retirement assets. No, they don't bury their money under a mattress, but they do something similar: They invest only in bank accounts, CDs, government and municipal bonds, fixed annuities, T-bills, money market funds and the like.

This choice does indeed meet two goals: You get current income, and your principal is safe. Unfortunately, a third goal is unmet (because it is unconsidered): the need to produce *higher* income in the future so you can counteract the impact of inflation.

But failure to consider the future can have a devastating impact on you. Consider Figure 23.6. It shows what happened to people who retired in 1982 and placed $100,000 into a one-year CD. As shown in Figure 23.6, their interest income that first year was 14.9% — meaning they would have received $14,900 in income that year.

But that rate changed annually. By 2013, the rate was only 0.32%, thus cutting the income to just $320, or a loss in income of 98%!

And it gets worse: Not only did their income tumble, but inflation also caused the cost of living to rise. By 2013, they needed $36,500 to buy what that original $14,900 bought in 1982 — yet their income was now only $320!

This is what happens if you choose only one type of investment: You're going to pick a safe one, and that means you're going to earn low returns — lower than the rate of inflation — and that, in turn, means the value of your account will fall in real economic terms. Stated another way, choosing nothing but safe investments means you'll go broke — *safely*!

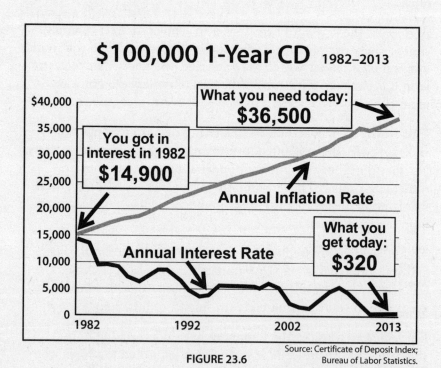

FIGURE 23.6

Source: Certificate of Deposit Index;
Bureau of Labor Statistics.

Ironically, those safe investments aren't always as safe as people assume. As discussed on page 48, bonds are sensitive to both interest rate risk and credit risk. Each can cause massive declines in value in remarkably short periods — the very type of declines that safety-conscious investors want to avoid.

Want an example? Consider a bond fund called the Pimco Corporate & Income Opportunity Fund. When interest rates rose in May 2013, the fund fell 15.75% in value. The Dow Jones Industrial Average was 14,840 at the start of that month; had it suffered that large a decline, it would have ended the month at 12,503, or a loss of 2,300 points!

Can you imagine the headlines? "DOW CRASHES!" "PANIC ON WALL STREET!" "CONGRESS HOLDS HEARINGS!"

Yet nobody paid attention to this fund's astonishing drop. Nobody, that is, except for the people who owned it.

This is why the best way to manage your investments after you've retired is to maintain diversification — because all the other ideas are much worse (too risky, too expensive and/or too little in return).

OK, so you agree that a diversified portfolio is the best approach. But what sort of diversification is needed?

It's a vital question, and fortunately you already have the answer! You reverse-engineered it six pages ago!

The rate of return that your analysis told you that you need to generate annually is your target, and all you need to do now is build a portfolio designed to meet that target, using a mixture of the *loanership and ownership* assets that we reviewed in Chapter 8.

Your mixture determines how much volatility your portfolio will experience and what rate of return it will produce. For example, since 1926, the average annual return for the S&P 500 Stock Index was 9.8%. And its standard deviation[76] — a measure of risk — was 19.1. The return and standard deviation for long-term government

[76]For a full description of standard deviation, see *The Truth About Money*.

bonds were 5.7% and 8.4, respectively — sharply lower risk and sharply lower returns.

Of course, we can't predict that these figures will remain the same in the future, so we'll just pretend that they will.[77] Figure 23.7 shows the results you would have obtained depending on your mixture of the two. As you can see, the more money you'd have placed in stocks, the higher your return would've been — and the higher your risk.

So you can choose the mixture that is most likely to produce the return you need (while keeping in mind that past performance does not guarantee future results).

History Shows That Investing Your Allocation to Stocks Makes Your Returns — and Your Risk — Go Up

Stocks/Bond Mix	Avg. Annual Return 1926–2013	Standard Deviation
0% in stocks/100% in bonds	5.7%	8.4
10/90	7.3%	9.6
20/80	8.0%	11.0
30/70	8.4%	12.0
40/60	8.8%	12.9
50/50	9.0%	13.7
60/40	9.2%	14.6
70/30	9.4%	15.5
80/20	9.6%	16.5
90/10	9.7%	17.7
100% in stocks/0% in bonds	9.8%	19.1

Source: Ibbotson and Associates

FIGURE 23.7

So, theoretically, if you need a 9% return, a mix of 50/50 would appear to be the best portfolio for you. Adding stocks would force

---

[77]Keep working with me here, people.

you to take more risk than necessary, and a mix with less would produce a return that's too low.

It's important to stress that the above is not meant to serve as the basis for creating a portfolio mix — it's just an illustration to aid your comprehension. Past performance is not certain to be repeated, and Figure 23.7 considers only two asset classes. Remember that we identified 18 asset classes and market sectors in Chapter 13, and when you construct a portfolio containing all of them, you not only increase your diversification, but you also increase the likelihood you'll obtain more consistent returns at ever-more predictable levels of risk.

> That's *consistent*, not necessarily *higher*. We regard consistent as better (even if not higher) because reliability is important — especially to retirees who are counting on the portfolio to deliver on its promises.

So there's your mission: The best way to invest your money in retirement is by building a highly diversified portfolio that's reverse-engineered.

You get it. Good. There's just one problem:[78]

If you build a portfolio containing a vast array of investments, including such asset classes as precious metals, commodities, foreign securities and emerging markets, how can you produce the income you really need?

After all, it's easy to get income from a bunch of bonds and bank CDs — they produce steady income at regular intervals. But by diversifying you're placing some, maybe much, of your money in investments that don't generate income. Emerging market stocks from South America, for example, pay no dividends. Neither does gold. Ditto for lots of asset classes. Thus, the overall amount of interest and dividends generated by a diversified portfolio is often a

---

[78] Aw, jeez.

lot less than the amount produced by a portfolio invested entirely in bonds and CDs.

And, making the situation even worse, some investments produce income unpredictably — both in the amount and frequency. Thus, you won't know how much income will be produced or when you'll get it![79]

So how are you, as a retiree dependent on income from your retirement account, supposed to maintain your lifestyle in a situation like this?

It's easy. And the next chapter tells you how.

---

[79]And this is supposed to be a better — no wait, the best — approach!

Chapter 24
The Best Way to Generate Income from Your Retirement Accounts and IRAs

When you're ready to start receiving income from your retirement accounts, you'll find that you have three choices.

The first is to simply receive whatever interest and dividends your account produces. But the income might be less than you need, it might be paid less often than you prefer (municipal bonds, for example, pay interest only twice a year) and the amount often does not increase over time to compensate for inflation. So this approach is not ideal.

Your second choice is to just withdraw money whenever you feel like it. This haphazard approach could easily cause you to spend more than your account can sustain. The result? You might go broke long before you die.

The above two methods are the most common ways retirees handle their money, but neither is very appealing. That's why you'll be happy to know there is a third choice. It's far more effective than the other two, for it creates a steady and predictable level of income (which you can change at any time), it preserves your ability to withdraw a lump sum at any time and it allows you to increase your income in the future to compensate for inflation.

This approach is called a *systematic withdrawal plan*, and it's remarkable both in its simplicity and its effectiveness.

When implementing a SWP,[80] you decline to receive the interest and dividends (and any other distributions your investments might produce, such as rental income from investment property), and instead reinvest that income back into the portfolio.

To compensate for the fact that you've given up the income, you simply arrange to receive a similar monthly amount from your account.

Figures 24.1 through 24.5 illustrate the difference between taking the income that a portfolio produces and operating a SWP. The first illustration shows what would have happened if you had invested $100,000 into a one-year bank CD (considered by many retirees to be a "safe" income-producing investment) and received the annual interest each year from 2003 through 2012.

As you can see, the CD's interest income fluctuated dramatically year to year (from $700 to $5,210) — creating havoc for the retiree who was depending on that income. The total income received over that ten-year period was $24,520, and the original $100,000 remained unchanged.

The other four illustrations show what would have happened if you had instead created a diversified portfolio along the lines we've discussed in this book. (For this discussion, we use a hypothetical portfolio containing equal amounts of long-term and intermediate-term government bonds, U.S. growth and value stocks, real estate, foreign stocks and gold.[81])

Figure 24.2 shows the results if your SWP had produced an income identical to that of the CD. But look! The value of the account at the end of the ten-year period would have been **$220,126 — more than twice the value of the CD**. With an account value twice as high as when you started, you could begin to produce income that's twice as much — helping you to offset inflation.

---

[80]Pronounced swip, not swipe.
[81]Represented, respectively, by Barclay's Long US Gov't./Credit, Barclay's Intermediate US Gov't./ Credit, S&P Growth Index, S&P Value Index, Dow Jones U.S. Select REIT Index, MSCI EAFE Index and London Gold Index. Note that this allocation is purely hypothetical. I am not suggesting you invest based on this asset allocation, and my firm has never placed any client in such an allocation. It is offered here solely to illustrate how a SWP might work.

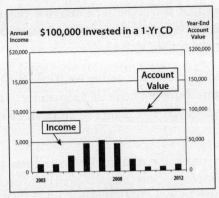

FIGURE 24.1

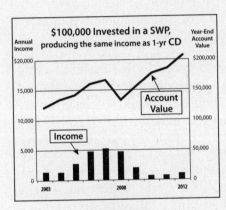

FIGURE 24.2

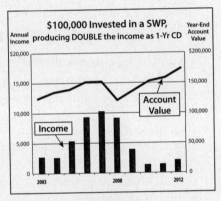

FIGURE 24.3

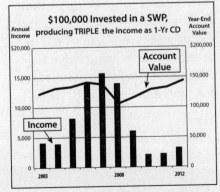

FIGURE 24.4

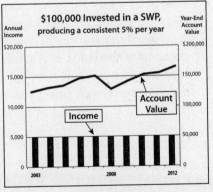

FIGURE 24.5

Figure 24.3 shows that you could have received **twice** as much in annual income as the CD, and your ending value would have been 83% higher than the CD's value.

Figure 24.4 shows the results of receiving **triple** the income of the CD. Even with this dramatic increase in income, your account would have ended nearly 50% higher in value than when you started.

Clearly, these are impressive results. But wait! There's more!

Simply matching, doubling or tripling the CD's income still would have left you with income that was inconsistent from month to month and year to year. To solve that problem, you could have arranged for your SWP to send you a consistent amount of income each month, just like you get from Social Security or a pension.

Figure 24.5 illustrates this: If you had decided to give yourself a 5% annual income stream, you would have received double what the CD would have paid, and your ending value would still have been $220,680, or 121% more than what you started with!

Please note these important disclosures: The results shown here reflect the results of a hypothetical portfolio over a specific time period. Different periods and asset mixes would produce different results; past performance does not guarantee future results. Also, notice in the figures that in some years the account fell in value, demonstrating that there are risks associated with this strategy. Finally, be aware that tax reporting can be confusing. With a SWP, you don't necessarily pay taxes on all the income you receive. Instead, taxes are based on the interest, dividends and capital gains the investments produce. We handle the tax record-keeping chore to keep it simple for our clients, and other good financial advisors do the same for theirs. But if you manage investments on your own, you'll want to keep this in mind.

Chapter 25
The Best Way to Transfer Your Retirement Accounts and IRAs to Your Heirs When You Die

Each time you open a retirement or IRA, you are asked a question: "When you die, who gets the money?" The person you name is your *beneficiary*.

> You can name more than one person. You can even name trusts and charities if you wish.
>
> If you name more than one beneficiary, you can state how much each gets, or you can let them split the account equally. It's entirely up to you.
>
> You can also change your beneficiary anytime, but you must do so in writing.

You will also be asked to name a *secondary beneficiary* (also called a *contingent beneficiary*). This person gets the money if the primary beneficiary predeceases you.

> Again, you can name more than one secondary beneficiary.

It's common for people to name their spouse as the primary beneficiary and their children as secondary beneficiaries. If you have done elaborate estate planning, you might have created a trust, and if so, you might want to name a trust that you've created as your beneficiary. Check with your estate attorney.

If you already own a retirement account or an IRA, answer this question: When was the last time you reviewed your beneficiary designation?

You need to see whom you named if (since you last reviewed it):

» family members have been born or died

» your marital status has changed

» your attitude about any family members has changed

If you don't name anyone as your beneficiary, your estate becomes your beneficiary. That means your heirs are determined by your will. And if you haven't signed a will, then (following your death) the money will be distributed by order of the probate court.

The result: You lose control over who gets the money — and the person or persons who get the money might not be whom you'd have selected.

Don't leave it to a judge to choose your beneficiary. Name yours by completing the paperwork when you open your retirement account and IRAs.

Here's an example of what can happen if you don't keep your beneficiary designation current. A gentleman participates in his retirement plan at work and names his wife as his primary beneficiary. They divorce a few years later. Fast-forward some more years and he gets married for a second time. They have a child and 10 years after that, the gentleman dies. When his widow contacts his employer, she discovers that the first wife — whom the deceased hadn't seen in more than 30 years — is still named as the beneficiary on his retirement account. Turns out the gentleman never thought to update it. The result: The first wife gets the money. His widow and their daughter get none of it.

Don't expect the courts to help in a case like this. The court case of John Hunter tells the tale. John was an employee of Marathon Oil, and in 1990 he designated his wife, Joyce, as his primary beneficiary for his 401(k). He signed a new document the same way in 2001. Neither time did he name a secondary beneficiary.

Joyce died in a traffic accident in 2004, but John didn't designate a new beneficiary. When he died the next year, the plan administrator, Eileen Campbell, distributed the money in John's account (more than $300,000) to his six brothers and sisters. She was aware that Joyce had two sons, Stephen and Michael Herring, and she was equally aware of how John felt about his stepsons: In his will, John left his entire estate to them, calling them his "beloved sons." But he had never legally adopted them, so Eileen concluded that the boys were not in the line of succession under the terms of the company plan. (As is often the case, accounts with no named beneficiaries are distributed in this order of priority: surviving spouse, children, parents, siblings and executor of the estate.)

> It's not a sure thing that your money will go to your designated beneficiaries. After all, the beneficiary is not required to accept your money. In rare instances, usually for estate planning reasons, beneficiaries disclaim the money (or a portion of it), meaning they deny themselves their right to receive some or all of it. Any money disclaimed by the primary beneficiary passes to other primary beneficiaries or, if there are none, to the secondary beneficiary or beneficiaries.
>
> Now you can see why a person might disclaim. Say you named your spouse as primary beneficiary and your children as secondary beneficiaries. If your spouse is financially secure and not in need of the money, he or she might disclaim the inheritance so the account can pass immediately to your children.
>
> Disclaiming should be done only with the advice of an estate attorney.

The boys challenged the distribution, claiming they were entitled to the money, citing their close relationship to Hunter as referenced in his will. The boys won their lawsuit.

But Eileen appealed, arguing that Marathon Oil's retirement plan gives the administrator "discretionary authority" to determine eligibility for benefits. The Fifth U.S. Circuit Court of Appeals (in *Herring vs. Campbell*) upheld her decision to give the money to John's siblings instead of Joyce's sons.

It took six years and tens of thousands of dollars in legal fees for the boys to learn they would not inherit the money in their stepfather's retirement account.

The lesson is clear: Review your documents to make sure that whomever you named as your beneficiary is still accurate.

Have you accidentally disinherited a child? You might have if you named only one child as your beneficiary, figuring that this child will split the asset with his or her siblings.

Not only might the IRS interfere with that plan (thanks to gift taxes), but the beneficiary might decide not to be as generous as you anticipated. And the beneficiary might have a spouse who has different plans too.

Bottom line: If you want certain people to receive a portion of the money in your retirement account, name them as beneficiaries.

You have three children, and you name them all as equal beneficiaries. All three children have children. What happens if one child dies before you do?

Some retirement plan and IRA custodians automatically assign the deceased child's share to your other children. In that case, the children of the deceased child get nothing. But other custodians default to *per stirpes*, which means "of issue." In this case, the deceased child's share goes to his or her children instead of going to his or her siblings.

So decide whether you prefer per stirpes or not, and then check with your custodian to make sure it handles your account the way you want.

Chapter 26
Have You Inherited a Retirement Account or an IRA?

Let's say you are the beneficiary of a retirement account or an IRA and the account owner has died. You are either the surviving spouse or a nonspouse. Let's explore what to do in each case.

If You Are the Spouse of the Decedent

If your husband or wife passes away and you are the beneficiary, you have four choices:

    A. Take the money from the deceased's retirement account, pay income taxes and spend the rest as you wish.

    B. Transfer the money to a new or existing IRA in your name, treating the account as if it had always been yours.

    C. Transfer the money to a Beneficiary IRA, which will be yours.

    D. Transfer the IRA assets to a new or existing IRA and then convert it to a Roth IRA.

Which answer is best?

Answer A is the worst, obviously, since taxes will be due on the distribution and the money will soon be gone. Sometimes, though, surviving spouses have no choice.

So on the hope that you don't need the money and can indeed leave it intact in a retirement account, Answer B is usually a better choice than Answer C, because B offers you more flexibility and potentially a lower minimum withdrawal requirement. Sometimes, though, Answer C is better; it depends on your spouse's age at the time of his or her death, your age, your income needs, and the type of IRA you inherit.

For example, if you are under age 70½ but your spouse was over 70½, Answer B lets you delay distributions until you reach age 70½. If you were to choose Answer C, you'd have to begin taking RMDs.

Say your spouse was age 70½ or older at the time of death. Did he or she execute the RMD for the year in which he or she died? If not, you'll have to do it (reporting the distribution under your Social Security number, not your spouse's, even though you'll calculate the RMD using your spouse's age and life expectancy, not yours. Go figure).

Answer C might be a better choice than Answer B if you are under age 59½ and need to access some or all of the money before you reach age 59½. That's because withdrawals in this case aren't subject to a 10% penalty — but they would be if you had selected Answer B.

When choosing a Beneficiary IRA (Answer C), the year when you have to take your first RMD (assuming your spouse died after his or her Required Beginning Date and did not yet take his or her RMD) will occur during the year of death and will be calculated based on the age your spouse attained when he or she passed away, not your age. It will, in effect, be handled much like he or she lived the entire year. Then, by Dec. 31 of the year following your spouse's death, the RMD amount to be withdrawn will be based on the greater of your spouse's age or your age, as found in the Single Life Expectancy Table of IRS Publication 590.

(If your spouse died prior to age 70½, you can delay RMDs until the year your spouse would have turned 70½, even if you are older than 70½.)

You getting all this?

If you transferred the money to a Beneficiary IRA and fail to take your distribution by the end of the year following the year of the original owner's death, you are subject to the *five-year rule*, which states that you can withdraw assets from an inherited IRA at any time, in any amount, provided you withdraw all the assets by Dec. 31 of the fifth year following your spouse's death.

We hate Answer D, although my colleagues and I grudgingly admit that there are a few circumstances where it might make sense. If you convert, future withdrawals will be tax-free. This notion is appealing, but there are lots of reasons not to convert, and I devoted eight pages to explain why in my book *The Truth About Money*. Here, highly condensed, are 13 reasons not to convert:

1. Converting won't necessarily increase your wealth.

2. Converting means you can't withdraw your money for five years.

3. Converting forces you to pay taxes today that you otherwise wouldn't have to pay.

4. Converting could push you into a higher federal income tax bracket.

5. Converting may subject you to an additional 3.8% Medicare tax.

6. Converting might cause your Social Security income to be subject to taxes.

7. Converting could increase your state income taxes.

8. Converting could cause you to pay a 10% IRS penalty.

9. Converting could require you to file estimated tax payments.

10. Converting means you might not know how much tax you will owe until next year.

11. Converting could increase your Medicare premium.

12. Converting could increase your taxes in retirement.

13. Converting could impact financial aid for your college student.

All that said, Answer D might be worth considering if you are in an unusually low tax bracket this year and converting won't alter that fact. This applies to very few people, which is why we tell most of our clients not to convert their IRA to the Roth IRA.

If You Are Not the Spouse of the Decedent

If the deceased IRA owner was not your spouse and you're not going to take the cash and spend it, you should create a *Beneficiary IRA (also called a Decedent IRA or Inherited IRA)*. If two or more people are beneficiaries, split the IRA into separate Inherited IRAs.

You must begin taking distributions from the account by Dec. 31 of the year following the IRA owner's death.[82] If the owner died on or after his or her Required Beginning Date, you base your withdrawals on the greater of your single life expectancy or the deceased IRA owner's life expectancy. If the owner died before his or her Required Beginning Date, you base your withdrawals on your life expectancy.

While you can withdraw as much as you want, a minimum requirement is defined by IRS actuarial tables. (If you fail to withdraw the minimum amount required in the first year, all the money must be withdrawn within five years.)

---

[82]Calculate the required amount by dividing the account balance (as of the prior Dec. 31) by the factor listed in the IRS Single Life Expectancy Table (Publication 590) for the age of the beneficiary. You must recalculate each year using the most recent year-end balance and the factor used in the first year, minus 1. Repeat annually until the IRA balance is zero or you die, at which point *your* beneficiary will take over (continuing with your math rather than being able to restart based on his or her own age and life expectancy).

Although complicated, these rules enable you to extend the life of the IRA, which can provide you with many years' worth of tax-deferred growth. It's worth the effort to gain the maximum benefit of these rules, so be sure to consult a tax or financial planner if you inherit a retirement account or an IRA — especially if you plan to leave the money to a trust, charity or other nonperson, because those rules are different and beyond the purview of this book.

"When I was young I thought that money was the most important thing in life; now that I am old I know that it is."

— Oscar Wilde

Permission of Harley Schwadron.

The Truth About Retirement Plans And IRAs

36 Key Take-Aways

Congratulations! You now know the truth about retirement plans and IRAs — and that means you're ready to improve how you contribute to, manage the money in, and make distributions from your accounts.

I invite you to use the information in this book to help you achieve your retirement goals. To make it easier for you, I've summarized the book's 36 key take-aways in this short, convenient list. Refer to it whenever you face a retirement plan or IRA question.

Thank you for spending time with me, and I wish you the very best retirement planning success!

1. Unlike many members of prior generations, you can't assume that your employer or the government will provide you with all the income you'll need in retirement. You must save for your retirement yourself.

2. And you need to start saving for retirement now.

3. The sooner you begin to save, the less you need to save each month, the more wealth you will accumulate, and the sooner you can quit saving and start enjoying a life of leisure.

4. Don't let anything stop you from saving.

5. You can accumulate wealth even if the stock market is falling.

6. Many employers offer free money to workers who save for retirement at work. If your employer is among them, make sure you do whatever you must to get your share of that free money — and if your employer isn't among them, consider changing jobs.

7. Ignore the bad advice offered by popular "money gurus," whose clever ideas can cost you hundreds of thousands of dollars in lost retirement savings.

8. To guesstimate how much money you'll need when you enter retirement, add a zero to the annual income you'll want in retirement and then double that figure. The result is a good indication of the amount you'll need in total savings and investments when you begin retirement.

9. Don't accidentally under-contribute to your retirement plan at work by letting your employer "auto-enroll" you into the plan. Instead, actively choose the amount you want to contribute to your plan — it'll likely be more than the amount your employer selects in the auto-enrollment process.

10. Your goal is to contribute as much of your pay to your retirement plan as you are allowed on a pre-tax basis. If you can't, just contribute as much as you can — even if all you can manage is $10.

11. Understand your plan's investment options before you start to invest.

12. Make sure you earn effective returns. Earning a low rate of return throughout your career is not going to produce the results you need.

13. Don't invest emotionally. Too often, this causes people to incur massive financial losses.

14. Ignore media hype about investing.

15. Don't mix money and politics.

16. Take advantage of dollar cost averaging.

17. If you own company stock in your plan, consider the NUA rule.

18. Place 100% of your current contributions exclusively into diversified stock funds. Invest your employer's contributions the same way.

19. Ignore mutual fund ratings.

20. Diversify your existing account balance extensively across all 18 major asset classes and market sectors on a global basis. The goal is to "own it all — all the time."

21. Periodically rebalance your portfolio.

22. Don't invest in a target-date fund unless you understand it and have confirmed it's your best option.

23. Supplement your workplace retirement plan with an IRA.

24. Do not contribute to a Nondeductible IRA.

25. Do not convert your current retirement accounts to Roth accounts.

26. Do not contribute to a Roth IRA unless you are in a low tax bracket.

27. If you leave an employer, move money from that workplace plan to an IRA.

28. Never borrow from your retirement plan.

29. If divorcing, never divide retirement plan assets without a court order.

30. Make sure you follow the rules for Required Minimum Distributions.

31. Determine how much money you'll need to withdraw from retirement accounts by reverse-engineering the process: begin at the end, by examining the amount you need. Then subtract income from other sources. Only the remainder should be withdrawn from your retirement accounts.

32. Maintain diversification in your retirement accounts and IRAs even after you retire.

33. Generate income in retirement through a strategy called a Systematic Withdrawal Plan.

34. Make sure you select the right beneficiaries for your retirement plans and IRAs.

35. If you inherit a retirement account or IRA, convert the money to your own account (if you are the surviving spouse) or to a Beneficiary IRA (if you are not).

36. If you have questions about retirement accounts and IRAs, contact us at 855-565-7249 — just like the folks on the following pages did.

RETIREMENT

One of the most popular features of my monthly newsletter, *Inside Personal Finance*, is the Q&A section. That's where I answer questions I receive from letters and emails, and callers to my radio and television shows. The following pages feature those dealing specifically with retirement issues; many might apply to your own situation.

And if you have questions of your own, you're invited to ask them: Call me at 855-565-7249 or email me at retirement@ricedelman.com, and I'll get you the answers you need for all your retirement planning needs.

Retirement Q&A

Q **I'm married with two children and am thinking of retiring when I'm 58. I have a portfolio with a value of about
$2 million. My home is currently worth $500,000. I won't
receive a pension, but I'll get Social Security in my 60s. Can I
realistically retire at 58 and maintain my present lifestyle —
which requires about $150,000 a year — without touching
the $2 million principal?**

Initially the answer would appear to be no. You have to plan to live
another four decades. If you need $150,000 a year, the rate of
withdrawal from your investments would have to be 7.5% a year,
which is not sustainable for that long. And because of inflation, in
20 to 25 years you might need $300,000 to equal the purchasing
power of $150,000 today.

But the prognosis isn't as scary as it may seem. Just because a 7.5%
withdrawal rate isn't sustainable doesn't mean your retirement idea is
a failure or that you're financially at risk. You're probably closer to
your goal than you think. Here's why:

You began with the premise that you don't want to touch the $2
million principal. Every retiree seems to say that like it's the 11th
Commandment: "Thou shalt not touch the principal." But in fact,
that's almost absurdly unrealistic and unnecessary. That is why you
have the money. Sure, you'd like to leave it for your kids and grandkids, but too bad for them. You need it, so use it.

Let's instead analyze it from the standpoint that we're willing to
allow the $2 million to be spent over the course of your lifetime.
Can we now generate $150,000 a year, adjusted for inflation? We
can't do the math here in 30 seconds (on the radio, talking with the
caller), but I'd say the odds are high the answer would be yes, you'd
probably be OK.

With more analysis, we can be definitive. We might find that, instead of retiring at 58, you might need to work until 60 or 62. If you've been earning $150,000 a year, your Social Security benefits will be more than $2,000 a month, not counting your wife's benefits. That brings you even closer to your goal.

Next, even if we discover you must work an extra couple of years, that doesn't necessarily mean full-time employment. It might mean taking a part-time job earning just $20,000 or $30,000 for a few years.

And, we haven't considered the worth of your home and how much it might appreciate over many years. It may not grow as fast as in previous years, but it will accrue value. Even if it stays at $500,000, it is another large asset that can generate income for you.

Thus, you are probably in far better shape than you think. I say *probably* because, to be certain, you need to discuss everything with a financial advisor, who will examine the money you have, how much you need to spend, when you need it, how long you will need it, your goals and objectives, and your risk tolerance. Once you do that, you'll have the definitive answer to your question.

Q **My company used to contribute 3% to our 401(k) plan. To get it, we had to put 6% of our pay into the plan. They just announced that now we have to contribute 10% of our pay to the plan in order for us to get their 3%. I suspect the motivation is that the company did this to save money because many staff can't save 10% and therefore won't get the total match. It seems counterintuitive to work harder than ever and yet end up with less in terms of retirement benefits. What's your opinion?**

At first glance, it indeed might seem that your employer is trying to save money. I doubt it, though. Most firms budget a certain amount of money for employee benefits. This figure includes everything from health insurance to the beer you drink at corporate functions. If costs become lower in one area, then those funds are often simply shifted to another area. Many firms don't retain the money saved from one area, and thus there is no windfall for the corporation.

Keep in mind that employers provide employee benefits for just one reason: to recruit and retain high-quality employees. As an employer, I know that it would be pointless to provide a benefit that no one wants; the firm would be wasting its money. So (at least in our organization), we work hard to determine what benefits you want and then we figure out how to provide them as best we can.

So if your boss isn't merely trying to save money, what might be the reason for asking you to save more in order to get the full match? As a financial advisor, I can think of a good reason for changing the employer match from "50 cents on the dollar" up to 3% of pay, to "30 cents on the dollar" up to 3% of pay.

The reason is this: If you save 6% of your pay for retirement, you will not be able to retire. You either will never retire or you will run out of money during retirement. You will be forced to go back to work — perhaps as a retail "greeter" or clerk at a fast-food restaurant. And your ability to keep working in your elder years assumes that your health will remain good enough to let you do that.

If you don't believe me, ask any financial advisor. Every professional will tell you the same thing.

Social Security will pay less than you hope, and you will have to be older than you anticipate before you will be eligible for benefits. Most workers will never receive a pension. And your expenses in retirement will not decline, so don't assume that you will be able to live on less than you live on today. (Sure, your expenses will change, but the amount will not. Commuting expenses will be replaced by health-care costs, and so on. You'll need as much money in retirement as you need today. Likely even more, due to inflation.)

You need to save 15% of your pay for retirement, and you need to start saving now. You don't have to save for college; your kids can repay college loans throughout their careers. And you don't have to save for a house; you can pay for it while you live in it (by making mortgage payments). But unlike college and homes, you must prepay for retirement; you cannot pay for retirement while you're in · retirement.

Therefore, you must start to save for retirement, and you must start right now. My research shows that saving 15% of pay in a properly diversified portfolio gives you a reasonable chance of accumulating enough money by retirement age so that you can quit working and still maintain your lifestyle.

To help you, your firm contributes money to your 401(k) account. Your employer places an amount equal to 3% of your pay into your account. But studies show that workers typically contribute only as much as is required in order to qualify for the employer's contribution. If you get the full match by saving 6% of your pay, then you'll contribute only 6%.

But saving 6% is not enough. You need to save 15%. Your employer's new policy, which requires you to save 10% of your pay to get the full employer match, will get you to 13% in total — close to the amount you need to save so that you can have a reasonable hope of retiring one day.

By the way, placing 10% of your pay into the plan will not cost you 10%. Thanks to the tax deduction you get, a 10% contribution will probably only cost you about 6.5%. Imagine: You place 6.5 cents into the plan and it's immediately worth 13 cents! You've doubled your money! And that's *before* you earn any investment returns!

Tell me again why you're complaining.

Oh yes, I forgot. You said many staff members can't afford to place 10% of their pay into the plan. I have two answers for them: Yes, you must; and yes, you can.

Yes, you must: As shown above, failure to place 10% of your pay into the plan will result in dire consequences for you at retirement.

Yes, you can: You might have to cut expenses elsewhere, but so be it. Life requires choices. If you do not believe you can cut your expenses, or if you don't know how or where to cut, talk with a financial advisor. If you don't have one, call us. We will help you. Stated more directly: We will take away your excuses. Remember: Excuses won't pay your bills in retirement.

If you remain unconvinced after all this, share this Q&A with your spouse/partner and your kids. Get their input before you decide not to put 10% of your pay into your retirement account.

Save 10% of your pay. Retire richer.

Q I've hit the maximum on my 401(k). Is it worthwhile to continue contributing on an after-tax basis?

It's great that you're contributing the maximum to your 401(k). All that money goes in on a pre-tax basis — a smart move. Make another, and don't put any after-tax money into your 401(k).

Once you reach the maximum, there's no benefit to putting more money into the 401(k). You don't enjoy a tax deduction on the excess, and the profits will be taxed at ordinary income tax rates, which are higher than capital gains rates. Therefore, it's better to invest that additional money in a taxable account.

Q My 27-year-old son lives with me, but he would like to move out and buy a house of his own. He doesn't have the money, but I could take the $60,000 or $80,000 he'd need for a down payment from my 401(k), and he could pay me back. I'm 57. Would it make sense for me to do that?

We wouldn't recommend it for several reasons.

First, because you're not yet 59½ years old and this is not a first-time home purchase or a hardship, you'd face taxes plus a 10%

penalty. For every dollar you took out, you'd have only 70 cents left for your son, which means you'd actually have to withdraw $1.50 in order for your son to get the dollar.

Another big concern is that, because you're in your late 50s, taking that much from your 401(k) could jeopardize your retirement. You might be reasoning that the real estate would grow in value faster than the money would grow in the 401(k), but keep in mind that the money you put into the house is no longer accessible to you. Should you need it later in an emergency, you couldn't sell a bedroom or a piece of the house; you couldn't demand that your son sell the house in order for you to get the money you need. You're much better off keeping it in your 401(k), where it's readily available to you.

At the same time, though it may not seem so to him, your son is better off financially staying with you and saving money. He should be able to accumulate enough for his down payment much faster than if he were to move out and pay rent. The process might be slower than he would like, but often there are good life lessons to be learned in delayed gratification.

It's good that he wants to buy a home and that you want to help him. But in the end, the fact is, he can't afford it yet; he's not ready. And it's simply not in your best interest to take money from your 401(k).

Q I'm 38 and my wife is 36. We're looking to put away some additional money for retirement. Right now, I'm maxing out my 401(k) and my wife is not working a full-time job, but she has some income from a jewelry sales business — about $20,000 per year. I'm trying to figure out if it would make sense for her to open a self-employed 401(k). She didn't set up an LLC and doesn't have any other retirement savings plan now. This seems like a way for us to put away money on a tax-deferred basis.

Yes, the solo 401(k) is a great option for you. It's for someone who's self-employed with no full-time employees. There are two components to the contributions: She can defer a significant part of her income and make a profit-sharing contribution of 20% to 25% as well.

Caution: You need expert help in establishing these accounts. Ask a financial advisor familiar with retirement plans for small business owners to help you, to make sure you don't run afoul of IRS rules.

Q **I set up a 15% contribution to my 401(k) plan at work, but in October I had to stop contributing because I hit the limit. Thus my paycheck got bigger in November and December. Is this going to cause a problem with anything, or does this really matter?**

Maybe. Some employers that provide a 401(k) match pay it as you contribute. If you don't contribute in a given month (because you over-contributed in prior months), you could lose that month's match.

Check with your employer to see how it pays its match. Some companies match your actual contributions as you make them; in that case, you're fine. But if your employer kicks in its match only in the months you actually contribute, you could inadvertently lose some of the match. That's literally throwing away free money.

Q **I'm a teacher. When I retire next spring, I'll receive my pension of about $65,000 a year. I also have the opportunity to roll my 403(b) account — about $220,000 — into my pension, guaranteed for life at a rate of $7.78 per $1,000. The advisor I use for my 403(b) says that wouldn't be wise — that it's better to keep it invested. What's your opinion?**

At first blush, it seems that your advisor is probably right, but we'd need to do some math to be sure. You need to do an "opportunity

267

cost" comparison to see which option is better. We'd compute the monthly income that the $220,000 would generate if placed into your pension and compare that amount to what we could generate if we invested that money elsewhere instead. Essentially, we want to find out which approach would produce more income.

But a proper analysis needs to go further, because rolling the money into the pension has these implications:

» The amount of money you'll get from the pension might never increase. If so, the income will be eroded by inflation over time. In a couple of decades, when you're in your 80s, the income will have half its current value based on historical rates of inflation.

» Rolling the money into the pension is an irrevocable decision. If you ever need the lump sum, you won't have access to it. This reduction in liquidity can be dangerous.

» Many state and local governments are experiencing significant financial challenges. Are you sure your teacher's pension will honor its promise to pay you the monthly income for life that you're expecting? Adding $220,000 to this promise seems like adding a bet onto a big bet you've already made.

» Adding the money to your pension will increase your monthly income. But do you really need that extra income? It might be better to invest it elsewhere so it can grow for years or decades, until needed. After all, if you receive income you don't need, you have to pay taxes on it anyway; if it's invested, you could have it grow tax-deferred until needed.

» When you die, the money in that pension is gone and the income you were receiving stops. Your surviving spouse and children get nothing. And if you try to preserve some inheritance for them, the only way to do it is to reduce (perhaps sharply) the income you'll get from the pension.

For all of those reasons, even before we do the math, you might conclude that rolling the money into your pension is probably not a good idea. But I emphasize the word *probably*. We'd want to examine your total financial picture in greater detail to make sure. Our analysis would not simply be a spreadsheet; it would evaluate your family's entire circumstances — goals, risk tolerance, need for income, life expectancy and other such matters from a complete financial planning perspective.

Therefore, while your 403(b) rep probably is right, I think his or her answer came a little too quickly because it's a very big, one time-only, irrevocable decision. That's why you should meet with an independent, fee-based, objective financial advisor; your rep is none of those. I suggest you consult with someone who is, to ensure that the opinion you get is truly in your best interest.

Q I work for the state of Connecticut for a nonprofit. Our workplace retirement plan has both an annuity component, TIAA (or Teachers Insurance Annuity Association, originally formed for schoolteachers), and a stock mutual fund component, CREF (College Retirement Equity Fund). I'm 60, and I expect to retire in two years. I have 65% of my money in TIAA and 35% in CREF. I'm wondering about the safety of the annuity, in case something happens to the insurance company. What is your opinion?

You're worrying about the wrong thing.

It is not likely that TIAA would incur an inability to pay income to you in retirement. Instead, you should be concerned about the limited liquidity offered by TIAA, the amount of the payment it offers you and the impact of inflation over the course of your retirement.

CREF's mutual funds provide rates of return that vary from year to year with the performance of the financial markets. You have the flexibility to shift your money among them as you wish, and at retirement you can withdraw the money in any amount whenever you wish. (You may withdraw all your money at any time, or slowly or not at all for many years.)

The annuity offered by TIAA offers a fixed rate of return. It is a low rate but has the advantage of predictability; you don't have to worry about stock market fluctuation or losses in value. But TIAA severely restricts your access to your money: Once you put money into TIAA, you can withdraw only 10% of your balance per year, meaning it would take you at least 10 years to get all your money back.

Most people reason that when they are younger they can afford investment risks; that makes them more willing to invest in CREF. But as they age, their willingness to tolerate risk declines. To reduce risk, they shift money from CREF to TIAA — often not realizing they've made a one-way decision: Once the money is in TIAA, you can't get it out any faster than 10% per year.

We don't like this restriction. TIAA says they provide full disclosure to investors, but we've encountered many instances where people say they didn't realize they were tying up their money for a decade when moving from CREF to TIAA.

You still have 35% of your funds in CREF. My advice is not to move that money into TIAA, since you're so close to retirement. Instead, move 10% a year from TIAA into CREF, so that by the time you retire in two years, you'll have half your money in CREF and half in TIAA instead of the current 35-65. If you are concerned about safety, realize that there are lower-risk choices available within CREF.

Q My friend is 71 years old and just retired from the Navy. She has a federal TSP (Thrift Savings Plan) account with $190,000 in it. What is she supposed to do with that 190 grand?

Usually, when you leave your employer (whether it's the federal government, the military, a nonprofit or a private company), you should roll the money in the employer retirement plan into an IRA.

There are two fundamental reasons for this.

First, IRAs offer you far more investment choices. In your friend's case, the TSP has just five choices. By moving the money to an IRA, your friend will have much more flexibility to invest in a more diversified fashion.

The second reason is simply that the IRA offers her better control over her money. The IRS rules are different for retirement accounts at work than they are for IRAs. Thus, when it comes time for her to make her distributions, it'll be easier for her to comply with the rules and she won't have to worry about the bureaucracy of a former employer.

If she moves her money properly, she shouldn't incur any taxes. She should talk to a financial advisor about an IRA rollover.

Q I'm a federal employee. Are ETFs available in the TSP?

No, but from a cost standpoint it doesn't matter. The investment choices in the federal TSP are the lowest in the industry.

The TSP's shortcoming is not that it fails to offer low-cost investments; the problem is that it offers too few choices (just five). That's why we recommend that our clients move their TSP money into an IRA when they leave government service.

Q I have about $1.5 million invested in my retirement account and other places. I just turned 66 but didn't apply for Social Security because I'm still working at a great job, and Social Security has not had any cost-of-living increases recently. I told myself I'd just wait another year or so. Waiting just one year increases my benefit about 8%. Did I make the right decision?

Not necessarily. We often recommend you take Social Security once you reach normal retirement age even if you are still working. If you wait, it will take years to break even, and who knows if you'll even live that long?

But be aware that the above does not apply to everybody. There are lots of situations where we'd recommend the exact opposite. For example, you shouldn't wait until age 70 to start taking benefits if you need the money to maintain your lifestyle.

In fact, in many cases we do advise clients to begin taking Social Security as early as age 62. Even though they get less than the maximum benefit, getting the money sooner is often of greater value — even if they don't need the income! (Investing those monthly checks can be a smart strategy.)

So, there is no general rule. Instead, you should talk to an objective, independent, fee-based financial advisor who can evaluate your specific situation.

Q **I heard your radio show discussion last week about the case of Verizon, which is transferring $7.5 billion in pension obligations to Prudential Insurance; Prudential will issue annuities to the retirees. Let me give you the real-life emotional point of view as one of the tens of thousands of affected retirees who have just been kicked out the door by the company for which I worked almost 40 years.**

What's the difference between getting paid by a pension fund or by an annuity? Well, annuities aren't covered by the Federal Pension Benefit Guaranty Corp. Is Prudential in danger of going broke and us losing our pension? I hope not. The real problem here for retirees is obligations and promises — both spoken and implied — being discarded.

A little history: All of the retirees covered by the now-defunct Verizon Pension Plan signed on with companies in the old Bell system in the 1940s, '50s and '60s. During those years, long before cell phones, fiber-optic, iPads and smartphones,

we installed and repaired plain old telephones and switch-boards. Most phone companies were subsidiaries of AT&T and part of the Bell system — a monopoly but a regulated one.

We were the folks who got up in the middle of the night to fix a line that was needed. We installed service when we promised. If you called for telephone repair, you were an-swered promptly and got an appointment usually for the same day. When there was a big storm, usually the only tracks out of a neighborhood belonged to a telephone company worker; that was our job — go fix what was broken.

It was a place where family and friends worked. In my case, three generations were "telephone people." We made it a point of personal pride to make things operate like they should — after all, it was our company too.

We didn't make large salaries, but we had job security, a chance to advance and, at the end of our career, a solid pen-sion with periodic raises and access to good health coverage. Ma Bell was a benevolent employer. Telephone people were respected members and leaders of their community.

Now comes the Justice Department and the breaking up of the Bell system. The company I worked for, the Chesapeake and Potomac Telephone Co., was bundled into several other East Coast companies and became Bell Atlantic, which later became Verizon. During this time territories changed, re-sponsibilities changed, the whole way of doing business became different. I had five different supervisors in an eight-month period. It was chaotic. The worst for some employees was when, because of combining or eliminating operations, they were deemed surplus and offered a buyout. That's the position I found myself in (after 30-plus years), along with several hundred others, but I was able to slip into a vacant job at a lower salary. I did so to protect my pension.

The way of life in the new telephone company changed forever. Profit began to overtake service as a mantra, and cost-cutting was the order of the day. Included was the pensioner — no more periodic cost-of-living raises for them. Those had been customary in the Bell system since the pension plans began.

I retired in 1989, one of the last years a pension was offered. In fact, I was given the option of taking the defined pension plan or a cash buyout. I chose the pension for the security of a regular check and the safety of the survivor option. Some of my co-retirees took the cash, and many who invested in high-tech stock lost it all when the bubble burst.

With the exception of one supplemental payment in the year 2000 (that, after taxes, amounted to less than $10,000), my pension payment remains the same as it began in 1989. And that's the rub; for all the years we worked, we received information about benefits present and expected, which painted a rosy retirement picture. Now here I stand in 2012, living on a 1989 salary.

A group of retirees for the past eight or 10 years has met with the officers of Verizon to plead our case for cost-of-living raises; it has been to no avail. Now Verizon has severed all ties with us by the shift of assets to Prudential.

That's the other side of the story.

Thank you for sharing your story. Your experience explains why we received Verizon's announcement with such astonishment and worry — and demonstrates why we usually advise our clients to take the lump-sum payment instead of the pension (when the choice is available, which it sometimes isn't). When you take the pension, you expose yourself to several risks:

» If the monthly check doesn't rise with inflation, you'll find it hard to keep up with the cost of living;

» If you need a large amount — say, for medical expenses or to help pay for the grandkids' college costs — you can't access the pension. All you can get is the monthly check;

» If you die, the income stops — placing your spouse at financial risk. To protect your spouse, you must agree to receive a smaller monthly pension;

» There is no inheritance for your children; the pension is for you (and maybe your spouse) only; and

» If the company goes out of business, the income might be interrupted, severely reduced or stopped entirely.

These risks can be avoided by taking a single, onetime payment, known as a lump sum, in lieu of monthly pension checks. You can invest as you wish, giving yourself a monthly income similar to what the pension would have provided. You can increase or decrease the income as you wish. You can access the entire balance anytime (subject to limitations that might be imposed by the investments you select), and any money you don't spend remains available to your spouse and children as an inheritance.

To decide which course of action is best for you, we advise those being offered pensions to consult with us or another fee-based, independent, objective financial advisor before making any decision. After all, this is a once-in-a-lifetime decision, you don't get to change your decision in the future, and you can't predict what might happen to that company during the 20 or 30 years you'll be living in retirement and dependent on them to honor their promises.

Make sure you make the right decision. A good advisor can help you.

Q **I got a buyout offer from my employer and am on the fence about taking the pension in a lump sum. I am lean-**

ing toward taking it and investing the money. You always say, "Do not put all your eggs in one basket." I know you invest in a diversified way, but still it would be in one basket. Can you discuss this?

You're right to be worried about concentration risk — having too many eggs in one basket. However, your view of the question is upside-down. Keeping the pension creates the very concentration risk I'd want you to avoid. If you keep the pension, you are entirely dependent on the company's ability and willingness to pay it every month for the rest of your life. Other huge companies have already demonstrated that this promise is fleeting: Many have reneged, reduced payments or simply gone bankrupt, ending the pension payments entirely (or forcing retirees to turn to PBGC, so they often end up with only a portion of what they were previously receiving). Indeed, leaving your pension in the hands of a former employer is maximum concentration risk.

By contrast, by taking the lump sum and investing the money into a highly diversified portfolio, your money moves from dependency on a single company to many thousands of companies and other issuers (including governments). This converts you from having all your eggs in one basket to having them spread among thousands of baskets — eliminating (or at least sharply reducing) concentration risk.

There's more too that you enjoy from this approach. By taking the lump sum, you retain full control over your money, meaning you can start, stop, increase or decrease your income at any time. (With the pension, you are limited to the one monthly check, with no future access to principal.) When you die, any unspent money goes to your spouse and kids. (With the pension, the income stops with your death; although you can continue income for your spouse after your death, you do so only at the cost of sharply reducing the income you'd get during your lifetime. Even then, your kids will still get nothing upon your spouse's death.)

But what about the concentration risk you'd incur by investing the entire proceeds through one advisory firm? I can't speak for other advisors, but at Edelman Financial Services we reduce that risk by implementing several safeguards for you. First, we have no access to or control over your money. Your account will be held at one of the largest custodians in the industry, and we have no control over or access to it (we merely serve as advisor to the account) — so you don't have to worry that something might happen to Edelman Financial Services. Your account will be invested in a variety of assets, further reducing concentration risk, and to guard against the risk that the custodian might fail, you'll enjoy protection from SIPC (which is to the securities industry what the FDIC is to banks) and supplemental coverage from the custodian that is virtually unlimited. (Keep in mind that this insurance, like FDIC insurance, protects against firm collapse; it does not protect against market losses in your account.)

In short, you are right to be worried about concentration risk — and that is exactly why you should take the lump sum.

Q **I just turned 70 years old in November. I have two IRAs. One is in a bank CD with a small amount but enough to meet the IRS required minimum withdrawal requirement. The other is in a brokerage account company and is worth a lot of money. If I withdraw the CD, does that meet the minimum withdrawal amount requirement for both accounts?**

If your math is correct, yes. But let's look more closely.

First of all, if you reached age 70 in November, be aware that you don't have to withdraw any money from any IRA this year. Or even next year.

The law says you can wait until April 1 of the year after the year in which you turn 70½. Since you reached 70 this past November, you turn 70½ next May. That means you have to make your first withdrawal by April 1 of the year after that. So you might want to get back to me in a year or so.

Assuming you're still with me, let me add more facts. If you wait until that April, you'll have to make two withdrawals that year: one for the prior year (which you've delayed until April 1) and another by Dec. 31 for the current tax year. (All withdrawals are taxable, so making two could push you into a higher tax bracket than if you spread them out across two tax years; for that reason, you might prefer to make one each year instead of two in the same year. But that would force you to pay tax a year sooner than necessary. And the higher bracket you'd incur in one year might be offset by the smaller bracket you'd enjoy in the other year, meaning two in one year might actually be better than one in each of two years. Isn't this fun?)

Also keep in mind that when you make a withdrawal, the amount you must withdraw is based on IRS tables. Those tables are based on your age (and more accurately, on your life expectancy and on the age of your spouse if there is more than a 10-year difference between your ages).

Furthermore, the value of your account is based on last year's Dec. 31, not the value of the account as of the date you actually make the withdrawal. (You following all this?)

Finally, the IRS doesn't care how many IRAs you have. It just wants to know the total value of all of them, and it wants you to make a withdrawal by the deadline for the minimum amount. So, yes, you can withdraw money from just one IRA to cover all your IRAs, provided that the amount you withdraw is enough to cover the minimum required for all the IRAs.

But here's an important caveat: You must withdraw the minimum required amount from each *type* of retirement plan. An IRA is different from a SEPP-IRA, which is different from a 401(k), a 403(b) or a 457 plan. If you have money in both a 401(k) and an IRA, you can't merely withdraw money from the IRA to cover the value of the 401(k); you must make separate withdrawals from each type of account. (If you were having fun before ... !)

If you make a mistake — taking the money too late, withdrawing too little or failing to withdraw from the proper accounts — you'll not only owe the tax, but you'll owe a 50% penalty as well (on the amount you were supposed to withdraw but didn't).

These rules are indeed designed to trap you. They are deliberately designed to increase government revenue. They're obscene, absurd and indefensible. But you either obey or suffer the consequences.

Q **I'm 73, so I've had to take several of those required minimum distributions from my IRAs. When I take those out, I've got to pay the tax on them. Is there any way to combine that with converting to a Roth?**

No, but nice try.

As you know, withdrawals from IRAs are both required after age 70½ and taxable. But withdrawals from Roth IRAs are neither required nor taxable.

So why not move money from an IRA to the Roth IRA?

Here's why not: To move the money, you actually withdraw it from the current IRA — and doing so makes that money fully and immediately taxable. So instead of withdrawing just a little bit from your IRA, you'll find yourself withdrawing all of it — dramatically increasing the tax bite.

When it comes to taxes, here's a general principle: If there is something you'd like to do because you think doing it will help you avoid taxes, you can be pretty sure the IRS doesn't allow it.

Like I said, nice try.

Q **The question I have is regarding the required minimum withdrawal from an IRA. When or how often in a year should I take the RMD — annually, semiannually, quarterly or monthly? I don't plan on spending the money.**

The IRS says you must begin to withdraw money after age 70½. It doesn't care when or how often you do this, provided you withdraw the correct amount by Dec. 31 of each calendar year. The frequency is up to you.

That means your decision should be based on your needs and goals. Some people need the income, so they start withdrawing money in January and they continue receiving money monthly.

But you said you don't need the cash. That means you'll simply move the money from an IRA to a taxable savings or investment account. It doesn't matter how you withdraw the money. You can take a single lump sum once per year or a series of payments over the course of the year. But whichever way you do it, maintain consistency. This way, you reduce the risk that market fluctuations will adversely impact the withdrawals.

Q My wife needs to take money from her IRA to meet the required minimum distribution. Is it best to do this during a week when the markets are up?

Yes, make sure you sell only at the highest price. Never sell at the lowest price.

That's a joke. Hope you found it funny.

Everyone, of course, always wants to sell at high prices. But no one knows when the "highest" price is reached.

So, let's get off that roller coaster. Your wife should simply liquidate each month 1/12th of the RMD amount. This way, she'll get the average price for the year. She won't get the highest price — but she won't get the lowest either.

And if she's going to reinvest the proceeds (after paying taxes), it doesn't matter when she sells or what price she receives. That's because she'll simply be moving money from an IRA to a non-IRA. Economically, the transaction will be a wash.

Q **I'm in my mid-60s and getting close to retirement. We believe our investments are well-diversified. How much money can we withdraw from our accounts and be sure our money will last the rest of our lives?**

That's an easy question to ask but a hard one to answer. It depends on how long you'll need that money. If you're married and both in your 60s, one of you can be expected to be alive at age 95. That suggests we need the money to last 35 years or more. We must consider inflation as well. All this affects the amount you should withdraw each year.

If preservation of capital is not as important (perhaps you have no spouse or children, or you don't like them very much), we can dramatically increase the withdrawal rate for you.

To be certain that you're taking the right amount, talk with a financial advisor.

Q **I just rolled over an IRA and decided to have my brokerage firm manage it for me. I can pay the fee externally by check or they can take it from the portfolio. I'm hesitant to have them take it from there because I'm not working anymore, so I can't put in any more money. I'm afraid that, when the market is down, they'll have to sell shares to cover the fee. What's the best way to handle this?**

It makes more sense to let them debit the account. Here's why:

When you take money from the IRA, it will be fully taxed, so a dollar in your IRA is worth only about 70 cents to you. If they take the fee from the IRA, it's really costing you only 70 cents on the dollar. You aren't taxed on that debit; the IRS says that a fee drawn from a retirement account is not taxable.

Handling it that way is more efficient too. It preserves your liquidity and minimizes the growth of the account — which, for tax purposes, is a good thing — while allowing you to maximize the growth of your non-IRAs.

Q **I have an opportunity to buy a percentage of a commercial building. It looks like a good deal, offering a fine return on the investment. My partners and I would pay cash for it. I have a dormant 401(k) with a former employer. Could I roll that over into a self-directed IRA to purchase the property?**

Can you? Yes.

Should you? No.

Because your money is in an IRA, you'll eventually have to start making withdrawals. But if the asset owned by the IRA is real estate, you'll have a problem. If you own stocks or mutual funds, you can sell a few shares. If you own bank accounts, you can withdraw a portion. But if you are one of many owners of a piece of real estate, you can't sell a portion of your investment. (Who ever heard of selling the living room but keeping the basement?) And if you can't sell, you'll run afoul of IRS rules. Think penalties — big penalties (50% of the amount you should have withdrawn, plus the tax itself).

Also, IRAs must be valued each year. That's easy for stocks, bonds, ETFs and mutual funds. But real estate must be appraised — and that's expensive to do every year.

No wonder few IRA custodians are willing to hold real estate in an IRA. The few that do this usually charge a lot of money — 1.5% annually is common, though I've seen fees as high as 3% per year.

And here's one final reason: When you put real estate inside an IRA, you lose all the tax benefits of real estate, such as depreciation and amortization. And the profits will eventually be taxed as ordinary income instead of capital gains. You also lose the ability to exchange the property for another tax-free option (known as a Starker Exchange) if the opportunity arose.

So, no, don't use the money in a retirement account to buy real estate. The investment might indeed be a good one, but use other funds to acquire it.

By the way, you referred to your account as "dormant." That pejorative term makes me think you're not happy with the returns you're earning in that account. (If you were happy, I doubt you'd be interested in moving the money to your real estate idea.)

You should send us a copy of your 401(k) statement so we can review it for you at no cost. The account there might be performing better than you think, meaning you should leave the money where it is. But if it's doing as poorly as you think, we can recommend improvements for you.

Q **My question is about the 3% inflation rate that often gets discussed. If I tell you I want $50,000 a year in retirement, you're going to tell me that, in 25 years, $50,000 at a 3% inflation rate will really be $100,000, and the rule of thumb is that you can't take any more than 4% out your first year, so therefore you need a nest egg of $2.5 million when you retire. I'm going to get really intimidated and depressed by that number and give up. Is a 3% inflation rate real? I just bought a pair of Dockers for about the same amount I spent for a pair 10 years ago. Also, I just booked a four-day trip to the Reno/Lake Tahoe area at a well-known casino, and the hotel bill for four days was just over $200. That's pretty cheap. I don't think it was *cheaper* than that 20 years ago. Obviously things like electronics continue to get cheaper — not more expensive. When I was in college in the late '80s, desktop computers were being sold from the campus store for $4,000 to $5,000. Now I can buy a computer for a couple hundred bucks. So I'm not buying the idea that everything in the future will cost more by 3% per year. My real-world experience says otherwise. Not everything gets more expensive. Have there been any analytical studies that show a more realistic rate that an investor can use for retirement planning?**

Great question.

Yes, the 3% figure is real. You're using a narrow set of anecdotal evidence to support your conclusion that prices have fallen. Sure, many clothes are still cheap because of cheap overseas labor. And sure, casinos are happy to let you stay for cheap rates to encourage you to gamble more. And even though electronics are indeed cheaper than they were 20 or 25 years ago, I'd argue that you're spending more on them than you did back then. After all, how much did you spend on all electronics in the late 1980s? Maybe you purchased a computer. Today that PC may cost less, but you also subscribe to cable TV, you own a smartphone (with monthly service charges), and you probably have an iPad or a Kindle plus electronic game devices for your kids, and much more. Add it all up, and it's a fair bet that you're spending far more on technology now than you once did.

Also consider that you didn't mention gasoline, which at this writing averages about $3.60 per gallon across the nation (about $1 more per gallon in some states, including California). Then there are postage stamps, food, entertainment (movies cost twice as much as 10 years ago), transportation, housing and health care (which is your biggest future cost threat).

Still, you don't need to be discouraged. In fact, you raise several important points that suggest your future won't be horrible. First, you agree that the key to retirement security is maintaining your buying power. Car prices don't matter because retirees seldom buy new cars, and few are still incurring college expenses. As a result, if you spend your money only on clothes and computers, inflation might not be the threat that some make it sound.

Second, inflation rates aren't certain to be 3% every year. Think back to the 1970s, when inflation was 13%. CD rates at the time were 18%. In 2013, CD rates are around 1% or less, but inflation is very low too. Thus, future inflation might be different from what it's been in the past. It depends on how the economy performs, and it depends on the goods and services you plan to buy. Because investment returns are often a reflection (to some degree) of inflation rates, don't assume that you can't keep up with high inflation rates. If you invest correctly, you can.

In our opinion, it's foolish to assume inflation will not be a problem for you. After all, you can't avoid spending money on something merely because prices have risen. Oil prices, food costs and health care are three good examples. And the costs of each have risen faster than the average rate, compounding the problem.

So instead of challenging whether 3% is a fair assumption for future inflation rates, simply recognize that inflation matters, and as rates rise (and fall) you need to have your assets rise to keep pace in order to preserve your financial security for your lifetime.

Q I'm 64 and plan to retire within two years. I'm sitting on $1.6 million worth of company stock, both inside and outside my 401(k) and in options. The stock is approaching an all-time high. Should I sell it all at once, one-half or one-third at a time or in smaller increments? And what about the options? Do I sell them now while the price is high or wait until they get closer to the termination date regardless of the tax consequences? I believe the income from this, along with my pension and Social Security, will be enough to maintain my lifestyle in retirement.

First, you deserve applause because you understand that you need to diversify. Those who don't diversify their holdings usually live to regret it. The challenge, of course, is knowing *when* to sell. You're probably asking yourself, "Do I sell it and watch it go up, or keep it and watch it go down?"

On a list of the world's problems, this one is a fun problem to have, but it's a problem nonetheless — one that can keep you awake at night or cause fights with your spouse. So let me show you how to resolve the dilemma.

You must approach the issue from a lifestyle-based, risk-based perspective. Avoid the "let's maximize the profit" approach, because that's how you can get into trouble.

I remember one client who had nearly all of his life savings tied up in a Fortune 25 stock. He'd worked for the company 40-plus years and didn't want to sell because of the company's reputation and his loyalty to it. But we all remember what happened to stocks during the credit crisis: His stock lost more than 50% of its value. It can happen to anyone.

The only reason you would delay selling all of it now is because you suspect that it might increase in value. But that's gambling. Who knows what's going to happen to the stock in the next 24 months? Anything under three years is a gamble. If you give me 10 years, I'll give you a good estimate of what you can expect. But if you're asking me what will happen in just six months or a year or two — well, in that short a time frame, no one has any idea what will happen.

Therefore, you should sell it all now.

You probably understand this intellectually. But emotionally, that might be very hard to do. You've been a loyal employee, you've seen the company do well, you still have high hopes for it and you are confident the stock will continue to do well. It feels almost like a betrayal to liquidate all of it, especially before retiring.

If you're feeling this way, here's an alternative: Just sell half or two-thirds now and sell the rest over the next two years. Be aware, though, that the longer you hold the stock, the greater your risk of loss.

Let's say you follow my advice and sell all of it tomorrow, and the day after the price rises. How will you feel? You should not berate yourself. Instead, you should congratulate yourself that you secured your retirement — and that's really what matters. Remember that the stock could just as easily have fallen the day after you sold.

If you prefer to sell gradually, you must remain disciplined: Decide the number of shares you will sell and the interval (monthly? quarterly?), and stick to your plan. Don't allow news reports or market activity to cause you to deviate from your plan.

How shall you reinvest your proceeds? This is an equally important question. We recommend you invest in a widely diversified portfolio that has the proper mix of all major asset classes and market sectors, to help you meet your income needs in retirement. Then rebalance that portfolio to ensure that your portfolio maintains its diversification. An independent, objective, fee-based financial advisor can help you accomplish these aims so that your retirement is everything you hope it will be.

Q Do you have an opinion on the Vanguard Target Retirement account?

Of course I have an opinion. I have an opinion on everything.

But I'm not going to share my opinion here because if I say I love that fund, readers might go buy it; if I say I hate it, everyone might rush to sell it.

What really matters is your particular situation — your needs, wishes, goals and risk tolerance. Tell me that, and I'll be happy to give you my opinion.

Glossary

72(t) See "Substantially Equal Periodic Payments."

401(k) An employer-sponsored retirement plan that allows employees to put a percentage of earned wages into a tax-deferred account. Employee contributions are usually tax-deductible.

403(b) A retirement plan similar to a 401(k), but available primarily to schools, hospitals and other nonprofit organizations. Annuity products are generally the only investment option.

403(b)(7) Similar to a 403(b) retirement plan, this plan allows participants to invest in mutual funds as well as annuity products.

457 Plan A retirement plan available primarily to state and municipal government employees, including police officers, firefighters, other civil servants and employees of some state universities and school districts.

Active Fund A mutual fund that hires a portfolio manager to buy securities that he/she believes will outperform the overall market and sell those that won't. Active funds tend to be higher in cost and risk than *passive funds*. Although these funds offer the potential for higher returns than the overall market, most fail to do so.

Adjusted Gross Income (AGI) Total annual income minus deductions, credits and other offsets including contributions to retirement plans.

Amortization The process of paying off a loan over time, where each payment consists of a larger portion of principal and a smaller portion of interest than the previous payment.

Annuitization Converting a lump sum of money into a series of monthly income payments for a specified period of time.

Annuity An insurance product that provides a tax-deferred return for a specified number of years.

Asset Allocation The distribution of money among a variety of investment categories, such as stocks, bonds and real estate. The result is called an *asset allocation model* or *investment portfolio.*

Asset Class A broad investment category, encompassing all securities of its type regardless of distinction. *Stocks* are an asset class, for example, with no distinction for type of stock.

Benchmark A point of reference, used to compare the performance of an investment to its peers.

Beneficiary IRA An IRA containing assets originally held by someone who died. The heir of the deceased is now the owner of the account.

Capital Gains Tax A tax levied on investment profits in the year an investment is sold.

Catastrophisizing Bias The psychological act of fearing that bad news will become the worst possible news.

Coincident Indicators Economic data that reflect the current state of the economy.

Commodities Basic materials or ingredients, such as food or metal, that are grown or mined for sale and eventual consumption.

Compound Growth The increase in an asset's value by growing not only its initial value but also the value of previously earned interest or growth.

Concentrated Fund A mutual fund that has most of its assets in a relatively small number of securities.

Confirmation Bias The psychological act of agreeing with data/information that supports the view you already had.

Contingent Beneficiary See "Secondary Beneficiary."

Cost Basis The amount you paid to purchase an asset.

Currency Risk The risk that the value of an asset might fall due to changes in foreign currency exchange rates.

Death Benefit The amount of money an insurance company pays when a policyholder dies.

Decedent IRA An IRA whose funds were originally owned by a person who is deceased. Also called a *Beneficiary IRA*.

Deductible IRA An IRA whose contributions are tax-deductible.

Default Risk The risk that an asset might become worthless if the issuer goes bankrupt.

Defined Benefit Plan An employer-based retirement plan where the employer is obligated to make monthly payments of a pre-defined amount to qualifying employees during their retirement.

Defined Contribution Plan An employer-based retirement plan to which the employer makes contributions on behalf of qualifying employees, but the future value of those contributions is unknown.

Depreciation A methodology used to determine the eroding value of an asset over its useful life.

Discretionary Authority The right of an advisor to buy or sell a client's securities without first obtaining the client's approval.

Distributions Money paid from an asset or fund to the account owner.

Diversification The concept of owning a great many assets, rather than a few.

Dividend A corporation's profit that is distributed to shareholders.

Dollar Cost Averaging The practice of investing a fixed amount of money into a specific investment at a specific interval.

Dow Jones Industrial Average A price-weighted average of thirty of the largest companies traded on the New York Stock Exchange.

Drift The shift in a portfolio's composition, caused when one or more asset classes rises or falls faster than others.

Drift Parameter The degree to which an asset's original value will be permitted to vary, both higher and lower. These limits are set by the investor.

Earned Income Compensation from wages, salary, tips and bonuses.

Edelman Online A web site that enables investors to determine which portfolio is right for him/her. Available at RicEdelman.com.

Employee Benefits Security Administration (EBSA) A division of the Department of Labor that is responsible for enforcing the Employee Retirement Income Security Act, which governs many retirement plans.

Employer Match The amount of money an employer contributes to an employee's retirement account based on the amount contributed by the employee.

Employment Retirement Income Security Act (ERISA) The federal law that governs how pension and retirement plans operate.

Exchange-Traded Fund A group of securities that is traded on the New York Stock Exchange.

Federal Deposit Insurance Corporation (FDIC) An agency chartered by Congress to insure bank deposits against bank failures.

Federal Reserve The central bank of the United States that regulates monetary policy.

Financial Industry Regulatory Authority (FINRA) A self-regulatory organization authorized by the U.S. Securities and Exchange Commission to regulate brokerage firms, stockbrokers and mutual funds.

Fixed Annuity An insurance product that offers a fixed rate of return for a specified period. The interest earned is tax-deferred until withdrawal. Withdrawals can be annuitized at the policyholder's option.

Fortune 500 A list of the 500 largest publicly traded companies in the United States, according to *Fortune* magazine.

Glide Path The shift in a mutual fund's mix of assets, from stocks to bonds, over a period of time.

Government Accountability Office (GAO) A federal agency that serves as the investigative arm of Congress.

Group Annuity An annuity purchased by a number of investors, typically a company's employees. By pooling their investments, they often can negotiate lower fees.

Guide to Portfolio Selection See "Edelman Online."

Herd Mentality Bias The psychological act of being willing to make a foolish decision merely because many others are making the same mistake.

Individual Retirement Account (IRA) A retirement plan that individuals can establish on their own, outside of any employer-based plan. Contributions may be tax-deductible; growth is tax-deferred and withdrawals may be tax-free.

Inflation The occurrence of an increase in the price of goods and services.

Inherited IRA An IRA whose funds were originally owned by a person who is deceased. The new owner was not the decedent's spouse.

In-Kind Transfer The transfer of securities from an employer retirement plan to an individual account.

In-Service Distribution The transfer of assets from an employer retirement plan to an IRA while still employed and contributing to the retirement plan at work.

Interest Rate Risk The risk that an asset's value will fall if interest rates rise.

Internal Revenue Code The federal tax law.

Knee in the Curve Period where exponential growth is about to trend upward dramatically.

Lagging Indicator Economic data that reflect past performance.

Leading Indicator Economic data that predict future performance.

Liquidity The ability to convert an asset into cash quickly and easily.

Living Benefit A guarantee offered by an insurance company to an investor of its annuity product, promising that the value of the annuity, or the income it provides, will not fall below stated minimums.

Market Sector A portion of an asset class. Where *stocks* is an asset class, *large-cap value stocks* is a market sector.

Master Limited Partnership An investment, typically in oil and gas, organized as a certain legal entity. MLPs often trade on the New York Stock Exchange. *Limited partners* invest money and hope for profits; their risk is limited to the amount of their investment. The *general partner* manages the enterprise, earns a portion of the venture's profits and has unlimited liability.

Modern Portfolio Theory The most commonly accepted basis for investment management in use today. MPT adherents diversify their investments among a variety of asset classes and market sectors. The goal is to generate above-average returns at below-average risks.

Money Something you'll never have enough of.

Morningstar An investment research company that compiles and analyzes mutual fund data.

NASDAQ An electronic stock exchange where investors buy and sell securities.

Net Unrealized Appreciation The increase in value between an investment's cost and its current price.

New York Stock Exchange A place where investors buy and sell stocks.

Non-Cash Compensation Employee benefits, such as employer contributions to a retirement plan, paid time off and health insurance.

Non-Deductible IRA An IRA where contributions are not tax-deductible, although annual profits are tax-deferred.

Non-Qualified Plan A retirement plan that is not covered by ERISA.

Ordinary Income Wages, salaries, commissions and interest. Profits from an investment are not included.

Participant Catch-Up Contribution Investors over age 50 are permitted to contribute more to retirement plans than younger people.

Passive Fund A mutual fund that buys all the securities in a given market, with the goal of producing returns equal to that market. Passive funds tend to be lower in cost and risk than *active funds* and have a record of generating higher returns than most of them.

Pension A monthly income, usually provided to retirees for life.

Pension Benefit Guaranty Corporation (PBGC) A federal agency within the Department of Labor that guarantees the pensions of some private companies and ensures that at least some of the promised retirement benefits will continue even if the company becomes insolvent.

Pension Fund A pool of money established by a company or union to provide monthly income to retirees.

Per Stirpes A legal definition whereby all heirs receive their share of an inheritance, even if an heir dies before the owner.

Plan Administrator An individual or company responsible for managing a company's pension fund or retirement plan.

Political Risk The risk of investment loss due to changes in public policy, including a government overthrow or nationalization of assets.

Portfolio Drift A change in the value of different assets, relative to each other within a portfolio.

Primary Beneficiary Synonym for *heir* or *recipient*. The beneficiary of a retirement plan, trust, annuity or insurance policy will receive the account's assets upon the owner's death. There may or may not be tax implications for both the deceased's estate and the heir.

Principal An investor's original capital, i.e., the money being invested.

Profit-Sharing Contribution Funds added to an employee's retirement account by the employer based on the company's profits.

Qualified Domestic Relations Order A court order that instructs a retirement plan participant to distribute money from his or her account to an ex-spouse.

Qualified Plan A retirement plan covered by ERISA.

Real Estate Investment Trust (REIT) A pool of money that invests in real estate or mortgages. Some REITs trade on the New York Stock Exchange; others are nontraded.

Rebalancing The act of selling a portion of some assets within a portfolio and buying more of other assets, to restore a portfolio's composition to its desired asset allocation.

Recency Bias The psychological act of assigning greater weight to recent events than to longer-term results.

Re-Characterization The act of converting a Roth IRA back to its original form of a Deductible IRA.

Required Minimum Distribution (RMD) The amount of money an individual must withdraw from retirement accounts in conformance with tax law.

Retirement Income – for Everyone Trust (RIC-E Trust®) A retirement planning tool created and patented by Ric Edelman that allows parents and grandparents to help a child save for retirement.

Rider Optional features you may purchase when buying an insurance product.

Rollover IRA An IRA that contains assets originally held in another retirement account.

Roth An IRA or employer-sponsored account that is funded with after-tax contributions. Withdrawals are tax-free in retirement.

Rule 72(t) See "Substantially Equal Periodic Payments."

S&P 500 Stock Index A list of 500 of the largest public companies in the United States.

Secondary Beneficiary Synonym for *heir* or *recipient.* The secondary beneficiary of a retirement plan, trust, annuity or insurance policy will receive the account's assets upon the owner's death, provided that the primary beneficiary has predeceased the owner. There may or may not be tax implications for both the deceased's estate and the heir.

Securities and Exchange Commission (SEC) The federal regulator of the securities markets, exchanges and investments and investment advisors.

Securities Investor Protection Corporation (SIPC) An agency chartered by Congress to insure brokerage deposits against failures by brokerages.

SIMPLE IRA An employer-sponsored retirement plan provided by companies with no more than 100 employees.

Small Sample Size Representative Bias The psychological act of using a small amount of data to reach a broad conclusion.

Solo 401(k) An employer-sponsored retirement plan for self-employed individuals with no full-time employees.

Spousal IRA An individual retirement account available to unemployed individuals whose spouse has an earned income.

Step-Up The setting of a new cost basis for an asset. This occurs when a person inherits an asset upon the death of another; the deceased's original cost basis is replaced by the value of the asset as of the date of death or nine months later, whichever is higher. This allows the heir to avoid paying capital gains taxes on the increase in value that occurred during the deceased's lifetime.

Structured Settlement An agreement to provide or receive specific payments over a period of time.

Subaccount Investment choices within a variable annuity.

Substantially Equal Periodic Payments A method of distributing money from a retirement account prior to the age of 59½ that avoids the 10% IRS early-withdrawal penalty.

Systematic Withdrawal Plan A method of generating income in retirement.

Tax-Deferred Investment income or profits that are not taxed until withdrawn from an account. Also called *Tax-Sheltered*.

Tax-Sheltered Annuity see "Group Annuity" or "Fixed Annuity."

Thrift Savings Board The agency that oversees management of the federal Thrift Savings Plan.

Thrift Savings Plan A retirement savings plan for federal employees and members of the uniformed services.

Trustee-to-Trustee Transfer The process of transferring assets, tax-free, from one retirement plan custodian to another.

Variable Annuity A type of annuity product where the return is based on the performance of the financial markets in which the money is invested.

Vesting The process by which employees accrue irrevocable ownership of assets contributed by their employers to accounts established for the employee's benefit.

Index

Page numbers in *italics* refer to charts and graphs.

Dychtwald, Ken, 219

early-withdrawal penalty, 96n14,
    169, 194–96
economic indicators, 58
Edelman Financial Services, 130
Edelman Online, 129–30
emotions, 55–61
    catastrophizing bias, 61
    confirmation bias, 58–60
    and crises, 68
    and media hype, 64
    and politics, 75–78
    and rebalancing, 133
    recency bias, 57, 60
    representative bias, 56–57
    and volatility, 59
Employee Benefits Research
        Institute (EBRI), 28–29, 31,
        43
Employee Benefits Security
        Administration, 168
Employee Retirement Income
        Security Act [ERISA]
        (1974), 5, 185–86
employers:
    company stock, 91–92, 94–96,
        285–87
    previous, inactive funds with, *see*
        dormant funds
    and risk of theft, 168
employer's matching contributions:
    and employee's maximum
        contribution, 267
    as free money, 36, 37–42, 267
    investing, 115–16, 118
    percentage of, 263–65
Enron, 91–92, 97
entrepreneurship:
    borrowing from retirement plan

for, 182
    and 401(k) plans, 266–67
    and IRAs, 10–11
    retirement accounts, *149*
ERISA [Employee Retirement
        Income Security Act] (1974),
        5, 185–86
estate, as beneficiary, 246
exchange-traded funds (ETFs),
        100–101
    and dormant accounts, 164–65
existing account balance, 117–46
    and asset allocation, 124
    and belling the cat, 119
    diversification, 122–29
    how to reallocate, 121–22
    investing in a mix of funds,
        117–18, 119
    investing in stock funds, 117–19
    and investment goals, 122–23
    owning it all, 129
    reallocating, 119–22
    rebalancing, 130–38
    resources, 129–30
    target-date funds, 138–46
    when to reallocate, 119–21
expenses, in retirement, 28–29
exponential growth, 13–16, *14*, 20
    doubling penny, 14–16, *15*, *16*,
        26, 27
    and knee of the curve, 27
    and rate of return, 51–54, *51*, *53*,
        54
exponentiality, nature of, 26
Exxon Mobil, 92

fear:
    books promoting, 72–74
    and rebalancing, 133
Federal Deposit Insurance

About the Author

Ric Edelman and his firm, Edelman Financial Services, have won more than 100 financial, business, community and philanthropic awards over the past 25 years.[1] Ric's commitment to teaching consumers about personal finance has established him as one of the most popular and accessible financial experts in America.

Acclaimed Financial Advisor

Edelman Financial Services has 95 financial advisors in 34 offices nationwide, and manages more than $12 billion for 23,000 clients.[2] Ric has been ranked the #1 Independent Financial Advisor in the nation three times by *Barron's*.[3] In 2013, *InvestmentNews* named him one of the industry's 15 most transformative figures over the past 15 years[4], and in 2012, the highly regarded industry website, RIABiz.com, named Ric one of the ten most influential figures in the investment advisory field.[5] Ric is a member of the Financial Advisor Hall of Fame, sponsored by *Research* magazine,[6] and the CNBC Digital Financial Advisors Council.

Ric graduated cum laude from Rowan University in 1980 and was awarded an honorary doctorate from his alma mater in 1999. In 2012, he graduated from the Executive Program at Singularity University. Ric has been featured in numerous articles, has appeared on hundreds of radio stations and every major television network, and has been quoted by dozens of newspapers and magazines, including *The Wall Street Journal*, *The Washington Post*, and *USA Today*.

Best-selling Author

Ric is a #1 *New York Times* best-selling author. Two of his eight books (*The Truth About Money* and *The Lies About Money*) have been named "book of the year" by the Institute for Financial Literacy. All told, his books have more than one million copies in print, have been translated into several languages and have educated countless people worldwide.

National Radio and Television Host and Newsletter Editor

Ric has been host of radio and TV shows for more than 20 years. His weekly radio show airs in 70 markets across the country and was ranked in 2012 as #2 as the Most Important Weekend-Only Talk-Radio Show in America by *TALKERS* magazine.[7] His television show airs nationally on Public Television. Ric also publishes a 16-page award-winning monthly newsletter and offers extensive financial education at RicEdelman.com.

Philanthropic Activities

Ric is former chairman of the board of his local United Way. He currently serves on the Southeast Board of the Boys & Girls Clubs of America and the Board of the Wolf Trap Foundation for the Performing Arts, and is a member of the American Savings Education Council. Strong supporters of nurses nationwide (who receive free financial planning services from his firm), Ric and his wife Jean provided the funding to establish the Edelman Center for Nursing at Inova Health Foundation and the Inova Center for Advanced Medical Simulation. They are also benefactors of the Edelman Planetarium at Rowan University, to excite children about science; in 2009, they provided funds to manufacture 15,000 telescopes and distribute them to elementary schools throughout the United States. Ric and Jean also encourage volunteerism and philanthropy within their firm; all employees receive one paid day off per year so they can volunteer in their communities, and the firm matches their donations to local charities. Millions of dollars have been raised and donated by Ric and Jean, the advisors of Edelman Financial and its staff.

[1]Throughout the firm's 25 year history, EFS and Ric Edelman have been presented with more than 100 business, advisory, communication and community service awards. A complete list of awards won can be requested by contacting the firm at 855-565-7249. [2]As of 12/31/13. [3]According to *Barron's*, "The formula [used] to rank advisors has three major components: assets managed, revenue produced and quality of the advisor's practice. Investment returns are not a component of the rankings because an advisor's returns are dictated largely by each client's risk tolerance. The quality-of-practice component includes an evaluation of each advisor's regulatory record." The rankings are based on the universe of applications submitted to *Barron's*. The selection process begins with a nomination and application provided to *Barron's*. Principals of Edelman Financial Services LLC self-nominated the firm and submitted quantitative and qualitative information to *Barron's* as requested. *Barron's* reviewed and considered this information which resulted in the rankings on Aug. 27, 2012/Aug. 28, 2010/Aug. 31, 2009. [4]*InvestmentNews – InvestmentNews* 15th Anniversary Issue, June 24, 2013, 15 Transformational Advisors selected by *InvestmentNews* using an internal methodology, which included a reader survey. [5]RIABiz's listing of the 10 most influential figures in the RIA business is in recognition of notable, driven and influential executives who are advancing their firms and are considered to be movers and shakers in the Registered Investment Advisor industry.[6]*Research* magazine cover story "Advisor Hall of Fame," December 2004 (based on serving a minimum of 15 years in the industry, having acquired substantial assets under management, demonstrating superior client service and having earned recognition from peers and the broader community for how they reflect on their profession). [7]*TALKERS* magazine ranking "250 Most Important Radio Talk Show Hosts in America" (April 2012) is based on courage, effort, impact, longevity, potential, ratings, recognition, revenue, service, talent and uniqueness of the talk show host.

GET MORE FINANCIAL EDUCATION FROM RIC EDELMAN

RADIO

Tune in to Ric's weekly radio show for the answers to all your financial questions, such as how to get out of debt; strategies to lower your taxes; whether to buy or lease your next car; and strategies for investing more successfully. Visit RicEdelman.com for station listings, podcasts and to listen live.

TV

Airing on public television stations across the country, *The Truth About Money with Ric Edelman* features audience Q&A segments, guest interviews, radio snippets, quick quizzes, and more all in a fast, fun and informative format that gives you information you need to help you achieve financial success.

MONTHLY NEWSLETTER

Inside Personal Finance, gives you the scoop on investments, taxes, insurance, estate planning, retirement, elder care, mortgages, home ownership and much more delivered straight to your home every month. This fast read explains everything in plain English. Visit RicEdelman.com to subscribe.

ONLINE

Check out all Ric's articles, podcasts and videos, and sign up for his weekly Email Update. It's all at RicEdelman.com.

RicEdelman.com

Ready to get started?
We're ready to help you.

We know how hard it can be to find the right personal financial advisor. Decades ago, Ric and Jean Edelman sought financial advice, but what they got was very disappointing. So they decided to teach themselves about personal finance, and then they created an advisory firm so they could share what they learned with others.

Today, Edelman Financial Services is one of the largest independent financial planning and investment management firms in America[1], serving more than 23,000 individuals and families, with more than $12 billion in assets under management.[2] We are ready to help you too, with offices nationwide. Come learn what so many of your neighbors have discovered, and see how we can help you achieve all your financial goals.

EDELMAN
FINANCIAL SERVICES

Financial Planning • Investment Management
Retirement and Institutional Services

RicEdelman.com/help   855-565-7249

[1] Based on a 2013 Financial Advisor Magazine survey of independent registered investment advisors that file their own ADV statement with the SEC, provide financial planning and related services to individual clients, and have at least $50 million in assets under management as of 12-31-2012. Only advisors that completed the survey are included in the rankings. Assets under management totals are taken from the total assets under management, as of 12-31-2012, reported on the firm's form ADV. Edelman Financial Services ranked 10th in assets under management as of 12-31-2012.

[2] As of 12/31/13.

Advisory Services offered through Edelman Financial Services LLC. Securities offered through Sanders Morris Harris Inc., an affiliated broker/dealer, member FINRA/SIPC.

Get Your FREE Retirement and IRA Account Review

Find out if you're on track to meet your retirement goals, from the advisor ranked three times by *Barron's*[*] as the #1 Independent Financial Advisor in the nation! As a reader of this book, you're entitled to a <u>free</u> review of your IRAs and retirement accounts.

Let the advisors of Ric Edelman's award-winning firm help you make your retirement everything you want it to be!

Get Started Now! Visit
RicEdelman.com/help
or call **855-565-7249**

EDELMAN
FINANCIAL SERVICES

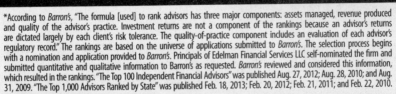

BOOKS BY
RIC EDELMAN

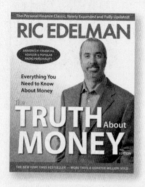

The Truth About Money

The 4th Edition is a comprehensive, practical, "how-to" manual on financial planning that's fun to read — critically acclaimed as the classic in personal finance!

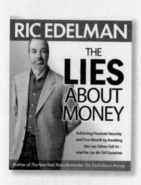

The Lies About Money

Ric shares his most valuable lessons gained through two decades of working directly with individuals and families — and reveals the lies others tell us, and the lies we tell ourselves.

Rescue Your Money

While pundits debate the economy, you're busy coping with bad investments, mounting losses and the realization that you've received bad advice. But you can fix it. This book shows you how.

Discover the Wealth Within You

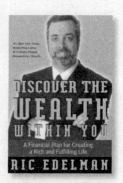

*A Financial Plan for Creating
a Rich and Fulfilling Life*
Ric shows you how to choose fun,
enriching and rewarding financial goals
and gives you a simple straightforward
plan for achieving them.

Ordinary People, Extraordinary Wealth

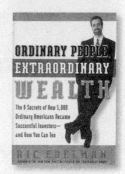

*The 8 Secrets of How 5,000 Ordinary
Americans Became Successful Investors
— and How You Can Too*

The New Rules of Money

88 Strategies for Financial Success Today
Ric shows you how to win in today's
economy, with proven strategies for
college, buying a home, saving taxes, and
choosing the right investments.

What You Need to Do Now

*An 8 Point Action Plan to
Secure Financial Independence*

Available at booksellers everywhere

The Other Side of Money
By Jean Edelman

**Living a More Balanced Life Through
52 Weekly Inspirations**

The Personal Side of Personal Finance

So much of our lives is focused on, or affected by, dollars. But too much attention to money can actually interfere with our wish to live a happy, fulfilling life. That's why personal finance is more personal than finance.

The Other Side of Money helps us reflect on how we are living our lives and suggests how we can see people and the world around us in a positive, loving way. From life's simple issues to our bigger questions, *The Other Side of Money* helps us find quiet and balance by turning inward so we can be in the moment. By looking at how we live our lives, we discover the lessons that let us become better people.

Available at Amazon.com

This page intentionally left blank.
(We ran out of things to say!)